UNEXPECTED
A NOVEL OF CHANGE AND FRIENDSHIP

FLORENCIA ROBERTSON

Raleigh, North Carolina
www.writewaypublishing.com

Unexpected
Copyright © 2024 Florencia Robertson

This is a work of fiction. Names, characters, business, companies, events, and incidents are the products of the author's imagination. Any resemblance to actual persons, living or dead, or actual events is purely coincidental.

No part of this publication may be reproduced, distributed, or transmitted in any form or by any means, including photocopying, recording, or other electronic or mechanical methods, without the prior written permission of the publisher, except in the case of brief quotations embodied in critical reviews and certain other noncommercial uses permitted by copyright law. Permission requests or information for bulk purchases should be sent to info@write-waypublishing.com.

Printed in the United States of America
ISBN 978-1-946425-93-5 (softcover)
Book layout by CSinclaire Write-Design
Cover design by author and Midjourney

Raleigh, North Carolina
www.writewaypublishing.com

CONTENTS

Prologue. 1

Breaking News. 5

If You Don't Know, Now You Know. 14

Like a Boss. 26

Moving Up, Stretching Out 39

You're Not One of These 20-Something-Year-Old Moms 44

The Awakening. 55

The BSG. 68

New School Playdates. 79

Old School Opinions. 93

Breastfeeding Detention. 98

Do Not Try To Do This in the Bathroom 112

Pumping and Dumping with Sober Sally 127

And the Story Continues 142

Daddy Daycare. 151

Return of the Mack 161

Fenugreek Tea with Breastfriends 168

TLC – Tender Love and Castor Oil 177

The Apprentice. 187

Overwhelmed. 195

The Pump Up Mix 205

Security 215

Heads and Ankles Will Roll 223

Confessions 235

Emotional Attachments 248

The Beginning of the End. 260

You Can't Control Everything. 271

All Good Things Must Come To an End. Or Do They? 282

Contingency Plan. 295

Emerge. 310

UNEXPECTED

Prologue

I plan everything. Well, not everything. I didn't plan this party at a posh restaurant that I am currently in the midst of, and neither did I plan for the guest of honor to be in attendance. I'm standing in a room full of giggling women with toilet paper being wrapped around my belly. The multicolored tissue paper hat created for me to wear is anything but flattering. I sneak a peek at the buffet, and my mouth starts to water. When will this be over?

Take a guess at what kind of party this is. Is it my birthday? Am I getting married? A farewell party from the j-o-b? None of the above. The correct answer is D. Baby shower! Yes, yes, I am going to be a proud mama. Again. The last time a baby and I were the guests of honor at a baby shower was a decade ago with Johnny, my second son. I am the lone female in my household, and I've survived fairly well. My boys make me so proud and have been easy to raise. And the *king* of my household, well, a girl couldn't ask for a better one.

The last piece of toilet paper is measured and some lady I only recognize by face has won the game. My belly is 56 inches in circumference. Woo-hoo! I have a date set with the gym seven weeks from now. Trust me, I will not miss that appointment. But until that time, this buffet and I are going to get to know each other in a personal way. This kid is hungry.

I have been opening the gifts, fifty percent of which were not on my registry. Some honorable mentions include the baby perfume, the clip on stroller fan, and baby knee pads. My mind drifted to this next child. Will labor go okay? With the first two, I pushed them out *au natural* and breastfed them both to the age of one. Am I still able to do that? Will this child look like me or like my husband? So many questions that I thought I would never think about again.

I'm 40-something years old. I have a 10 year old, a 13 year old, and a 15-year marriage that have filled my life with meaning and adventure. I'm a boss, and a pretty good one at that. I'm purposeful with all of my decisions and devise plans that I am confident will ultimately end in success. But this situation, I did not foresee. Totally out of character for me. Maybe the looming big 5-0 caused some type of panic in me that threatened my sense of youth, but this last year has been filled with some pretty reckless choices. One of which landed me here, at this baby shower, in honor of me and my third child. They say women reach their sexual peak in their thirties. I'm a late bloomer and a victim to that saying.

"So, mamacita, how are you feeling?" my good friend Lisa whispered.

"Hungry. Is it time to cut the cake?"

"After you thank all the ladies for coming to the party, you may cut the cake and send them all on their way."

Don't get me wrong, I love all of my guests, but this near middle-aged body was not intended to carry around all this additional weight. I was uncomfortable. My feet reminded me of one of Cinderella's sisters when she tried to shove her foot into the glass slipper. Not pretty. I was trying to figure out what I was doing here. And by *here*, I meant pregnant. Control over my life was slipping away as the months in this pregnancy were flying by. For this moment, I try to shake these thoughts and blame them on the hormones, but what if it's not just the hormones going to my brain? What if this is the beginning of a downward slope into a place where

I have no control, no influence, no meaning?

My panicky thoughts are put on hold by the sound of applause. I have opened and admired the last gift. It's time to give my thank you speech. I ungracefully stand up and open my mouth to say thank you. Before I get a single word out, I look down at my swollen feet and watch as amniotic fluid begins to puddle around the cute shoes I bought specifically for this occasion. The room ignites with excited panic. All kinds of instructions were being delivered, and people started scurrying around the room. I was grabbed by both arms and swept out of the restaurant into the backseat of Lisa's car. My cousin Jackie hopped in the front seat and frantically called my husband, ordering him to meet us at the hospital.

As I watched the traffic rush by from my backseat window, I couldn't help but think that the descent had begun.

Breaking News

It all began with a urine sample. I don't think anyone enjoys presenting them. I wasn't applying for a job or being convicted of a crime. I made an appointment with my gynecologist because I thought I was in perimenopause. I hadn't had a period for four consecutive months. They'd been irregular for the past two years. I hadn't felt my best lately. I thought I was having hot flashes, and I felt faint a lot of times. My appetite was changing, and I wasn't losing any weight. My mood was a little off, and I couldn't get my hair to do right for anything. I considered myself to be a bright person. So with the assistance of the internet, I self-diagnosed myself as being menopausal.

My mother passed away when I was a preteen. Apparently she didn't share a lot about her medical history. My aunts were clueless when I asked them about Mom's medical history. Dad wasn't much help either. I'm an only child, and my parents were happily married to each other. I assume Mom must have had some gynecological issues that prevented her from having more than one child. She absolutely loved children. But there's only me.

My long time GYN (and OB when I was childbearing), Dr. Branch, peered at me over her glasses like a librarian who takes her job too seriously and said, "What brings *you* in?"

I gave her the spiel and, as I was explaining my perimenopausal theory, I couldn't help but notice she repeatedly perused my chart. I summed up my symptoms and looked at her. I was intrigued about what was in my chart.

"Let me complete your pelvic exam, Lonnie. You'll have to have some blood work as well."

I assumed the position that all women dread at the GYN's office. She finished up and said, "All of the symptoms you described can be symptoms associated with menopause. But they are also associated with other conditions as well. And in your case the condition could be pregnancy. Your urine sample tested positive, and your uterus definitely has something in it."

All I could do was stare at her. Speechless. I shook my head and tried to say something, but my brain was so busy computing all the odds that this could be true that no words came out. She looked at me. I looked at her. The silence grew awkward.

"Lonnie, if you truly are pregnant, it's not the end of the world. Women your age have babies all the time, and it'll be just as rewarding as raising your boys." She rested her hand on my shoulder for a second and then left me alone in the room. I still hadn't said a word.

The nurse came in and escorted me to the lab to get the blood work done and schedule me for an ultrasound. I was so engulfed with my thoughts that the phlebotomist had to ask me twice which arm I wanted her to stick. I just laid my left arm on the armrest. I felt tears welling up, but they were short-lived as the novice phlebotomist kept fishing around for a vein, repeatedly poking me.

When I got back to my car, I rested my head on the steering wheel and tried to come to terms with this news. If I truly was pregnant, that would change everything. In four years when my oldest left the nest, I would have a child starting preschool. This would delay my empty nest plans by *years*. I tried to do the math in my head, but I couldn't compute. Whatever the answer, it would be too many years. I thought of all the time I'd put into raising my boys, looking forward to the end goal of being alone with my husband, enjoying the rest and achievement of having raised productive children in this society.

Now, the thought of starting over was so depressing. Diapers! It'd been years since I'd changed a diaper! And the college fund! Having a child at this stage could put us at a disadvantage financially. We had more years behind us than we did in front of us. What could I give a child in my middle years, approaching my final years? What if something happened to me or David and we weren't there for this child?

I managed to work myself into a sobbing mess, but then my tears came to an abrupt end when I realized *I hadn't received my blood test results yet.* This could be a false positive. Yeah. I decided to put my focus there so I could make it through the rest of the day. I wouldn't mention this to anyone since there was no definitive evidence that I was pregnant just yet. I wiped my face and headed back to work.

As soon as I got back to my desk, my boss, Will, came into my office all excited with the news that he's been promoted to Senior VP, and he was recommending me for his position as assistant vice president. We both had been with this company for a long time, before my boys were born, actually. Will and I had seen a lot of people come and go and had shared many promotions over the years. This took the cake. I wished I could be excited, but if I was pregnant, would I be able to manage an AVP position? He seemed to think I could do the job in my sleep. I agreed. But if I had a baby keeping me *sleepless,* how good would I be?

Will was probably confused by my lack of excitement. I told him I was just sad that he'd be leaving the branch to take this new position. He started talking about how he could make the company better in his new position. Any other day I would have been totally engaged in this conversation, but not today. When he got to a good place for me to interject, I jumped all over the opportunity. I gave him all the attaboys he was looking for, and it was good enough to get him out of my office. After he left, I took five to have an emotional breakdown in the restroom before my eleven o'clock meeting.

After the boys were in bed and David and I had a chance to talk, he was happy when I told him about the promotion possibility. So happy he wanted to reward me with sex, ha ha. Of all nights. I almost never refuse sex, because I honor my marriage. But I weaseled my way out of it tonight given the circumstances.

With everything on my mind, I couldn't go to sleep. Maybe if we had had sex, I'd be snoozing right now. I decided I might as well get up. Maybe listening to my favorite podcast would help settle me down. It usually helped me focus my thoughts and motivated me to do better. I slipped out of bed, grabbed my phone, and headed to the living room.

> *Top of the morning everyone! This is Dan. Joining us today is life coach Cindy J. She's going to talk about ways to discard that mental buildup in order to move forward with your life!*

Well, this oughta be good.

> *Dan, thanks for having me on the show. In today's society, it is so easy to have our minds clogged with all of the stressors of our daily routine. One of the first things I have my clients do to expel some of this buildup is journaling. I know it sounds old school, and you'll be hard pressed to find a diary with a lock and key these days, but writing or recording the thoughts that keep your mind from being in its most productive state frees you up to think more clearly.*

That made sense. I'm an action-oriented person. I stopped the podcast and switched my phone to its record setting and began to talk. I decided right away that voice alone wouldn't do it, so I switched from the voice setting to the camera. I spilled the beans to the phone as if I were in a therapy session. When I hit the red button to stop the recording, I felt much lighter.

Turns out Cindy J. was right. Getting all my thoughts out *was* very therapeutic. I was ready for some sleep.

Will's promotion and the AVP position opening were announced today and applications for the AVP position were opened up. I sent an email immediately expressing my interest. I know, I know. Yesterday I couldn't get excited about this, but I'd gotten some sleep, and I was a little clearer. I definitely wanted a shot at this position. I'd done some exceptional work for this company.

While I was putting the finishing touches on my email, my cell phone rang. Well, blood work don't lie. I was pregnant. I had a one thirty appointment tomorrow with my now OB/GYN.

I think I went into shock with the blood work news. The next thing I knew, I was in the restroom, hanging over the toilet. This wasn't morning sickness. This was my body in shock. My work productivity was minimal the rest of the day.

By the time I headed to my car, I was past the denial stage and fully into the anger stage. As I threw my briefcase and bags in the passenger seat, I decided that I wanted a retest. I didn't have time to be pregnant. I wanted this promotion.

In the midst of all this upheaval thinking, I was going to be late picking up Johnny from baseball. I hate being late! Especially when it involves my kids. This whole pregnancy had me off my game. I couldn't afford to have my thoughts blurred for months by extra hormones. And then there would be brain cell loss from lack of sleep and continued hormonal changes after the baby came. Ugh!

And I had to tell my husband. This was . . . this was just beyond me. I began to cry, one of those uncontrollable ugly cries. I reeled it in to a whimper. I needed to leave the parking lot and pick up Johnny.

"Do I say 'Hello'?" David asked as I began recording his response to the news that he would once again be a daddy.

"No, I'm the only one looking at this. I figure this video diary will give me a few laughs when this baby graduates from high school."

"Well," David said as he leaned in closer to the phone, "we're having a baby! I'm surprised but happy. We have two wonderful sons, and I know this baby will be perfect, just like them." He leaned over and kissed me as I stopped the recording.

"We'll be fine, babe. I'll call the financial planner in the morning."

He saw the uncertainty on my face and grabbed my hand. "Lonnie, we're still young and hot for each other. Isn't this what happens in passionate relationships?"

"No! This happens to people who have unprotected sex. I have no idea why we were so stupid."

"Stupid in love."

"Sex and love are not synonymous."

"Well, since you're already pregnant, let's be stupid and have unprotected sex."

"I can't *believe* you're suggesting that right now! This is so serious. Our lives are never going to be the same!"

"Today was different than yesterday, last week was different than the week before it. Things are never the same, they always change, and we always grow as a result of change. I can see this has you troubled. Sex will take your mind off of it."

I smacked him with the nearest pillow and threw myself face down on the bed.

"Lonnie, this is the beginning of a surprise chapter in our love story. I am embracing it. We've made it through difficult times, but I don't see this as something disastrous. This baby is something we created, together, in love."

"In stupidity," I murmured with my face buried in the comforter.

"The video journaling continues here in the ultrasound room," David said, impersonating a TV game show host. "Here we are getting ready for the ultrasound." He turned the camera so the ultrasound screen and I were in view. "The ultrasound tech has asked not to be recorded. Drum roll please." He got no drum roll. "No, really, babe, give me a drum roll, I'm filming."

I tapped my fingers rapidly on the exam table, cringing as that cold gel was squirted on my belly. Images began to pop up on the screen, and my heart was racing.

"Is that the baby's head?" David asked.

"No, sir, it's your wife's ovary."

"Is that the baby's leg?" David sounded even more excited.

"Uh, no. But you're getting closer. It's the baby's arm. Now, we don't know how far along you are, so we may not be able to tell the sex of the baby yet. Would you want to know the sex if we can see that?"

"Yes!" we replied simultaneously.

"Okay, we'll start by getting some measurements, so we can see how old this baby is."

After a brief silence, I learned I was about 18 weeks pregnant. I could feel David's palm getting sweaty. Neither one of us could say anything.

"I'm not finding a penis, guys. And here's the folds of the labia."

Tears start rolling down my shocked face. David squeezed my hand while he continued to record us.

A baby in my forty-plus-year-old belly. I didn't know how to describe how I felt. I was totally out of my element. I do plan almost every detail in my life. I try to anticipate curveballs and make minor adjustments to keep us on track. But now I felt like we'd derailed and fallen into some uncharted territory without a compass to guide us back to a familiar place. It felt like a bomb had exploded, and I was dazed from the impact. I couldn't even hear, but I could tell David was calling my name.

"Lonnie. Lonnie, are you okay?"

"I'm sorry, I think I blacked out."

"Wow, babe! We made a girl."

I rolled over on the table and began sobbing. David and the technician both went into comforting mode. She grabbed a tissue and shoved it into my clenched hand while David stroked my hair and said how excited he was. All while the camera was still rolling.

Little did he know that these were not tears of joy, but tears of fear. What do I do with a baby girl? I have boys. And I'm over forty! I think I'm going to vomit.

We got the remainder of my visits for this unexpected turn in life scheduled and made our way to the car. It was a good thing David was with me, because there was no way I could have driven myself anywhere.

"I know this isn't what we planned," David said as he started the car, "but we can make the adjustment. You're an amazing woman. You surprise me daily. All the things you manage to accomplish and your ability to make something good out of less than fortunate circumstances is incredible. We'll succeed raising three children just as we have so far with two. And I don't know about you, but I'm still young. The other day at the gas station, this lady asked me if I was the boys' older brother!"

I pinched him because now he's lying.

"Oww! Okay! Maybe she didn't say their *brother*, but she was definitely indicating that I don't look my age. Life is never fully mapped out, babe. You have to anticipate the unforeseen. I love you *and* this baby. I'm happy, and I need you to send my baby happy vibes. All you have to do is what you've always done."

"David, this isn't like ten years ago when we had Johnny. I'm considered high risk because I'm over forty. What will the boys think? We have to put away money for another child's education. We'll need to work longer to have enough for retirement. You're gonna need a cane to walk her down the aisle."

He laughed. "How about this, I'll call Will's secretary and let her know you won't be in this afternoon, and let's go get frozen yogurt. Does that sound good?"

I agreed to frozen yogurt, and we headed to Guppies, one of our favorite spots. It was actually the same place where I told him we were having our first son. This is our spot when we want to make a memorable moment. I guessed this was memorable. Tears welled up in my eyes again. I couldn't even put into words how this moment would be remembered. Would it be the worst season of my life or my greatest triumph? I couldn't fathom feeling any less in control, so I'll call this one of my lowest points and rebound from here. This could be good, right?

The weather was beautiful, so we sat out on the patio. I ordered cookies and cream and David ordered some seasonal flavor that didn't sound appetizing to me.

"Let's have both families over this weekend for dinner, and we'll break the news to everyone."

"I don't know about that. It means I have to cook and clean, David."

"Potluck."

"That might work."

"It's settled. Dinner at our house Sunday afternoon. Can you get excited?" He gave me puppy dog eyes.

"Yes, I can get excited," I said, reluctantly.

"I can't wait! I get a baby girl! A princess. I bet she'll look like you, because the boys look like me." His giddiness was slightly annoying.

As we walked back to the car, the thought of his family and mine at the dinner table hearing that we were having a baby girl began to cause me anxiety. I felt like vomiting again.

If You Don't Know, Now You Know

I called Dad to tell him about dinner at the house on Sunday and asked him if he could bring the meat. When I told him Jackie, Lisa, and David's family would be there, he asked if we were celebrating something. I said that it had just been a while since all of us had been together. Dad sounded a little suspicious, but said he would bring chicken, beef, and fish—something for everyone as he put it. I thanked him with my spoiled little girl tone and told him I loved him.

Dad is a fantastic cook. He always says my mom taught him well. Since I grew up without my mom or siblings, it was Dad who made sure my life was full and happy. He catered to my every need and most of my wants that were within reason. He'd be so excited about the news. I was sure this little girl would consume his life just like I had.

David called his mother and put her on speaker phone. Just like my dad, she asked if there was some occasion for the family get together. He said we wanted to see everyone's faces. His mom mentioned his grandma was asking about him, so she would extend the invite to Mom Mabel as well. She reminded David to call his sister Joanna to invite her. Lizzie, his other sister was out of town, so she'd get the news secondhand. I thought this was all going to come together.

David's family is very different from mine. Everybody knows each other's business, and they can be cliquey at times.

I've earned my way into the clique over the years, but I also made my stand against the "need to know" mentality they carry.

In the beginning of our marriage, his family was too nosey. They were so used to knowing all the details about his sister Lizzie's marriage that they thought they would treat us the same way. Lizzie's husband ended up leaving her, partly due to certain overbearing family members. I think Joanna never married after watching her sister go through a divorce.

There was no way I was losing my marriage, so I put my foot down and closed the door to our personal lives. It was rocky in the beginning, but smooth as butter now. His grandmother is a hoot. His aunts are evil, but I've learned to tolerate them. We save ourselves the headache and only invite his aunts to select events. This wouldn't be one of them. I was already trending negative emotionally, so I didn't need any Negative Nellies pushing me further down that path.

I felt the need for another therapeutic moment after all this, so after everyone was off to bed, I made my way to our home office. I gathered the videos I had taken previously and put them all in one spot before I hit the red button.

> **Well, it's a girl. We're having the family over for dinner Sunday to share the news. Seeing as how I'm halfway through the process, if I don't say something soon, his family will announce it for me. I love them, but they can be so intrusive. I'm lucky David's grandma hasn't seen me in a while. She'd call it a mile away. What am I supposed to do with a girl? I grew up with my dad. I spent time with my girl cousins and my friends have girls, but I've never had to develop a girl. This is just ... my life. This is my life now.**

I let that marinate in my psyche a moment. I looked back at the screen with a little more confidence.

> **This is my life now.**

David and I had bought each of our boys a special gift for the dinner. We were going to tell everyone that the gifts were for the boys making the honor roll this quarter, but I knew that when they opened the gifts, they'd realize these gifts were for big brothers, which would lead into the announcement.

The boys were excited about having everyone over, and David could hardly contain himself. He's no good at keeping secrets, which is partly the reason we were announcing this as soon as we could. My friend Lisa and my cousin Jackie arrived early to help me get dinner set up. They could tell I was up to something, but I just kept deflecting and changing the subject when they asked what was going on.

My dad arrived and popped a rotisserie chicken and a pot roast in the oven, and then began preparing the fish. I was glad this was keeping him occupied. Next, David's parents, Sheryl and Jerry, came in bearing dishes of food. His dad greeted me with his usual hug and his mom with her usual pleasantries. They had Lizzie's son Jordan with them. He ran off to be with his cousins. The doorbell rang again. I expected it to be Joanna, but when I open the door, my heart dropped.

"Lonnie."

"Mom Mabel." I greeted her with a hug.

"You look good, dear. Where's David? He owes me some money. I bet that's why he hasn't called me in a few weeks. I told him his sorry team was gonna lose in the conference championship. David!" she yelled, tossing me her jacket as she walked off to find David.

"Hello, Lonnie," said Aunt Teresa, the source of my heart drop. This woman is the most bitter thing you'll find this side of the Rocky Mountains. Her sister is the most bitter thing on the other side of the mountains.

"Wow. Aunt Teresa, how nice to see you. David didn't say you were coming. What a surprise. And Uncle Larry, it's been a while."

They stepped into the foyer. Aunt Teresa looked around the house.

"Well, David failed to tell us about this little shindig. Mother didn't want to drive at night to get home, so we volunteered to drive her. She made this to bring." She shoved a warm dish at me. "I don't know why she used her good dishware. Please make sure it is handled properly," she said as she walked to the living room with Uncle Larry following quietly behind her.

"Will do." This was not going the way I planned.

Joanna came running up to the door before I closed it.

"Hi, lady!"

"Hi, Lonnie," she said as we embraced. Joanna and I went to the same college. She is the reason David and I met.

She leaned in close to me and whispered, "Who invited Aunt Teresa?"

"She invited herself."

I carried Mom Mabel's dish to the kitchen. I've always loved the sound of a bustling house. Conversations going on about current events and sports, laughter, and children playing. Although I experienced that at family gatherings when I was young, I went home to a quiet house with just me and my dad. We talked about any and everything, but the excitement of having lots of people in a home is something I cherished then and still cherish now.

"All right, everyone, dinner is served," David announced.

Once everyone got settled at the table and my father-in-law blessed the food, David made his little speech.

"Now before everyone digs in, I'd like to present my boys with a gift," David said with pride. "They are such stellar students, and they have once again made the honor roll!"

Everyone applauded and congratulated the boys. Our nephew Jordan urged them to open the gifts. The boys unwrapped the gifts to reveal silver chains with two dog tag pendants.

"What do the tags say?" yelled Mom Mabel from the other side of the table.

"It has my name on one tag and big brother on the other tag," DJ said.

"What does your say, Johnny?"

"The same thing," he replied nonchalantly as he reached for the macaroni and cheese.

"Let me see." Sheryl looked at the tags Johnny handed her. "Why does Johnny's say big brother? Shouldn't it say little brother?"

"No, it's correct. Johnny is a big brother," David said with a big smile

Everyone at the table looked at me, and I give them a sheepish grin.

"Lonnie, are you pregnant?" Jackie shrieked.

"I'm having a girl."

Joanna screamed with excitement. Jackie ran around the table and embraced me. Dad was in tears, the boys were jumping up and down, and Jerry slapped David on the back as men do when they are proud of an accomplishment.

Mom Mabel pulled a whistle out of her ever-present purse and blew it loudly. That got everyone's attention real quick.

"This is a historic moment," she said as she stood up from her chair. "My first great-granddaughter. Let's toast to the new baby girl!"

Everyone raised their glass. Mom Mabel pulled a small bottle from her purse and poured its contents into her glass before raising hers.

"To the baby girl," she proclaimed.

All eyes were on Mom Mabel as we joined in the toast. My dad, Jackie, and Lisa struggled to hold back their laughter. Sheryl dropped her head in embarrassment.

"Mom Mabel, can I have some of that juice you're drinking?" Johnny asked. Mom Mabel reached in her purse.

"No!" yelled all the other adults at the table. Then the laughter erupted.

"Well, Lonnie, what will *you* do with a baby girl? All you

know is how to care for boys. Girls require different things," said Aunt Teresa.

Jackie got an offended look on her face and opened her mouth, but I signaled for her not to respond.

"Well, Aunt Teresa, I'm capable of learning what it takes to raise a girl. I have done wonderfully with my boys. I'm quite sure I'll do exceptionally well with a girl. Plus, I have Sheryl, my friends, and family. We'll do it together."

"You're no spring chicken, dear. How will you keep up with the demands of motherhood? Your children must come first. You all are so busy. It would be a shame for the daughter not to get the attention she deserves."

"Aunt Teresa," said David, "my wife is a very capable woman. And I'm confident we'll raise a very well-rounded young lady." His facial expression and tone said that the conversation was over. Aunt Teresa picked up her fork and began eating.

"So, when can we expect the little angel," my dad asked as he came around to hug me once things settled down a bit.

"I'm 18 weeks."

"What!" exclaimed Lisa. "You're halfway through the pregnancy, and you're just now sharing."

"We just found out this week," I said.

Mom Mabel dropped her fork and said, "Honey, this isn't your first rodeo. Don't you know what it feels like to be pregnant?"

"Mother!" Sheryl blurted, giving it two syllables. "Every pregnancy is different. I'm sure Lonnie probably has irregular cycles, and that's why they're just finding out."

Uncle Larry's bite of chicken went down the wrong pipe, and he coughed it up across the table. It landed in Jordan's plate and in his surprise he accidentally knocked over his cup and juice flowed across the table into Uncle Larry's lap. Aunt Teresa let out a disgusted sigh and began feverishly wiping Uncle Larry's pants. He just sat and let her do this, almost like he was enjoying it.

The rest of the visit was relatively smooth. David's family and Lisa left after dessert and coffee. My dad and Jackie stayed to clean up, so David and I could have time with the boys. They were excited and full of questions.

"What will her name be?" asked Johnny.

"I haven't thought about it."

"You should name her MacKenzie. I like that name."

"Where'd you come up with that?"

"There's a girl in my class named MacKenzie, and I like her name."

DJ interjected, "I think Chloe would be a good name for her."

"Daddy and I will keep those in mind. So how do you two feel about adding a sister to our family?"

"I think it's great. I get to be a big brother like DJ! It's my time!"

We all laughed.

"What about you, DJ?" David asked.

"I'm excited! She'll be good looking just like me. I'll teach her everything she needs to know. Look at what a great job I've done with Johnny."

I love this kid. So confident, sometimes a little too confident. But it gave me comfort that I'd be able to raise a confident little girl. And I'd have help from a great support system (minus Aunt Teresa, who's no help at all).

My dad and Jackie finished up in the kitchen and joined us in the living room.

"Girl, we have to plan a baby shower! Pink frills and hair bows, and you know I can teach you a thing or two."

"Your skills might be rusty. Your girls are grown," I joked.

"I still do their hair from time to time. I'm a pro."

"You know I have some skills with hair too," my dad chimed in.

"Dad, when was the last time you did hair?" David asked.

"It's been a while, but it's just like riding a bike."

We couldn't help but laugh at that comment.

"It's been real, family," said Jackie. "Lonnie, I'll call you later this week. I'll let Mom and the sisters know the great news. Love you guys." She gave everyone hugs goodbye, and I walked her to her car.

"David's aunt is rude," said Jackie.

"I know. We've had many run-ins. She never thought I was good enough for him, but that man wouldn't be half of what he is without me in his life."

"You're right about that." She gave me a high five. "I can't believe you're pregnant. And it's a girl!"

"That makes two of us."

"I can't think of a better woman to have a baby at our age than you. You handle every situation you face with such grace. Don't stress, Lonnie, you'll be an awesome mommy to a little girl."

"Thanks, Jackie." I gave her a hug, and she hopped in her car, waving as she drove away.

When I came back in, my dad was inquiring about David's lost bet with Mom Mabel.

"How much do you owe her?"

"Fifty bucks! I don't know why I bet against her. She wins every time."

"I can't believe she pulled that bottle out her purse." Dad burst into laughter.

"What was in her bottle, Dad?" asked Johnny.

"You're too young to know what was in her bottle," said DJ.

"Okay, DJ, what was in her bottle?" David asked.

"It was one of those drinks on the commercials. Why don't they show old ladies drinking that stuff? Mom Mabel would be great in one of those commercials," said DJ.

"I can just see her now, getting out of a cab with some of her Bunco buddies, walking the red carpet into a club!" David said.

"All right, I see where this is going. There are children present."

Dad and David continued laughing while I sent the boys to bed.

"I saw your tears of joy earlier," I said as I walked with my dad to his car.

"Lonnie, when you said you were having a girl, I had a flashback to when you were born and the doctor said, 'It's a girl!' I cried at that moment too. I knew how much I loved your mother and how wonderful a woman she was, and I knew at that moment I would love you just as much. I'm going to spoil this baby, just giving you a heads up," he said happily.

"I think we all will, Dad. I love you. Thank you for bringing the meat. You never disappoint."

"Love you too, sweetheart. I'll talk to you later."

When I got back into the house, David was watching ESPN. He heard me come in and turned off the TV.

"It's public knowledge now," he said.

"It is, but I don't want my job to know. Not yet anyway. I'm still applying for this promotion, and I'm afraid they may discount me because I'm pregnant."

"They technically cannot do that, but I do see how that could happen."

"I want to go through the process and get the position before I share that I'm pregnant. I want a fair shot."

"How long do you want to stay home after the baby is born?"

"I don't think I'll be able to do a full twelve weeks with a new position, but at least six."

"What about childcare? It's been a while since we've had to trust someone with a baby. And I'm feeling different these days about leaving a baby with just anyone."

"I'm sure we wouldn't leave our baby with just anyone. After this job thing is settled, I'll start asking around. Thank you for suggesting we have a family dinner today. I would have dragged my feet and probably come home from the hospital with a newborn before anyone knew I was pregnant."

"That's why our relationship is so successful, babe.

We know each other's strengths and weaknesses, and we step up in the areas where the other is weaker."

"That's a great comment to end our evening." I wrapped my arms around him and smooched him real good. "I'm going to bed. You coming?"

"I'll be up in a few. I need to check the bank account to make sure I have enough to cover what I bet on the game. Mom Mabel talks too much trash. I had to put some money on my team to shut her up."

"All right. You better not lose your children's college money to Mom Mabel."

"I'll get it back with my inheritance," he said jokingly.

I got to my desk Monday morning and quickly sifted through the usual emails, but one caught my attention.

> Thank you for your interest in the Assistant Vice President position with Mendallmen Corporation. Your documents for consideration have been received and reviewed. We are pleased to inform you that you are a qualified candidate for this position. Please contact me at 800-737-1111 x 321 to set up an interview. Again, thank you for your interest in the position and the best of luck to you during the interview process.
>
> Lynn Murray, Recruitment Specialist

Just as I picked up the phone, Julia, the director over Production Services, knocked on my door. I signaled her to come in.

"So, what did you think about the meeting last week?"

"I'm super excited for Will, and I hope we get the right person to fill his shoes. We have a great team here. I'd hate to have a poor leader with such an exceptional group of people."

"I agree. Did you apply for the position?" she asked.

"I don't think it's wise to discuss that among ourselves,

as many of us would be qualified to step up into that position."

"You're right. There are many of us who are qualified. Well, if you did apply, good luck to you."

"Same to you, Julia."

I'm not sure what she was trying to get out of me, but she wasn't getting it. I don't give up information to just anyone, and she was not on my need-to-know list. I dismissed our conversation and proceeded with my phone call. Lynn scheduled my interview for the next Tuesday. I gathered my things for my morning meetings, but I was interrupted yet again. This time it was Leonard, director of Account Services. Mentally, I rolled my eyes.

"Hey, Lonnie. Just stopped by to have you sign a form for one of your designers."

"Thanks, Leonard. How are Connie and the kids?"

"They're good. How about your husband and boys?"

"Fantastic." I signed the form and handed it to him.

"So, do you know who from our branch applied for the AVP position?"

"Leonard, I'm really not . . ."

"I heard Julia and Mike in Creative already have interviews."

"Wow, umm, I . . ."

"If either of them get the position, I may have to put in my two week notice. Do you think I should apply?"

"Leonard, I'm late for my nine o'clock. Thanks for bringing that form by." I scooted past him and out of my office. If this was what the next few weeks would be like, I was not looking forward to them.

Next Tuesday showed up quicker than I thought it would. I felt prepared for my interview. Well, mostly prepared. I didn't think to buy a new outfit. My clothes were starting to fit poorly, but I found a few pieces that would work. That wouldn't last much longer.

I arrived a little early to the corporate office. After some small chat with the receptionist, I took a minute to look over my talking points. I heard a familiar voice and looked up to see Julia coming out from her interview. Julia greeted me and continued on her way. Lynn, the recruiter, appeared at the door of the conference room and motioned for me to come in. She ushered me to sit across the table from three individuals, John Bianco, the CEO of the company whom I had met once out of all the years I'd worked here, Brian Leach, the newly promoted General Manager, and Will, who was stepping into Brian's former position. I shook each person's hand before I sat.

I won't bore you with my talking points, but trust that I knocked the interview out of the park. We ended with a little chit chat about our families and congratulatory banter for Will and Brian on their new positions. I was confident in my performance, and Will gave me a nod indicating that I had done well. I left the room feeling much lighter than when I went in. As soon as I got to my car, I sent my thank you emails to John, Brian, and Will and treated myself to Guppies on the way back to the office.

Like a Boss

A few weeks went by before word started trickling in about the interviews. Leonard was the one to break the news to me.

"Julia and Mike are out. They got emails today thanking them for applying, but excusing them from the next phase of interviews. That's a great way to start off the weekend. Did you get one too?"

"You know, Leonard, I haven't had a chance to check my email, but when I do, I'll let you know my fate."

Sure enough, when I did check my email there was one from Lynn, the recruiter. It was requesting a second interview. Yes! I immediately called her and set up the next interview. This one was going to be an informal dinner with her and Brian on Monday. I ran out to my car and called David. Too many sensitive ears and people in the building. He praised me for the accomplishment. I kept our conversation short and tried not to draw too much attention to myself as I came back to my office. Wouldn't you know, Mike from finance was standing outside my office.

"Did you get an email?"

"I did get an email."

"What did it say?"

"I'd rather not share right now."

"Why are you being so secretive?"

"I'm not trying to come off that way, but my email

is personal, and I don't wish to share the details of it. I hope you can respect that."

Mike gave me a look and walked away. I knew this was going to come back around, and I was sure rumors would begin to surface, but I was going to remain neutral in the process and not reveal anything until the process was over.

Thoughts about the interview and dinner with Lynn and Brian stayed on my mind. I arrived at the upscale restaurant on the other side of downtown after work on Monday, ready for what the evening would bring. Lynn was standing outside, talking on the phone, so I gestured to her that I'd be inside. I had never eaten at this place, so I grabbed a menu and took a seat near the door.

"Sorry about that," Lynn said. "That was Brian, he got turned around, but he'll be here in about five minutes. Let's go ahead to our table."

We were seated next to a window where we could see the river that flows through downtown. That and the beautiful Mediterranean decor gave a sense of being somewhere far away. We gave our drink orders and studied our menus.

"Have you eaten here before?" I asked Lynn.

"Yes. I frequently bring clients here."

"What's good on the menu?"

"I always start with the hummus trio for an appetizer. All of the salads are good. I generally stick with chicken. All of the chicken dishes here are good. I've heard others say the fish is good as well," Lynn said as she raised her hand a little to catch Brian's eye.

Brian took his seat just in time to put in his drink order as the waitress dropped off ours.

"Forgive me for being late. I've never been in this area. This is nice," he said.

"Totally understandable, Brian. Do you want to start?" Lynn asked.

"Sure. Well, Lonnie, you are one of our strongest

candidates for this position. You've been with the company over fifteen years and you have a strong understanding of our industry and how we fit in the local market. One of the things we love about your branch is the cohesiveness of the team and the seamless interactions between departments. We want an AVP who is able to handle not only the business side of things but also work well with our people.

"As you know, Will did an excellent job of promoting pride in what you all do and maintaining very high job satisfaction among the team at your branch. If you were given the opportunity to take this position, how would you motivate your staff to increase productivity while maintaining high job satisfaction?"

Brian and Lynn seemed quite impressed with my ideas and responses to the questions. I felt pretty good when I left. All I could do now was wait. Lynn indicated that a determination would likely be made next week. AVP, here I come!

The waiting room at the OB's office was packed today. At the front desk there were two sign-in sheets, one for OB patients and one for GYN patients. I quickly sign myself in on the appropriate sheet.

I got called to the back, dropped off my urine sample, and got weighed. The visit was a typical second trimester visit, nothing exciting. The doc listened to the heart beat and talked about my weight. They sent me out with a parting gift of that lovely glucose solution. They would be testing me for gestational diabetes my next visit.

I got to the office just in time for my first set of Tuesday meetings. During a short break, I ran back to my office to grab a few documents before my lunch meeting with Will.

"Lonnie, how are you feeling?" Julia asked from my office doorway.

"I'm great. How about you?" I responded with a little suspicion in my voice.

"Nothing new going on? You look a little different."

"How so?" I asked as I printed my documents, trying not to acknowledge her.

"I can't put my finger on it. You're just looking a little different. Just asking." She walked away.

I hate it when people waste my time with meaningless conversation. I grabbed what I needed and rushed off to my lunch meeting. Will had lunch with each director every other week. Of course, we discussed my interview, his promotion, and the highlights of what was going on in my department. As our meeting went on, I thought about how much I would miss Will. We started working at Mendallmen at the same time, same orientation class. He started as a manager in the operations department, and I was a minion in the marketing department. We've come a long way since then.

I was so close to getting the job, but I was beginning to question if it was really what I wanted. Could I handle such a big position with a newborn? Would it affect my marriage, my relationship with my boys? I didn't want to be that parent who works ten hours a day and gives their family only a few hours in the evening. But the other alternatives, not working or staying where I was, wouldn't be fulfilling. At least not for me. Being at home was just as much a fulltime job, but it was twenty four hours a day. At least working outside of the home, you could break up the time you performed in your role as mom and wife.

As the days went by, my thoughts compounded to the point that I picked up the phone to follow-up with Lynn about this job. But at that very moment *she* called *me*.

"Lonnie Peterson."

"Hi, Lonnie, it's Lynn. How are things going?"

"Going well." Quit with the small talk, tell me I got the job!

"Brian and John have finished their interviews, and we're all pleased to inform you that you will be the new Assistant Vice President over South Branch."

"Thank you!" I could barely contain my excitement. I was so overwhelmed I was holding back tears.

"Brian and I would like to do lunch tomorrow to discuss the details and salary. Would the same restaurant where we met before work for you?"

"Definitely will work."

"All right, see you tomorrow at noon. And congratulations."

"Thank you, Lynn. See you tomorrow."

I fumbled my phone in my hands and my fingers were trembling as I called David.

"David."

"Lonnie, are you okay? What's wrong!"

"I got the promotion."

"Oh, sweetie, that's awesome! I knew you'd get it! Guppies tonight!"

"Maybe not Guppies. We've had a little too much of Guppies lately."

"I'm so proud of you."

"David, I'm a little anxious. Did I do the right thing pursuing this being pregnant? I know I can do the job, but can I do it with added responsibilities at home? I don't want to kill myself, our marriage, or my relationship with the boys."

"We'll take on your promotion as a family and do whatever is necessary to share the responsibility. You've earned this, babe. You'll be successful, even with a little baby girl."

"Thank you, David. You are priceless."

"Okay, I gotta go, but I'm taking you out tonight. Call your dad and see if he's off tonight, so he can watch the boys. I'll call my mom as a backup."

"I'm on it. Love you."

"Love you, AVP."

I immediately called my dad. He had a night off and agreed to keep the boys. My next stop was Will's office.

"Will, I just heard from Lynn!" I whispered with great excitement.

He got up to shut his door. "Finally! They told me yesterday. I've been waiting for them to tell you. Congratulations!"

"Thank you, Will. And congrats again to you. We're both very deserving."

"I'm setting up an All Call meeting in an hour to share the news with everyone."

"Are you going to train me?"

"After you sign your papers tomorrow, you will become my apprentice. You'll still hold your duties as Director of Marketing. We'll just set aside time each day to get you up to speed."

"What about my position?"

"They'll post a notification for your job just as they did mine. Do you have anyone in mind that you think can fill your shoes?"

"I haven't given it any thought, but I will tonight."

"Good. Congrats, Lonnie. I have a conference call in a few minutes. See you at the All Call."

Everyone showed up the last hour of the work day for the All Call in the large conference room.

"Good afternoon, South Branch!" Will exclaimed. "Doesn't everyone love an unexpected All Call at the end of the day? First, I want to make sure we acknowledge a few new employees and a couple of birthdays."

Will took the time to honor birthdays and warmly introduce our newest employees. This kind of time to celebrate and connect all of us is part of why he was so good managing South Branch.

Will continued, "Now most of you have heard that I'm being promoted to Senior Vice President, and I want to share with everyone what that will entail. I will no longer be at South Branch, which saddens my heart because we are truly the better half of the company. My new office will be at Main Branch. My last day will be this time next month. I will retain all of my normal duties during this time in addition to training my replacement."

My heart started racing. He was getting ready to break the news.

"After an outside agency's thorough candidate search followed by a series of interviews by our company for my replacement, we were overjoyed that the best candidate was one within our branch."

Now I could hear whispers and see intrigue on many faces.

"I'm pleased to present the new Assistant Vice President of South Branch, Lonnie Peterson!" The applause and cheers as I made my way to the front surprised me. "Lonnie, give us a few words."

"I wasn't expecting to say anything, but I do want to say that I'm excited to serve you all as AVP. Will is a tough act to follow, but I've got a few tricks to add to his act." I stepped aside to hand the gathering back over to Will.

"Now, I'd like to take any questions anyone may have, suggestions, things we may need to address."

Julia was the first to raise her hand.

"First, I'd like to say congratulations to Lonnie. Not just on your promotion to AVP but also on your new baby!" she said with sarcastic joy. The whole room buzzed, and Will gave me a puzzled look. "Will, my question to you is what were the criteria for choosing the new AVP?" She sat down with a vindictive sneer on her face. I wasn't sure I was prepared to handle this.

"Well, Julia, I know you are aware of the criteria, but for those who are unaware, I'll share those with you."

"*. . . you obviously didn't meet them,*" I whispered under my breath.

Will went into the details of the hiring process for the position while fellow employees were gesturing to me from across the room, wanting answers about a baby. I ignored them all. How did Julia find out? Is this what her comments earlier were about? Ugh, who has time for this foolishness?

Now I had to break this news to my superiors, and they were going to question whether they made the right decision. It was going to happen anyway, but I would have liked to break the news in my own time, not under these circumstances. I still had to sign my papers, so I wasn't even technically promoted yet. I wanted to get up and walk out, but that would be a major sign of immaturity. I sat through the rest of the questions, none of which pertained to me, thank goodness.

As soon as Will closed us out, I moved as quickly and calmly as I could to my office. I accepted a few congratulations in passing but refused to stop to speak to anyone. I wanted to gather my things and get out of the building, but Will was the first person at my door. He closed it behind him and just looked at me.

"It's true, Will, but I don't want to talk about this right now. If you'll excuse me, I need to head out," I said with minimal eye contact.

"Let's talk tomorrow morning."

He opened the door, and I walked out into a crowd of questions. I felt like a famous actress trying to get through a mob of fans. I smiled and said, "I'd love to stay and talk, but I need to get going." I kept my legs moving until I finally found myself at my car. I got in and sped off, almost hitting a lamppost on my way out of the parking lot.

I drove to Johnny's practice and took a seat on an empty metal bleacher alongside the field. My head was swimming. What was Julia thinking telling the whole branch? If she was upset about not getting the job, go have a drink. Don't include me in her desperation. And how did she find out? Why must my life be so complicated right now? I watched Johnny make a catch, and I gave a weak cheer from the stands. He looked over and waved proudly.

"Aren't you going to ask me how my day was?" Johnny said on the ride home. I guess I took too long to ask.

"I'm sorry, J. How was your day?"

"I got an A on my math test!"

"Awesome! That's better than last time. I told you could do better with a little studying."

"Let's focus on the A, Mom, not the studying. I told my friends that I finally get to be a big brother. They were giving me pointers on what to do when I become a big brother."

"Oh, really. What kind of pointers?"

"Well," Johnny said, "if something breaks, say your little sister did it."

I told him that wouldn't work until she got older.

"Josh said I should sing to the baby while she's in your tummy, so when she's born, she'll know my voice, and she'll do everything that I say. And Ms. Miller overheard us talking, and she told me to tell you congratulations. She said I should help you and Dad as much as I can around the house and that will make me a good big brother."

"Wow. That's all interesting advice. Ms. Miller's is the best. You should ask *your* big brother what big brothers are supposed to do. Think about what he does for you and what you do together and that may give you a good idea."

"Sometimes he makes my lunch. He never lets me win at basketball. He plays video games with me. If I'm sad, he makes me feel better."

"He'll teach you everything you need to know."

We went back and forth jokingly until we reached the house. It was a nice mental break from the drama at work.

Dad arrived shortly after Johnny and I got home, and David and I got ready to go out for dinner.

We chose a small Thai restaurant, intimate but not formal. Perfect for a much needed date night. I shared the details of my day, and he was just as blown away as I was.

"I'm afraid they'll say that I won't be able to handle the position being pregnant and then having a newborn. They may go back and hire the next best person. I knew I would have to tell them eventually, but before I did, I wanted to show I could do well in the position."

"First of all, they can't disqualify you because you're pregnant. Second, our child will be a year or two old before there's evidence that you are good or not good in the position. All you can do is be honest and focus on what you bring to the table. You'll need some time off after the baby comes, and they have to give you at least the minimum six weeks, right?"

"I guess," I replied, feeling somewhat defeated.

"Listen. You interviewed for this position, and you beat out all the other candidates. Being pregnant does not change the level of expertise you bring to this position. You're a hard worker, and we'll do whatever it takes as a family to make you shine. You're going to sign the papers tomorrow. Julia's little diatribe won't stop the show. Now eat your curry. My child needs nourishment."

"You're right, babe. I've earned it." I devoured my curry and took in the serenity of the moment.

That night I was awake with my never-ending thoughts. I mentally rehearsed what to say to Brian and Lynn. I also rehearsed what *not* to say to Julia. I ended my midnight think session with a blabber session on my video diary. I closed the entry on this comment:

It just so happens that these two major events of life have coincided, and I'm ready and able to tackle them both.

For my morning commute, I chose some upbeat music to pump myself up for this day. It was supposed to be an exciting day for me, and I was confident it would be. I walked into my place of work, head up high, still deflecting questions about being pregnant, accepting all inquiries about the promotion, and ready to defend myself. I completed my usual routine of preparing myself for morning meetings and answering emails. I responded to Will's request to meet at ten. My game plan was to tell anyone asking about the baby that I'd share details later.

I made it through the nine o'clock meeting and went to Will's office.

He was on the phone. He motioned for me to have a seat as he walked to his door and shut it as he finished his call.

"Well, this is a turn of events. I know you didn't plan this. Please tell me this wasn't planned."

"You know me too well. I did not plan this, but I'm ready to move forward as both a new mom and AVP."

Will gave a big sigh. "I knew you would say that. How far along are you, if you don't mind me asking?"

"About 5 months."

"You've been holding this for that long?"

"I just found out a few weeks ago, around the same time I applied for the position."

"Your training technically doesn't begin until after your meeting with Brian and Lynn. Be the first to mention the pregnancy and tell them what you told me, as far as being ready to move forward in both roles." He leaned back in his chair. "You're a brave woman. This isn't going to be easy for you."

"I know, but it is what it is. And I am who I am. So I won't fail."

"They can't take the opportunity from you, but trust me, they will watch you like a hawk to make sure you're performing up to their standards. And that little show Julia put on yesterday, well, you can expect more. Be honest whenever there is something controversial that becomes public. The people will respect you when you come clean. And be prepared to say something, or they will put words in your mouth. The administrative part of the job isn't that difficult. It's the people part of the job that takes finesse."

"Thanks, Will. I've got to get ready for my meeting to sign myself into your seat."

He smiled and gripped his chair arms. "I'm taking this seat with me."

When I arrived at the restaurant, Lynn was at the same spot, on the phone, like our first meeting. She motioned for me to go in. I was more nervous today than I was any time during this whole process. I stood to shake Lynn's hand as she came in the door.

"Hello again."

"Congratulations, Lonnie. If this were an evening meeting, I'd treat you to a drink. That was Brian. He'll be here shortly."

We sat and placed our drink orders, nonalcoholic for both of us. We shared small talk about our families until Brian arrived.

"I gotta stop being the last one to show up. You all might start spreading rumors," he said. "Congratulations, Lonnie. We're very excited to have you as our next AVP at South Branch. You come highly recommended not only by Will but by those you supervise and others on your level of management."

"Thank you, Brian. There is one detail I'd like to make known before we get started. During this interview process, I found out that I am pregnant."

Brian frowned and Lynn gave me a puzzled look.

"I'm aware that this position and being the mother of an infant both carry heavy responsibilities, but I am prepared to move forward in both roles."

"Wow. I didn't expect the meeting to start off like this," said Brian as he pulled out his tablet. "Having a newborn will add complexity to your experience as AVP, but I don't doubt that you will be able to handle this." He slid the tablet over to me. "Here is your job offer and the salary we are proposing. Any negotiations will be handled here and finalized before we leave. Look over the document, and if there are items or terms you wish to negotiate, speak now or forever hold your peace."

I looked over the document, negotiated the salary and terms, and signed on the dotted line. We discussed my maternity leave. Brian recommended I take only six weeks, but he made it clear that I had a choice to stay out longer. He told me to follow-up with Will regarding who would cover me during maternity leave.

"It's our goal to help you be successful in your position.

If there is something you need to do your job better or to improve your branch, let us know sooner rather than later," Brian said, closing the negotiation part of our meeting and moving us on to enjoy our lunch.

When lunch concluded, we all stood, shook hands, and went our separate ways. It was done! I was the AVP! It didn't go south as I'm sure Julia hoped. Now, on to bigger and better things. I called David on my way back to the office to share the details of my meeting. He offered to take me to Guppies yet again, and I told him no thanks. My waistline expansion should be strictly due to pregnancy, not gluttony. I still needed to meet with Will again before closing out my day. His guidance during this transition would be invaluable.

Moving Up, Stretching Out

Will's formal promotion shindig was at a swanky restaurant downtown. The upper echelon in the company and branch leaders were invited. I had a hard time finding something to wear, but finally found something I could fit my second trimester body into.

About 20 minutes into the meal, Brian stood and tapped his glass to get everyone's attention. He congratulated Will and invited him to say a few words. Will, being the person he is, said more than a few words and managed to give me a little shoutout in his monologue.

The evening was a great opportunity to acquaint myself with people I had only seen cc'd in emails and mentioned in company publications. I was able to engage in conversations at strategic and casual levels and make memorable encounters with pacesetters and decision-makers in the company.

My last encounter of the evening was one that I was not expecting nor one that I would forget. I was standing in the lobby waiting for David to pull the car around when Julia entered the lobby.

We both faced the window, not speaking. I decided to take advantage of the awkward moment and air out the All Call situation.

"It was a great party, wasn't it. Will is leaving behind a great legacy that I plan to build on," I said.

"It'll be interesting to see the difference in leadership styles. I hope you can handle the added stress."

"I'm quite capable of managing home and work. This is a growth opportunity for me, and I plan on capitalizing on it. How did you know that I was pregnant, Julia, and why were you inclined to share that with our branch?"

"I go to the same office as you for my GYN care, and who doesn't get excited about new babies? I knew the branch would be ecstatic for you."

"I found it disrespectful, and it seemed there was a motive for you sharing that information."

"What were your motives behind concealing your pregnancy? I'm sure if the powers that be knew prior to the interview process, you would've been nixed from the list."

"Pregnancy nor parenthood hinder a good worker or leader from fulfilling their duties. If you thought sharing that information was going to hurt my opportunity, or increase yours, you were mistaken."

"Everyone knows you and Will are '*old friends.*' I'm sure that's what got you the position," Julia sneered.

"I leverage all my business relationships to find opportunities for growth or promotion, Julia. But my experience and skills are what got me the position. And my skills must be on point, because they gave the job to a pregnant woman."

And with that, I walked out to our car. David opened my door and, as I stepped into the car, I called out to Julia, "See you bright and early on Monday." She turned away from the window.

"So, you two best buds now?" David asked with a grin.

The more I thought about Julia's words, the more my blood pressure began to rise. The thing she said about handling the added stress lingered in my head on the drive home. It was not a question of *whether* I could handle the stress, but *how* I would handle it. Julia was trying to get a rise out of me, but she wasn't going to get it. She wanted to see me fail, but she would be disappointed. I was still in the driver's seat of my life, and I didn't intend to let anyone or any situation cause me to give up the keys.

I ended my night with a video diary session and then headed off to bed. David was waiting up for me. He told me how beautiful and powerful I looked tonight. I knew his words were sincere, but I was waiting for the smooth move that would lead to getting our groove on. And just like clockwork, he turned on the smooth, and we end the night in the groove.

My transition into the AVP position moved into phase two. Today was my first day on my own. It was packed with director meetings and interviews for my previous position as Director of Marketing. Naturally, I had to meet with Julia. She was scheduled at the end of the day, just in case I needed to fire her.

As my meeting with Julia approached, I tried to prep my mind and emotions so I wouldn't be caught off guard. She knocked on my door, right on time. I expressed to her what we would cover in our meeting and asked if there was anything she wanted to address before we began.

"I'd like to say that I apologize for any embarrassment I may have caused by sharing your news. I'd like to move past that and focus on the continued success of our branch."

You better had. "I appreciate the apology and accept it. I agree that focus on the work we do here is imperative."

And with that said, we actually had a productive meeting. Day one was in the books.

After dinner I sneaked away to video the details of my day. I was far enough away from my first video that I could go back and watch it and find humor in my despair. David occasionally sneaks on my phone and records a message to encourage me.

I slept well that night, which was a good thing, because my ligaments were beginning to cave in under the pressure. And given my advanced age, getting out of bed was a chore.

I hobbled into work late due to my slowed pace. I don't know if it's okay for pregnant people to use Bengay, but I smelled like a walking jar of menthol. I got a few jokes about my fragrance of choice for the day, but most people were sympathetic to my "condition." I failed to remember I had a meeting with the execs and a few directors from Main Branch this afternoon. I didn't have time to wash this stuff off and was sure using the hand soap in the bathroom to freshen up would be a little uncouth. Or would it?

I tucked myself into the car smelling of antibacterial flowers and headed to Main Branch. This meeting was simply to acquaint myself with this group and determine if there were any areas where we could collaborate. Main Branch handles all of the broadcast advertising, while South Branch focuses on print and outdoor advertising. Although I would love a collaborative project, developing myself as the leader of my own branch was my only priority right now. So this meeting was pointless. I popped back into the office for one more meeting before it was time to pick up Johnny from practice.

At home the guys had been brainstorming about where we were going to put the baby. At the moment our inn was at capacity, with each bedroom spoken for. Today's discussion involved closing off an area in the basement for a bedroom.

"So, who's going to do the work? That's a major construction project." This seemed pressing to me.

"We can use the guy who finished Lisa's basement."

"I don't know, honey. That guy was a little sketchy."

"Well, I could get a few friends together, and we could knock it out over a couple of weekends."

Now, I won't say this out loud because his sons are in the room, but my husband is not a handy person. And he rolls with a bunch of other non-handy men. Why he was posing this as an option was beyond me.

"Babe, you know this is not in your realm of strength. We need to just pay someone if we decide to go this route."

"I'm offended," he said with his hand over his chest like a Southern belle whose been insulted. "I've got the tools to get it done. And whatever I don't have, I know a few guys who might have access to what I need."

"Having the tools does not equate to doing the job properly and timely."

"I disagree with you. I think this will be a great bonding experience for me and the boys."

I dropped my head. "Given the short time frame, should you spend your time on a big project like this?"

"It's not that big of a project, Lonnie. I think we can handle it. We'll start this weekend. I'll have Jacob come over tomorrow to help me get measurements. He's good with that stuff."

Jacob is an architect of the computer engineering type, not the kind that builds structures. I was not in agreement with this! But David was already corralling the boys down to the basement. I heard them throwing around ideas. I hit the record button on video to capture this moment.

I'm going on record. This is not a good idea.

What a day. I lay my achy body down in my bed and for the first time, I addressed the girl in my expanding midsection.

"Everyone is excited for your arrival," I told the baby. "They have every right to make a fuss over you. But you and I know we have some unexciting, late nights ahead of us. But we'll have each other." I closed my eyes and fell sleep.

You're Not One of These 20-Something-Year-Old Moms

Lisa wanted to drag me all over town today to plan for the baby shower. As I searched for something to wear for this foray, I realized I did not have anything that fit. Maybe I'd better get in some retail therapy before Lisa came to pick me up. I threw on the only pair of sweatpants I owned and a t-shirt emblazoned with *Best Mom Ever* and headed to the car.

"Where you going, Mom? I thought Ms. Lisa was coming over," Johnny said as I was halfway out the door.

"Your sister is growing, and now I can't fit in my clothes. I'm going to go pick up a few things to wear. I'll be back soon."

I headed to the nearest chain store that had maternity clothing. I picked up several things and carried them to the dressing room.

"That's a cute top and I picked up those pants myself last week. They fit pretty nice," the lady attending the dressing room said. Her hair and makeup looked as if she had just come from a photo shoot. She walked from behind the small counter to hand me a hanger indicating the number of items I'd be trying on. You could see her cute little baby bump peeking through the same pair of pants I had over my arm.

"Well, I hope they fit me as well as they fit you."

"When are you due?"

"Beginning to middle of August."

"Well, you and I are in luck. The summer line for

maternity is the best. Preggos gotta be cute too."

I cracked a smile and headed back to the dressing room. She was correct about the pants. They felt fantastic. I quickly tried on the other items and was quite pleased. This preggo *will* be cute! Now I was ready to take on baby shower shopping.

Monday rolled around and this cute preggo walked confidently into the office with clothes that fit. My day ran long with meetings and a successful interview for my previous position. As I got up to leave, there was another knock on my office door.

One of the managers on a big account reported we had an unhappy customer who was threatening to take their business to one of our competitors. I got all the details on the situation and told the manager to pack up and go on home. I started two emails. One was to Will asking for advice on how to proceed and the other to Travis, the director over that department. I was upset now. I had met with Travis earlier and none of this was discussed. This issue now became the priority for my Tuesday.

As I lay in bed, I ran through tomorrow's itinerary in my head. I also recalled that I had an OB appointment. Aghhhh! I didn't have time for this! *No offense, baby girl*, I thought as I rubbed my belly. I had that glucose testing tomorrow. I hopped out of bed and left a sticky note on the fridge to remind me to take the glucose solution at the prescribed time.

I crawled back into bed and began planning how to address the issue with the customer. What does a pregnant person in leadership wear to convey power? Did I have anything in my closet that said, "You better fix this mess or you're fired"? I got out of bed again and raided my closet for something with a little authority. I pulled out a combo that would at least get me in the I'm-the-boss ballpark and then got back into bed, ready to close my eyes this time.

The meeting about our unhappy customer actually went well. Earlier in the year we had renewed a contract with a billboard supply company that unexpectedly raised its rates due to a supply shortage on their end. Every month we were paying more and more for supplies and passing that price increase along to our customer. Now that we understood the problem, we put together a game plan to redeem the customer's confidence.

I walked back to my office and noticed the unopened glucose solution on my desk. I went into panic mode because now I had to drink this stuff before I went into my appointment. I snatched the bottle and chugged it down.

My OB appointment was routine. Listening to heartbeat, poking around on my belly, and measuring the baby girl, all the usual. The doc asked about work and sleep and warned me to maintain balance and get rest. I was able to tell her that I actually felt pretty good, well, outside of the ligament stretching. Overall, she was impressed with how I was doing and sent me on my way, reminding me that I was to come back every two weeks now.

The last day of the school year was this week. I'd been so consumed with work, I had totally forgotten about DJ's middle school graduation. I couldn't believe he would be in high school next year.

"Do you want to go out for dinner after graduation, DJ?"

"Yes! Let's go to that place Dad took us after Johnny's tournament. Their food was so good!"

"I think that will be great. I'll check with your grandparents to make sure they are still coming."

The boys continued discussing their day. I could hear the excitement of summer break in their voices. Just when they've gotten old enough to do things for themselves and stay at home alone for an hour or so, we'd be back trying to find babysitters for every adult outing. It's like getting the go-to-jail card in Monopoly, don't pass Go, do not collect $200, and you can't get out until you get lucky or you've done your time.

You're Not One of These 20-Something-Year-Old Moms

All the grandparents and Mom Mabel were in attendance at the graduation. We cheered our big guy on as he walked across the stage. I couldn't help but be emotional. The next time I saw my first born walking across a stage to receive a diploma, he'd be graduating from high school and leaving me! That thought and the pregnancy hormones led to a short ugly cry when I got to hug my son after the graduation. So many milestones and emotions were going on in my life right now.

"Lonnie! Are you expecting?" gasped Pam, the mom of one of DJ's close friends.

"Hi, Pam. I actually *am* expecting. We'll add a little girl to our crew in a few months." I gave her friendly hug.

"Wow! You're more woman than I am, girl, having a baby at our age."

"Life happens. Gotta take it by the horns."

"Well, keep me posted. I want to make sure I get something for this special little girl. Are you going to stay home?"

"No. I was recently promoted, so I'll go back to work after maternity leave."

"Really, Lonnie? Girl, take it easy. You're not one of these 20-something-year-old moms with all that energy and good joints. Take time to enjoy your baby. I'll catch up with you later. Will DJ be going to the freshman prep sessions over the summer?"

"He will. I'll see you around, Pam."

This conversation, believe it or not, was not the only intrusive moment of the night. I got lots of looks from other moms. And there were the conversations where people couldn't maintain eye contact because their eyes were drawn to my bump. Mom Mabel had to check one lady who was standing a ways off from me and commenting on me being pregnant.

"Why are you worried about what's baking in her oven? You're just mad nobody's up in your kitchen," Mom Mabel said to this woman with a glare as we walked away.

When we made it to the restaurant, I told everyone to go in and I would be there in a minute. I sneaked in a video entry just to clear my head. I made it short and to the point. I stepped inside just as the family was being seated. Mom Mabel was in rare form. It always amazed me how well she performed under the influence. The boys get such a kick out her. We all did. The reality of having four generations at this table was real to me at that moment and so special.

Once everyone's belly was full, we gave our hugs and headed home. David and I spent some time with DJ before he went to bed, sharing with him how proud we were and our excitement about him going to high school. We embraced him for a long moment and then said good night. We gave Johnny some nighttime love and then headed off to bed ourselves.

I woke on Saturday morning to the smell of coffee, the sound of hammers, and the voices of my dad and David's dad. Two more people that should not be touching tools. I threw on my robe and headed down to the basement.

"Dads, what are you doing?"

"Fixing up DJ's room. What are you doing out of bed? Shouldn't you be resting?" asked my dad.

"I'm as rested as someone approaching the third trimester can be."

"What's your plan for getting to the hospital when you go into labor, Lonnie?" asked Jerry.

"We haven't discussed that yet, Dad," David interjected as he pulled a bent nail from a 2x4.

"If the baby comes while Mom is at home," said Johnny, "I'll call 911."

"You won't have to do that," said DJ, "I'll drive her to the hospital, 'cause it's not that far."

"You do realize you need to have a driver's license, don't you, DJ?"

"Grandpa, I watched this video of a kid Johnny's age driving. I've watched Mom and Dad almost every day of my life.

I'm getting ready to go into high school. I'd be a great driver."

"I'm not quite ready for you to be driving, DJ," I said. How about we leave that part up to your dad or grandpas. Please be careful with the tools everyone." With that I left them and went back to bed.

When I woke the second time, I lay in bed cherishing my sleep-in moment. Wouldn't be too many more mornings allowing this time, so I grabbed my phone and shot a quick video. I caught up on my podcasts and by then my brain was in active mode, shooting out signals to my muscles to get out of bed. Apparently the connection was bad, because my body was not moving. But what began to move was my belly. The little lady started kicking at the walls of her temporary dwelling place. The sleep-in moment was over.

The guys were taking a break and Johnny asked, "Mom, what's the baby's name going to be? We talked about it, but I don't think we picked one yet."

"Out of all the ones we've talked about, which is your favorite," I asked curiously.

"I like Jade. It's a cool name."

"Wow, I don't remember talking about that name."

"I know. She's a character on this game I play. What do you think?"

"I think I'll think about it."

We had thrown around a few names, but there was one I always came back to. My dad's name is Evan, and I'd been thinking about the name Eva. David and I talked about names that evening. I pitched the name Eva to David and he liked it. We agreed that her middle name would be my mother's name, Carolyn. I thought Eva Carolyn Peterson was perfect. So it was settled, that's what her name would be.

It was a lazy weekend. It's good to have those every now and then. As I prepared for my work week on Sunday evening, I began developing my maternity leave plan. Will would be onsite once a week and would approve budgets. Julia and Mike were the most senior people in my branch, so I was delegating most tasks to them. Things had been surprisingly smooth with Julia. Mike, I wasn't so sure about. I had a feeling he might skip out on me since he didn't get the AVP position. I'd hate to see him go since he did an excellent job. His department ran like a well-oiled machine.

I hadn't put any time into researching childcare. I couldn't leave my baby just anywhere. The best places had wait lists months long. I researched every daycare between work and home. I made a list of typical questions one might ask a daycare provider and added it to a list of daycare providers that might work for us. I shared the list and the questions with David and asked him to start calling for me. I regretted not putting more time into this crucial part of the plan. What if we couldn't get her into a good daycare? Maybe I was overreacting. It wasn't like we were applying for college.

On Monday between meetings, Mike stopped by my office and, just as I suspected, he had found another position and was resigning. I gave him my congratulations on his new venture, but when he told me he was going to work for one of our competitors, I got nervous since he was the Director of Creative Services with our company. I let him know that I wanted to speak with him again later that day. As soon as he left my office, I called Will.

"What do I do? He's good at what he does, and he has intimate knowledge of our branch's accounts."

"I doubt we can offer him more to stay than what the other company is offering, and we currently don't have any positions open that we could promote him to," Will said.

"I planned for him to be one of my fill-ins while I'm on maternity leave. Do you think we can offer him some type of incentive to stay until I come back? That's months from now. Do you think he'd bite?"

"It's worth a try. What do you have in mind?"

We discussed different incentives and later that day I explained them to Mike. He agreed to think the idea over and get back with me. I hoped I'd averted a crisis. On Friday, Mike agreed to our counter offer. He said he would stay on during my maternity leave and for two weeks after my return, making his departure the middle of October. Boom! I had a plan.

It had been weeks since my employee crisis in Creative Services was averted. Our new Director of Marketing was fully on board, and everything had been running smoothly. I was now in the thirty-fifth week of pregnancy, looking like I could give birth any day. I left my heels behind several weeks ago. I was allowed to park in a handicap spot, so I didn't have to walk so far. My branch jokingly offered to rent me a scooter, but my pride would never allow that.

My OB appointments were weekly now, and my OB was proud of how my 40-plus-year-old executive body was handling this pregnancy. The baby was growing just as she should and keeping me up at night as if she were already here. The room addition was coming along, and the electrical work was done. It looked like general contractor David should be done by B-Day. The countdown began.

Lisa and Jackie had been all in on preparing for the baby shower. They'd booked the venue, prepared the guest list, and were ready to party. David and I had chosen a daycare that had great reviews and a spot available the week I'd return to work. Everything was going the way it should. The way I planned.

The day has finally arrived. Baby Shower Day. David dropped me off at this posh restaurant, and I made my way to the room that was already buzzing with girly excitement. Baby shower games commenced, and the last few guests wandered in. Although this was exciting, I was uncomfortable today, the-end-of-pregnancy discomfort of a body just being tired and stretched to its limits.

I waddled around greeting as many people as I could, sneaking in the occasional snack here and there. This whole thing had been extremely fatiguing. I was ready to go home and rest. But I guessed the pregnant lady couldn't just up and leave with the guest of honor. After the last gift was opened, I stood to give my thank you speech, which I had prepared with a dramatic finish, tears and all.

Well, there was no speech, and I ruined my new shoes with amniotic fluid. I just stood there. Everyone else in the room was apparently just as shocked as I was. This wasn't supposed to happen for another two weeks! I'd never had my water break on its own, so this was a surprise for me. Restaurant napkins were being thrown at my feet, reminiscent of the palm branches being thrown at Jesus's feet when he entered Jerusalem. Lisa and Jackie grabbed my arms and practically dragged me out of the restaurant. I was about to walk into a serious situation, a 40-something mother of a newborn.

Someone shoved me into the back of Lisa's car. Jackie hopped into the front and called David. She told him my current situation and to get his behind to the hospital. She called her sister who was helping with the shower and gave her instructions on how to proceed. She turned and looked at me slumped in the backseat.

"You just couldn't wait, could you?" she scolded.

"I'm in labor here!" I said with a controlled forcefulness. The contractions kicked in, and there was no turning back. This child is coming and soon.

We pulled up at the hospital, and Jackie and Lisa got me out of the car and into a wheelchair. What a sight this had to be. Two excitable middle-aged women running through the ER with an equally aged pregnant woman in a wheelchair trailing amniotic fluid behind her. The ER staff did what they do and got me up to labor and delivery.

David arrived shortly after they got me in the room. I wished I could think straight, but that was impossible with the contractions. They hooked me up to the dreaded monitor that gauged your already decimated abdomen. It revealed a steady heartbeat and off the chart contractions. I had never been a screamer during labor. I thought I might make a different choice this time.

They checked my cervix. The nurse went running out of the room.

"What's wrong?" I yelled.

"It's fine, babe," David said as he grasped my hand and rubbed my head.

"Nurses don't run out the room if everything is fine!"

She quickly returned with another nurse who introduced herself and put on gloves.

"The doctor is on his way, but he may not get here in time. I know you are having very strong contractions, but I need you to try not to push."

"Have you lost your mind! I have no control over whether my body pushes," I yelled at the nurse through a strong contraction.

"I understand, but if you could . . ."

"Nurse whatever-your-name-is, I am 40-something years old. This vagina and uterus don't have the muscular integrity of somebody who's 20! Put your mask on and deliver this baby!"

She complied with my order, and three pushes later, a screaming baby entered the world. At that point, the doctor came into room.

"Looks like I missed all the action," he said. "I'm Dr. Jones. I'm on call this weekend. It looks like you have a baby girl here. The nurses are going to give her a look over, and I'm going to give you a look over while they're doing that. It looks like you usually see Dr. Branch. I'll be chatting with her shortly to let her know Baby Peterson has arrived."

David left me to go observe Eva. I lay there in the bed, my eyes closed, completely exhausted, ready to kick this doctor for pressing on my belly and demanding I push out the placenta. *Reach in there and get it yourself. I'm done.*

I opened my eyes and David was standing there with our daughter in his arms. His eyes were filled with tears of joy as he handed her to me. I held my daughter for the first time, a person I never expected to have in my life. She was beautiful. Not just because she was a newborn. We all know that every newborn is not beautiful. But she truly was. I held her close and closed my eyes. I felt David's face next to mine. All I could do was exhale.

The Awakening

I opened my eyes in the middle of the night to a faintly familiar sound. Before I could orient myself to what I was hearing, I became distracted by this nagging pain in my loins. It was all starting to become clear, that sound, this pain, OH MY GOODNESS, I JUST HAD ANOTHER BABY!

I stumbled out of the hospital bed, groping for the bassinet that I could not reach because my nurse left a blood pressure cuff strapped to my arm. As I reached for the bassinet, eyes half opened, I heard another familiar sound. A voice so deep and calming, speaking encouraging words. Could it be? My knight in shining armor, my wonderful husband of fifteen years?

Unfortunately not. It was my night nurse Joyce, with the little hairs above her lip.

"Lonnie, you better lie back down. I have the little one here. Just changing a diaper for you so you can rest. You look like you could use some more sleep."

I made my way back to the bed, grateful to lie down again. I began to recall how paralyzed with disbelief I was at the report of the doctor when she told me I was pregnant. I had thought I was going through menopause, so I'd gotten a little reckless. It had been so long since I'd had a baby. I'd started to panic because I wasn't really sure I remembered how to do anything. Joyce interrupted the melodrama being displayed on the back of my eyelids.

"Lonnie, I think the little one is hungry. Time to whip out the girls."

The *girls*. They'd been exclusively available to my hubby for the last fifteen years, minus years I breastfed the boys. What he does with the girls and what a baby does to the girls are polar opposites. The girls will miss you, honey. They'll see you in a year. There's no telling what they'll look like, but they'll be back.

I obediently popped out one of the girls to feed my baby. My brain dug deep to remember all the tricks to get a baby latched on, and Joyce was right in there with me like a third hand.

My breast was the size of this baby's head. I was really struggling with how this was going to work. Why was I drawing a blank? I'd done this before. A whole lot of times. Joyce grew impatient with my attempts to get this baby to latch on and took it upon herself to grab my frontal real estate, squeeze the darkened area around my nipple, and push it into the baby's mouth.

"I know it's been a while for you, but you gotta get back in the swing of breastfeeding. You make a 'C' with your first finger and thumb, with the thumb as the top of your 'C'. Then you put your 'C' over the areola and gently squeeze. Now you're ready to present the breast to the baby. You rub the nipple across the baby's lips to activate the baby's rooting reflex, which should lead to a latch and then sucking."

"Joyce," I asked with eyes still closed, "what time is it?"

"It's 3:40 a.m."

"Don't you think it's a little early for a tutorial on breastfeeding?"

"If you could see how poorly you were doing, you'd sign *yourself* up for my tutorial," she said with a little sass in her voice. As she walked out of the room, she added, "Don't forget to keep a record of when you feed her and when she has a dirty diaper."

Joyce wasn't out of the room more than thirty seconds before Eva lost her suction and out came the nipple. Now I was forced to put my tutorial to work. I followed all the steps, and Eva even tried to do her part, but she wasn't latching on very well. This went on for a few minutes, and then she began to cry.

"I don't blame you, little lady." And I started to cry too. I laid her on my chest and stroked her back in an attempt to calm her down enough to try again. I whispered in her ear, "We have to work together to be successful." I tried again to get her to latch on, but I'd soothed her to the point of sleep, and she was no longer alert enough to participate in feeding.

I looked down at my sleeping baby and recalled the words I've said to so many other new moms . . . enjoy every moment.

I opened my eyes, again, to that same sound. The weak precious cry of a newborn. I better enjoy this because once those lung muscles strengthen, she was going to sound like a toddler having a tantrum in the toy aisle. I'd spent the last forty eight hours feeding, eating, sleeping, changing diapers, caring for my postpartum body, and feeding again. Cooped up in these four walls with a baby and my thoughts. It helped that the room was large with dark wood floors and a soothing decor. My room faced the west, so I had a beautiful view of the downtown area from my window. But this was the last day I'd get to enjoy the view. The little lady and I would be busting out of here today. I turned toward the door in response to the "shave and a haircut" knock. It could only be one person.

"How are my girls?"

"Dad!" I sat up in the bed and received his big warm hug.

"How's she doing? How are you doing? Bet you never thought we'd be here again."

"Don't rub it in, Dad. I'm still trying to wrap my head around it. Did you just get off work?"

"I did. Stopped and picked up some coffee for you and

one of those chocolate raspberry scones you like from the bakery by your house."

"Dad, I don't think I should be drinking that coffee, but you can hand over the scone. You're the best, thank you." I scarfed down the delicious baked creation, crumbs flying everywhere while Dad perched at the foot of my bed.

"So when are they releasing you two to the world? Don't they make old people like you stay longer?" He chuckled at his own humor.

"Wow, Dad. I think I'm going to call the nurse and have you escorted out of here." I finished the last piece of the scone and made my way to the bassinet. I picked up Eva and walked back to the bed. I carefully exchanged the sleeping baby to the arms of her grandfather.

"This never gets old," he said as he looked at Eva and touched her nose and caressed her hands. "Seeing yourself reproduced over and over again. Another person to influence and train and send out to impact the world. I'm so proud of you guys. I'm blessed to have such a great daughter, son, and grandkids."

I put my arm around him. Our moment was interrupted by the door opening, and in came the most skilled pediatrician I know, Dr. Looneski. I know, the name sounds ridiculous, but he is the best pediatrician in the region. This was his third hospital visit with me following the birth of my children. He's been the pediatrician for both boys. A little loose with his words, but a good doctor nonetheless.

"Well, well, well. I didn't know you had any eggs left. Is this an immaculate conception?" He motioned to my dad to hand over the baby.

"Don't you have to knock when you enter a patient's room? I'm going to write a nasty comment about you on my satisfaction survey," I snapped back.

He reached over and gave me a quick hug. He laid Eva in the bassinet and looked her over. "Well, it looks like she's got all the necessary tools to be a female. What's this one's name?"

"Eva."

"Eva," he said, holding her up in the air, "you've chosen a great family. Your brothers are going to train you up right." He handed the baby back to her grandfather and sat on the couch across the room. "I spoke with your nurse and she said you're having trouble breastfeeding. Eva's weight is down, and that's normal right after birth. But to stay ahead of any additional weight loss, I'm going to have you see one of the lactation consultants when you come in for Eva's first follow up visit."

"A what kinda consultant?"

"Lactation consultant. We have one full-time in the office. I'm sure you haven't noticed since you've had no need for that service until now. She'll walk you through breastfeeding to make sure you're using a technique that works for you and Eva. You'll probably communicate more with her than with me the first month or so."

"Doc, forgive me for being blunt, but what else is there to know. Joyce has already given me a crash course. I think Eva and I just need some more practice."

"From what I hear, you need practice and a coach. Hence, I'm recommending the lactation visit." He stood and reached out his hand to shake my father's hand. "Congrats on another healthy grandbaby, Mr. Lee. See you in the office, Lonnie. I'll have the girls at the nurse's station set up your appointments with the lactation consultant and me. Do you have any questions?"

I was annoyed at this point, so my answer was "No."

"Great. Have a safe trip home. See you in a few days." And with that, he was gone. I loved him, but I hated him.

"Dad, you're on baby duty. I need a shower before we go home."

After my shower, Papa and Eva were asleep on the couch, so I climbed back into bed to catch a final snooze before I had to depart my maternity sanctuary. As I closed my eyes, I heard a light knock on the door and some voices I loved to hear. In came the rest of the men in my life.

My husband brought me a small white bag. "I got you one of those chocolate raspberry scones you like from the bakery by our house."

I smiled. "You're the best, thank you." I devoured my second scone. Doesn't get much better than this.

My dad and David were in the corner laughing about how David struggled getting the base to the car seat setup in the truck. The boys were showering their sister with love. Johnny was holding her for the first time, and DJ was barking orders on how to hold the baby. The nurse came in for the final time to get us out the door. I asked her to take a picture of us all. This was definitely a moment to remember.

It was three a.m. and the little one had decided it was now meal time. I already missed the nursing staff at the hospital. I picked up my bundle of joy and settled in for our three a.m. snack. Once we were settled, I shared a little secret with Eva.

"These three a.m. meetings don't work for me. Don't get used to this. Six a.m. will work better for me." Eva looked at me with milk dripping down the side of her face. I wasn't really sure she was drinking any of it. She lost suction and began to cry. My husband rolled over and sat up in the bed.

He rubbed Eva's head. "Hey, lady, cheer up. At least you're not me for the next six weeks." I kicked him beneath the comforter. "Oww!" he whispered.

"Do you think I'm doing okay, you know, with feeding her?"

"I'm no professional, Lonnie. It's only been four days. Give yourself and Eva some time. Maybe the doc is right. It won't hurt to have someone coach you through this."

He took the now wailing baby from me and walked around to the bassinet to change her diaper. "I know Eva was not planned like her brothers. That makes her extra special. Our lives are so structured, I think she came to shake things up a bit. I don't want you stressing about this breastfeeding. I want you to enjoy being a new mom again."

I wiped away tears and took the baby-fresh girl into my arms and got in position to feed her. I make my "C," squeezed the areola, swept the nipple across her cheek, and she turned the other way.

"Hey now," said David, "if you're not going to drink your milk, move over. I do recall that milk is sweet."

"Okay, you're fired. I'll rehire you in a few hours when you get some sleep."

I gave it another try, and we had success. "Finally," I sighed. I closed my eyes, hoping she would drink enough. My breasts were engorged. I looked forward to feeding time more than she did. Just not at three a.m.

David put Eva back in the bassinet, and we both rolled over to go back to sleep, but I was too consumed with thoughts to drift off. I guessed he was right. I shouldn't let breastfeeding ruin my new mom experience. I'd successfully breastfed two other children. I knew I could do this. Granted that was years ago.

I started to tear up as I thought about the visit with the lactation consultant. What if she said, "Give it up, middle-aged woman," or even worse, what if I wasn't making enough milk? I could start pumping milk, but I did that with DJ, my oldest child, and I made so much milk, the poor kid was choking every time I fed him.

The waterworks really began as I thought about having to use baby formula. I know nothing is wrong with that, but I'm a strong believer in breastfeeding and that mother's milk is the best thing for a baby. David felt the sobbing motions of my body and turned over and wrapped his arms around me. We didn't exchange any words. I just lay there in his embrace, sobbing. My tears eventually ceased, and we both transitioned into much needed sleep.

I woke a few hours later, minimally refreshed. I made my way to the bathroom, taking special care not to wake the sleeping child. I stood in front of the mirror horrified at the sight of my eye luggage and disheveled hair. I turned on the water and let it fill the sink bowl while I studied my face in the mirror.

Get it together, woman. You're no amateur. I bent over and scooped the water into my hands and gently splashed it over my face. As I wiped the water from my eyes, I glanced again at my face. I saw bewilderment and a sense of loss in my eyes.

"You're not a loser, girl!" I said fiercely and dunked my face into the water. I immediately came back up, water dripping everywhere. This time when I looked into my eyes, I saw determination. Satisfied, I went back to bed with the goal of getting as much sleep as I could and making this day mine. The baby blues had no place here. I had a baby to nurture and a life to reorganize.

I walked into the pediatrician's office on Friday with Eva in her carrier. I had forgotten how heavy and bulky those things are. Why didn't I bring the stroller? I needed a personal assistant. Shortly after I signed us in, we were escorted back to one of the treatment rooms. After Eva was weighed and measured by the nurse, in walked Dr. Looneski.

"Well, Eva," he said as he lifted the baby from my lap and laid her on the exam table, "you're not gaining your weight back at a rate that I like. Is your mommy feeding you?" he whispered loud enough for me to hear. "Has your milk come in, Lonnie?"

"Yes. And she's been eating regularly, just not long enough."

He lifted Eva off the paper-lined table and cradled her in his right arm. He turned to me with a serious look in his eyes.

"I know your stance on formula, and I respect the views of all of my parents. But you know that my patients come first. You may need to supplement your breastmilk with formula to make sure Eva is getting what she needs."

Eva started crying, and I began tearing up.

"Doc, I respect your opinion, but . . . "

He held his hand in the air to signify he didn't want to hear what I had to say. "I know we can get into a heated debate on this issue, but I need you to do more than respect my opinion. I need you to honor it."

There was silence between us for a few awkward seconds, then the wailing baby brought us out of the moment. He handed her to me.

"You have your lactation appointment directly after this appointment." He stood up and put his hand on Eva's head. "I know you'll be a chunky monkey the next time I see you, Eva." He patted me on my shoulder as if he were giving condolences. "See you next week, Lonnie."

The nurse came back in and gave me her little progress report and led me down to a room where I was to wait for the lactation consultant. There was a comfortable rocking chair with a rocking ottoman. I assumed this was for me and took a seat. I laid Eva across my lap and rubbed her back. She started to calm down. As I looked around the room, I saw a scale on a table, all kinds of pumping supplies, and nursing pillows. The room was cozy, the lights were dimmed. It all seemed right to get a little nap out of the situation. I closed my eyes and rocked us into a deep, calm state. Only to be interrupted by a professionally friendly voice.

"Hello, Mrs. Peterson, I'm Sandra, the lactation consultant," she said as she wiped sanitizer on her hands and then reached to shake my hand. "Can you show me what you've been doing and tell me about how long she feeds when you nurse her? Maybe there are some techniques I can share to make this easier for you two."

With that, we went into forty-five minutes of feeding, burping, positioning, and fondling my breast.

"Don't be offended by this, but it's been a decade or so since you've done this, and I'm sure it'll come back to you, but to reacclimate you to breastfeeding, I want you to go to our breastfeeding support group in addition to our sessions. The group is run by Mary, one of our nurses. She'll weigh the baby and answer any questions you have. This allows us to track Eva's weight to make sure she's gaining and to tweak your feeding sessions, if needed, to ensure Eva's getting what she needs. Mary usually does a little education for the whole group every time the group meets."

My bottom lip dropped to the floor. It's like I'm on probation! I just needed some practice, that's all.

"The socialization will be good too. Meet other moms, some that might be your age."

Okay, lady, now you're pushing the envelope. I'm two seconds from lighting you up with a poopy diaper.

"The group meets here every Tuesday morning at eleven. I'll see you next week, Mrs. Peterson. So glad to have the new Peterson here. Call if you have any questions."

And before she finished her last sentence, she was out the door. I was appalled. Breastfeeding is not something you forget how to do. All babies lose weight and gain it back within the first week or so. Why did she think this was necessary? Ugh. I should do what was best for Eva, and if the doc and this chick thought we needed this, we'd try it.

I knew my focus was supposed to be on this baby, but to take my mind off breastfeeding, I checked my work emails once I got us settled in the car. Most were the usual day-to-day communications, but there was one from Mike that was marked with high importance. I slumped down in my seat and grabbed my head in total disbelief. HE RESIGNED. After all that effort and extra money! I immediately called Will.

"Lonnie! How are you and the little one?"

"We're good, Will. Have you spoken with Mike? I got an email saying he's resigning!"

"Lonnie, I have been made aware of Mike's resignation, but I am not discussing this with you as you are on maternity leave."

"Will, I can . . ." He cut me off.

"You can enjoy your time with your newborn, and I will handle this situation. The only time I want you calling is to say hello. Tell David I said congrats. No worries, Lonnie, the branch will survive while you are on leave."

"Thanks, Will," I said in defeat.

"You're welcome. Talk to you soon."

Now I was angry. How did this make me look? I was gone one week and this dude bailed on me! If I see him on the street, he better cross over to the other side, because I'm going to take him out. This was a disaster. And there was nothing I could do. I hated this feeling. I didn't even know what to do to change my disposition. I drove home, emotions running high.

As I pulled into the driveway, the truck suddenly cut off and came to a stop halfway into the garage. I looked at the dashboard. The gas gauge needle was under the E. I never let the tank in my car get this low. Why did I pick this day to drive David's truck?

Now my anger and hopelessness turned to sorrow. All I could do was cry. I couldn't breastfeed, I couldn't lead at work, and I couldn't even pull my vehicle all the way into the garage. Eva joined me in the pity party and cried with me. I would have continued sobbing, but I couldn't endure her cries.

I got us out of the truck and into the house. I settled us on the couch and put my training from a few hours ago into practice. I dozed off during the feeding. Sometimes sleep is the best medicine. Thirty minutes later I opened my eyes. Eva was sleeping. I have no idea if she ate long enough. I was supposed to switch sides during our feedings. If she fell asleep, I was supposed to wake her and keep feeding. I didn't know what the rules were if I fell asleep, but I was breaking protocol. I carried the sleeping baby to her bassinet and laid her down.

I went to the home office and sat at the desk. I needed to get this out of my head or it was going to overtake me. Time for a recording session. Verbalizing my thoughts and feelings once again took the weight of the situation off my shoulders. I sat back in my chair and closed my eyes in an attempt to bask in the moment of release. I heard David and the boys come in. David was rushing to each room looking for me. He finally found me in the office.

"Are you okay?"

"I'm fine. What's going on?"

"The truck is halfway in the garage, and it's parked at an angle. Did something happen?"

"Oh. I totally forgot about that. It ran out of gas as I was pulling into the garage."

"I'm so sorry, babe. I've been driving the truck and didn't think to put gas in it. I'll run out and get some gas for it right now. Are you sure you're okay?"

"I'm fine."

"I'll take the boys with me. Do you want anything while I'm out?"

"No. Thank you."

"Okay. Call me if you think of something." He kissed me on the forehead and headed back out.

I returned to my moment of peace. Only for a second because Eva woke up again. The thought of maintaining this uncontrolled routine was growing more concerning. I couldn't keep this up and remain sane. Knowing it would get better as the baby grew older didn't help. I couldn't wait for that before I pulled myself together. If I didn't establish a sense of control, her infancy would reduce me to simply a purveyor of fine breastmilk and all-inclusive diaper changes.

I made a stop in the bathroom to revisit the mirror. One look at my tired face and I was reminded that no one was going to do this for me. I had to pull myself together and get my head in the game. I was well able to handle this.

I stood there and looked at myself until I believed the words, then I went to pick up my crying baby. I sat on my bed and got her latched on. After a few minutes when she tried to doze off, I woke her and switched to the other side. She ate for a good while, and this time when she dozed off, I was sure she'd had enough. I put her in the bassinet and then followed suit and went to bed myself to get some much deserved sleep.

My family had been preparing meals for us. Tonight David's parents were on kitchen duty. I woke from my much needed sleep to the sound of their voices down in the kitchen. I looked over in the bassinet. Eva was not there. I must have been sleeping really good if I didn't hear her. As I sat on the edge of the bed, David walked in with Eva.

"I kept her happy as long as I could. I wanted you to get some sleep. My parents are here working on dinner and the boys are working on laundry. Is there anything else we can do?"

"Not that I can think of. Thank you."

"When I came home earlier, it scared me to see you like that. I could tell you weren't yourself."

"I've got it together. At least for the moment. I just needed some sleep."

"When will you start pumping so we can help with feeding?"

"I can start now, but the thought of having to clean all that stuff and the bottles is overwhelming."

"I don't want you overwhelmed. Don't worry about washing bottles. There are plenty of hands around here that can do that. You're not alone in doing this. You don't have to push yourself to do everything you did with the boys." He grabbed my hand and looked me square in the eyes. "*We* can do this."

"We can do this," I repeated in an attempt to solidify the thought in my brain. "If you bring me the pump, I'll pump after I feed her. And she can go back down with your parents for a while if that's okay."

"It's okay," he said, reassuring me that it really was okay.

The BSG

It was Tuesday, ten thirty a.m. Eva had chosen to forget everything we knew about breastfeeding today, and I was frustrated. Not because she was having infant amnesia, but because I couldn't figure out how to gain control of this situation. I was contemplating *not* going to the support group since we had such a good weekend. But now I was frustrated again. This group might be my salvation. Maybe they'd teach me a trick or two I hadn't tried, and I wouldn't have to go back again. I'd go today, pick up the tips I needed, get Eva weighed, and I'd graduate and not have to go back.

I entered the pediatrician's office and followed the directions scribbled on a chalkboard sign positioned on the check-in desk. I went down the hall to a room in the back of the office. There was a sign with a silhouette of a breastfeeding woman on the door. It read "Breastfeeding in Progress."

I opened the door and found myself in a room with about twelve women. The group leader saw me come in and instructed me to sign in. I watched her as she weighed a baby and talked with the mom. I wrote our names on the sign-in sheet. There was an option to sign-up for a newsletter from the support group. I signed up. Maybe they'd have some good info in them that would keep me out of here.

I took a seat and looked around the room. I planned to beeline to the leader as soon as she was done with that mom. Maybe she could get me in and out. As I thought through my game plan, I got a tap on my shoulder.

"Hi. I remember those pants!"

I was caught off guard by that statement. Almost offended, as if some man just rolled up on me insinuating he's been in these pants.

"I think we met at my job. You were shopping for maternity clothes."

It started to come back. It was the pregnant lady from the store when I went on my impulse shopping trip.

"Yes, I remember you. These pants were a good buy. So, you had your baby too. Congratulations."

"Thank you. I did a few weeks ago." She held up her baby for me to see. "Her name is Scarlett."

Scarlett had on this audacious pink bow that was the size of her bald head.

"So, how does this work? Do I wait in line or wait for her to come to me? This is all new to me."

"Wow, I didn't think this was your first baby."

"Oh, she's not my first. She has two older brothers. But they are much older. I've never been to a breastfeeding support group, so I'm not sure what to do here."

"Well, this is my second time coming. It's pretty cool. Mary weighs all the babies and answers any questions you have, then we sit and share anything new that might be going on with our babies. Mary or another mom may give advice on what to do. I'm sure you have a ton of knowledge you can drop on us."

"I'm hoping I don't need to come back."

Scarlett began to get fussy. As her mom put on a blinged out nursing cover, it dawned on me that I didn't know her name. "I'm Lonnie. I don't think you've shared your name."

"I'm Sasha." She fumbled under the nursing cover to get her baby latched on.

I looked around the room to see if there was anyone else familiar. As I scanned the room, my attention went to the sound of a choking baby. There was a younger lady across the room whose baby had milk running all down his face. He was coughing to clear his little lungs. A lady who could be the baby's grandmother was there and slightly panicked, rummaging in a bag for a cloth to wipe the baby's face. My heart melted as I saw the desperation in the mom's eyes. In my mind I returned to the moment I held a baby choking on milk that flowed too strongly from my breast. But unlike her, I sat alone with my oldest child, not knowing what to do and having no real support.

I heard Mary call for Eva. I picked up my baby and made my way over to the scale and changing table.

"Lonnie, correct?"

I nodded.

"Strip her down please. I want to weigh her without the diaper. How has feeding been going?"

I shared our difficulties and how our feeding sessions were very short. She asked me to feed her during the group session so she could see how Eva was latching on and then she'd weigh Eva once more to see how much she drank.

"All right, mommies, let's get started." Mary took a seat near her changing table workstation. I took a seat near Sasha, who was deep in conversation with another mom. I glanced at the young lady with the choking baby. She was looking to Mary with her baby boy laid across her lap, all tuckered out from feeding.

"We have a few new moms here, so we'll go around and introduce ourselves and our babies."

A well-put-together woman across the room stood with a baby that looked like he was close to being able to walk.

"Hello, everyone! I'm Tish and this is Micah. He just turned seven months a week ago. I have twin girls and another son. I'm a great resource for any new moms in the room. Welcome."

I checked out of the introductions for a moment as Eva began to get restless. I broke out my black, no-frills nursing cover and got Eva ready to feed. Mary caught me out of the corner of her eye and came rushing over.

"Keep going with the introductions. I'm going to assist Lonnie for a minute," she said as she peeped under my cover. She watched the latch, gave me a thumbs up, and scurried back to her seat. Once Eva was sucking, I turned my attention back to the introductions. The next mom had one foot up on the chair next to her, breast out in the open as she fed her baby.

"My name's LeeAnn, and this is Wind. He's my second child."

Wait. Did she say Wind? Who names their baby Wind? I couldn't even focus on her introduction secondary to her flashing us all with her breast and exposing her crotch with her foot up in the chair next to her. And this woman was not young. She looked like she was closer to my age.

Sasha leaned over, "Did she say Wen, like short for Wendall?"

"No. She said Wind, like *Gone with the Wind*."

Sasha had a confused look her face. I nudged her because it was her turn for introductions. She introduced herself and held up her daughter for everyone to see. The only thing you really could see was the bow and her shiny bald head.

It was my turn. "I'm Lonnie. This is Eva. She was born last week. She has two older brothers."

"How old are they?" asked Tish from across the room.

"My oldest is thirteen and my middle child is ten." I got a few stares as if I had to explain the enormous gap between my kids.

"Did we get everybody?" Mary asked.

"I haven't gone yet." It was the young lady with the choking baby. "My name is Grace, and this is Jackson. He's three weeks old."

"Well, welcome to all our newcomers and welcome to all our faithful veterans. Anyone have an issue with their little one they want to throw out to the group?"

Grace sheepishly raised her hand. "Jackson did okay the first week and a half, but now every time I feed him he starts choking. The pediatrician said I probably have a strong letdown. I don't know what that means. She just told me to come here and see the lactation consultant. This meeting was first, so I'm hoping I can get some help." She started to tear up.

"This is called overactive letdown. The milk comes out forcefully in large quantities. It's difficult for the baby to drink that much milk that quickly," Mary explained. She instructed Grace and the group on a few techniques to overcome the overactive letdown.

After the discussion, I returned to have Eva weighed. Mary informed me that Eva drank two ounces. Mary instructed me to make sure she was feeding about every three hours. After I got our things ready to go, I couldn't help but reach out to Grace. I walked over to her and introduced myself.

"Grace, right? I'm Lonnie. I just wanted to let you know that I had the strong letdown with my oldest son. It was difficult. But as he got older and my milk supply stabilized, it got better. Definitely try those techniques Mary recommended. Don't quit." She thanked me and I thought she looked a little hopeful.

"So, will I see you next week?" asked Sasha.

"I don't know. We'll see how this week goes. It was good to see you again."

I got Eva settled in the car and sat for a minute mentally recapping my support group experience. I had mixed feelings. Honestly, it was refreshing to know I was on the right track with feeding this little girl. Those little weight checks and Q&A with Mary without having to pay a copay would be priceless. But having to endure frontal nudity and conversations that didn't necessarily have anything to do with my situation for an hour of my life every week seemed a questionable use of my time.

I headed home, making sure I pulled the car completely into the driveway. I got us both into the house and headed to the office to recap my support group experience in my video diary. I mentioned my reunion with Sasha, the baby named Wind with the flasher mom, and Grace with her son Jackson. I hit my red button when Eva began crying.

I picked her up to cuddle on the couch. Looking at her little face, I thought about how selfish I'd been since she'd been here. Just interacting with her out of necessity and not because I adored her. This was my daughter. Our attachment to each other started here and now.

"I love you, little princess," I whispered and kissed her nose. She passed gas and gave a little smirk.

A few days later there was an email from the support group. The message contained a recipe for lactation cookies and encouraged everyone to come out next week. I thought about it briefly and then moved on to checking my work email. I noticed that Will had given Julia some added responsibilities. I hoped she was enjoying it. I'd be back soon. The thought of returning to work triggered me to think about daycare. I hadn't contacted the daycare provider to let them know I needed Eva to start two weeks earlier than I expected.

I quickly called the SmartStart Early Learning Center. When I explained my need to bump up my start date, I was told my original start date was the earliest they could take Eva.

My brain went into overdrive. Did I extend my leave, look for another daycare provider, or have David take some leave? Just then I got a call from my dad. He could hear the concern in my voice and asked what was troubling me. I shared the daycare situation with him.

"Honey, I'd be glad to keep her for a few hours those two weeks. I don't want you stressing. Just give me a few hours to catch a nap, and then I can come over."

"Are you sure, Dad?"

"Anything for my girls. Let's talk about it closer to that date, okay."

"Dad, what would I do without you?"

"No need to wonder. I'll always be here for you."

That man is priceless.

As the week went by, I got cabin fever and decided Eva and I were getting out. Maybe I'd buy her one of those oversized bows that Sasha's baby wore. I totally was not going to do that! People peep into your baby's car seat to see a beautiful princess and all they can see is this big bow with rhinestones all over it. I really needed to pick up more diapers and a few other household items. I could send David, but it was time Eva and I had an outing. My world was feeling restricted with just driving back and forth to the pediatrician and checking emails.

After breakfast and micro managing the guys in the basement, I got Eva dressed, packed our bag as if we were going on a day trip, and headed out to the baby store.

The diaper aisle was my first stop. Store brand, name brand, organic brands, even cloth diapers were displayed. There was a day when I'd have gone for a cloth diaper, but I'm not that committed anymore. Maybe if I chose the organic diapers I would get the best of both worlds. I threw a pack of organic diapers in the basket. I also needed more nursing pads. The last thing I wanted was an involuntary entry into a wet t-shirt contest.

"Lonnie!"

I turned at the sound of my name and saw Sasha. She waved me down. I made my way over to greet her. Another lady I remember seeing at the support group was with her.

"We keep running into each other around here. Do you live close by?" Sasha asked.

"I live about ten minutes from here."

"I live a little further out, but the store discount makes it worth the drive. Looks like you have a sleeping beauty," she said as she peeped into my carrier. There was no point in me peeking into her carrier because there was a bow blocking any view of her child.

"I don't think I met you at the support group, but I remember your face. I'm Lonnie," I said to the other woman.

"Hi, Lonnie. I'm Rachel."

"Rachel and I work here. Our coworkers had gifts for us, so we both swung in today. What brings you in?"

"Just picking up some basics."

"Have you decided whether you'll come back next week? You should come. It's good to socialize with other moms. And you get to make sure your baby is growing and healthy. For free!" said Sasha.

"She has a good point," Rachel chimed in. "Our insurance sucks, so any opportunity to get free preventative care, I'm first in line. I'll be there every week. I want to be successful at this breastfeeding. Everything I've read says it's the best for our babies."

"It's settled. We'll see you on Tuesday, Lonnie," said Sasha.

I didn't recall agreeing to anything. But what else was I doing besides being a 24-hour breastaurant.

"Well, I thought my peer pressure days were behind me, but maybe I'm mistaken. I will likely see you all on Tuesday," I said.

"Awesome! Oh, Lonnie," Sasha said pointing at my basket, "those organic diapers leak some kinda terrible. I'd go with the store brand. They're just as good as the brand name diapers and way better than this organic brand."

"Thanks for the advice. I'll change them out." I dropped my nursing pads in my basket and headed back to the diaper aisle.

Back at the home front, DJ's room was ready for move-in, so I joined them in the basement as they carried his furniture down.

"Wow, DJ, you'll be down here all by yourself," I said.

"It's a rite of passage, Mom. I have to be able to prove myself in the basement to prepare for my own place when I graduate high school," said DJ with great confidence. His dad snickered.

"Living in your parent's basement is not an indicator of whether you're ready to live on your own. We have plenty of time for rites of passage, but this is not one of them," David assured DJ.

"So when DJ graduates, I get to move into this room, right?" Johnny asked.

"There's no need for you to move down here. You have a room upstairs," said DJ.

"You don't need a room if you don't live here," Johnny said with a little agitation in his voice.

"Whatever, J. Mom and Dad will always save me a room, and this will be it."

"Actually, I planned on turning it into a workout room the day I drop you off at college," David said with all seriousness in his voice.

"Dad!" the boys said simultaneously.

"Okay, everyone. To celebrate the completion of DJ's room, we're going out to dinner tonight. Where do you want to go? I want Guppies for dessert," said David.

"Can we have pasta for dinner?" asked Johnny.

"Sounds good to me. Go upstairs and get yourselves cleaned up," David instructed. "You headed out early this morning, Lonnie. What did you and Eva buy?"

"I just needed to get out. I was feeling like I was on house arrest."

David laughed.

"I forgot to tell you that the daycare can't take Eva two weeks earlier, so my dad said he'd watch her for those weeks."

"Well, okay. Are you sure about that?"

"What else are we going to do? It wouldn't be worth it trying to find another daycare provider for two weeks. He's off during the day, and he offered."

"Let me see if my mom can help him out for those two weeks, and I can flex my schedule so we can make it work. Do you want my mom to come over one day next week so you can go out by yourself for few hours?"

"I think I should take you up on that offer. Maybe I'll take Wednesday. I go to the probation, I mean the pediatrician's office, on Tuesday for the breastfeeding support group."

"So you decided to go back?"

"Yeah, it a free check-up, so why not?"

"I think it's a good idea to keep going. Can't hurt."

"I know it's a good idea. Maybe it's just pride that makes me resent it. And the thought of giving Mary peep shows every week doesn't excite me."

"I'd like a peep show." And the wet t-shirt contest began. I wish my breasts knew the difference between a hungry baby and a horny man.

Before we got to the restaurant, I had David stop at a grocery store. We'd forgotten Eva's pacifier, and I wanted to enjoy this outing. I ran in and grabbed a pacifier. While I was in the checkout line, there was an argument brewing near the entrance to the store. A lady with a baby was sitting on a bench, and the store manager was trying to calm the lady.

"Ma'am, I respect your rights, but we have customers complaining," pleaded the manager.

"That's not my problem. And if you want me to deprive my child of nourishment because of a few insecure customers, I'll make sure the city and the media hear about your insensitivity toward a mother feeding her baby," the lady retorted.

I recognized the lady. It was the flasher from the support group with the baby named Wind. I paid for my pacifier and hurried over to the scene.

"Hi there. Is there anything I can do to help?"

"This manager is committing an act of discrimination by refusing to allow me to feed my baby in this store."

"Ma'am, I am not saying you cannot breastfeed your baby in the store. I'm simply asking that you cover up. We have customers who are uncomfortable with you exposing yourself and there are *children* in the store," the manager said discreetly.

I dug in my diaper purse and pulled out my nursing cover. "I know you don't own one of these, but you can borrow mine. Just use it so that you can finish feeding Wind, and this gentleman can leave you to your breastfeeding," I said as I handed her the nursing cover. She must not have recognized me until I mentioned her son's name. She looked at me and reluctantly took the cover.

The manager thanked us and quickly walked away.

"I shouldn't have to cover anything. I'm just feeding my baby," she said with frustration in her voice. "I remember you from the support group, but I missed your name."

"It's Lonnie. I didn't catch yours either."

"LeeAnn."

"I'll see you Tuesday, LeeAnn. I can get the cover then."

"Thanks," LeeAnn said as she draped the black cloth over her shoulders.

I left her there and headed back to my family. All I could think of was how she has tits of steel to breastfeed in public with no cover. I knew it was a controversial topic, but I'd stay on the safe side of the controversy. I respected her position on breastfeeding, but I didn't want to see her breasts, and I breastfeed!

I got in the car and we headed off to dinner. I kept the incident to myself as a conversation about exposing your breasts in public seemed an inappropriate topic to share over dinner with one's family. But I for sure completed a video diary entry on the situation, sharing my opinion on the matter.

New School Playdates

I was actually eager to go to the support group when Tuesday came. I wanted to know how the grocery store incident ended. I also was hoping the young lady with the overactive letdown would be there. I couldn't stop thinking about her. The despair on her face was imprinted in my memory. I had walked in her shoes, and I knew how discouraging that season was for me. When I arrived, Tish was getting everyone's attention.

"Good morning, mommies, Mary is in a consultation and running a few minutes late. I thought I'd get us started today. It doesn't look like we have anyone new, so we'll skip introductions. Are there any topics anyone wants to share?" Tish asked.

"I have one," said LeeAnn. "What is it with people complaining about breastfeeding in public? It's legal, it's natural, and why should feeding a child be seen as offensive?"

"I'm assuming you've had this experience," said Tish. "Did you use a nursing cover? I notice you don't use one here."

"No, I did not use a cover, because I'm not required to. No one is telling the chicks with the see-through tops and push up bras to cover up. They'll pay money to see that, but when a mom is feeding her baby, they want you to cover up," LeeAnn said passionately.

"Well, my personal opinion is that moms should be discreet when nursing in public," said Tish.

"You mean discreet like our friend over here," LeeAnn

points to Sasha, who has a nursing cover that could double as a disco ball it had so much shine. "There's nothing discreet about that."

"We should probably move on before this turns into a political debate," said Tish.

"Well, I'd like to comment," I interjected. "I think all of us feel strongly about the necessity of breastfeeding or we wouldn't be here. Maybe I use my cover out of insecurity about my own body. I only want trusted people to see that part of me. Okay, I only want my husband to see that part of my body."

"I am in no way insecure. It's just right not to expose yourself," Tish piously replied.

"Why is feeding a baby seen as an exposure of your body? Breasts have glands that produce milk. Babies can only drink milk in the early months of life. It seems to me like the breast and the baby go together. And they don't go together when it's convenient for everyone around us. They go together when a baby signals it's time to eat!" LeeAnn protested.

"We all have our own thoughts and practices when it comes to breastfeeding, but we shouldn't impose them on others. And with that, is there anyone else that has a topic they'd like to share?" Tish asked, putting an end to the topic of public breastfeeding.

"You can always carry a copy of the laws stating your right to breastfeed in public," said Rachel.

"Moving on," said Tish. She signaled the lady sitting next her to speak as she raised her hand.

"Has anyone tried any of the organic diapers? I'm concerned about the chemicals in the regular diapers," she said.

"That's a great question, Bobbi. Does anyone have any experience with the organic diapers?"

"I've never used organic diapers, but if they can hold as much fecal matter as Tish, I'd try them," said LeeAnn. "Why are you here anyway? Your kid is like two."

With that comment Tish rose from her chair, looked around the room, and turned to LeeAnn and said, "I will have you know that I have supported this group with every child I have brought into this world. I am the most experienced mother in this room when it comes to breastfeeding, and I've earned the right not only to be here but to lead when necessary."

"You're not the most experienced mother in the room. Lonnie is," retorted LeeAnn. Everyone in the room turned their attention to me.

"Well, take the floor *most experienced* mom," Tish said angrily, staring me down.

"I don't profess to be the most experienced mom in the room, but to answer your question regarding the organic diapers, I've heard they leak." Everyone continued to look in my direction as if I had more to offer. Then Mary came in. "And here's Mary. Who'd like to have their baby weighed first?" I asked, directing everyone's attention away from me.

"I apologize for being late, ladies and babies. What'd I miss?"

"Just talking about public breastfeeding and organic diapers," Sasha chimed in.

"Those are great topics. NIPing is always a fun one. Who's up first? I won't have time to do our usual group discussion, but I'll chat with everyone individually during weigh in. Good thing you all started out with that."

"I got us started, Mary. I wanted to make sure we maximized our time together," Tish said proudly.

"Thanks, Tish."

"Wait, Mary, what's NIPing?" asked Rachel.

"Nursing in public."

The lightbulb went on for everyone in the room.

Sasha and Rachel, well mainly Sasha, begin whispering about Tish. I noticed Grace was having trouble again. Her little man was choking on that milk. I walked over and sat next to her. Eva had fallen asleep during the dramatic discussions, so I left her on the other side of the room in her car seat.

"Have you tried expressing some of the milk right before you put him to the breast?"

"It works sometimes," she said with discouragement.

"And have you fed him sitting up so his head isn't back while he's drinking?"

"Not all the time."

"Are you pumping milk?"

"Yes. I want to make sure I have enough stored up for when I go back to work."

"That might be part of your problem. You may be overproducing and the baby can't handle all that milk. What might help is pumping out the first bit of milk and then putting him to the breast. Then he won't have to overcome that initial letdown. When he's done, then you can pump whatever is left."

"That sounds like a lot to do every time."

"It is, but he's worth it. He grows every day. A few weeks of that, and he may be able to take the letdown, and you won't need to do all of that."

She looked at her baby with tears in her eyes, "He is worth it. I'll try to do it every time."

"Is there anything else bothering you? Do you have the baby blues?"

"I've got the life blues. His dad is denying that he's the father. I had to take a semester off from school, and I don't see how I'm going to finish. I think I've lost my scholarship and how does somebody go to school and be a mom? My job didn't have maternity leave, so I'm currently not working." Tears were streaming down her face now.

"Grace, I haven't dealt with all that, but I can tell you that things have a way of working out. It won't always be easy, but you must keep your eyes on what's important in your life. It sounds like your son and finishing school are important, so keep those things firmly in mind."

"Thank you, Lonnie." She moved Jackson into a sitting position on her lap and attempted to feed him again. This time with success as he happily sucked at his mom's breast. I wrote down my number and left it with her, "Call me if you have any questions or just need to talk." I headed back over to Eva and began to gather our things.

"We're having a playdate on Friday. You wanna come?" asked Sasha.

"Playdate? They can't even hold their heads up or roll over to look at each other."

"It's the exposure that counts. You have to start them early. Come on, it'll be fun." I was feeling the peer pressure again.

"I'll let you know tomorrow."

"If I don't hear from you, I'm going to call you," threatened Sasha.

LeeAnn was finishing up her visit with Mary. She caught my attention as I was packing up. "You wanna go get some tea? I know a great place a few blocks from here."

I have to be honest. All these new relationships were overwhelming. Relationships with people require time and commitment, neither of which I was prepared to give. But when I thought about my relationships prior to this baby, none of them were new. They all had history. Maybe I should embrace all this newness and open myself to experience new friendships. "Um, sure. As long as you don't get me arrested for indecent exposure."

"Very funny. The place is called Hot Spatula. I'll text you the address. What's your number?" I gave her my number and we packed up Wind and Eva and drove separately to the cafe.

Hot Spatula turned out to be a quaint, earthy little place. I could see why LeeAnn would choose this spot. We chatted and laughed for about an hour, sharing surface level info about our lives, kids, and husbands. I left there with that excitement you feel when you start something new. LeeAnn was older than most of the other ladies in the group but a little younger than I. Her perspective on life seemed so different from my own, but that intrigued me.

When we said goodbye, I added that I would see her next week. I had to laugh at her reply.

"I'll be there. Somebody's got to put that chick in her place." Referring to Tish, of course.

Back at the Ponderosa, the boys had just returned from school shopping with their dad. The start of a new school year was always an exciting time. Especially with DJ going off to high school this year. As they showed me all of their supplies, Johnny finished up a sandwich, leaving the crust on the plate.

DJ said, "Eating the crust is a sign of maturity, Johnny. You see how I ate *all* of my sandwich. One day you'll realize the crust is quite delicious."

"Speaking of maturity, Eva is going to be three weeks old this week." David picked her up from her bouncy seat and sat on the couch with her. "What did you do today, little lady?" he asked Eva.

"She was invited to her first playdate this Friday."

"Playdate? What does an infant do at a playdate?"

"I have no idea."

"No boys at this *playdate*, right?"

"Not this time, just girls."

"So, are these other moms from 'the group'?"

"Yes. They're younger, first time moms. I guess I fit in their category since it's been so long since I've had a newborn."

"It's good for you and Eva to get out. Just make sure their babies aren't sick. I don't want my princess under the weather," he said as he kissed her little feet.

"Oh, did your mom let you know if she can help my dad watch Eva the first two weeks I'm back to work?"

"Yes. She said she can do Thursday and Friday both weeks."

"Awesome!"

"She also offered to watch her some the week before you go back so you can get prepared to get back into the swing of things."

"That will work. It'll take me some time to get through emails and meetings with Will to get me up to speed. Wow, I only have about three weeks left. I need to touch base with

Will and schedule a few phone meetings before I get back in the office."

I sent a quick email to Will requesting two phone meetings the week before I return and asked how things were going in the office. If I really wanted to know, I could ask Leonard, but that was a door I did not care to open. Will quickly responded with two dates and times he was available that week and assured me everything was going fine. However, he divulged no details regarding the office. I accepted the meeting dates. Eva was beginning to fuss.

I sat next to David on the couch and took Eva from his lap and put her to the breast. Much to my surprise, she latched on the first try. Breastfeeding had improved, but it still wasn't seamless. She popped on and off the nipple and didn't eat as long as she should have. This made her fussy. We'd started introducing the bottle a day or so ago and that was looking promising. I wanted to keep breastfeeding, but I knew when I went back to work that it was going to be hard to maintain. I did have some pumped milk stored up. I'd probably rev up my pumping sessions over the next few weeks to stay ahead of the inevitable drop in milk supply. For now, I was just going to enjoy this moment of success. I had three more weeks before I had to think about maintaining a healthy milk supply.

"Babe, I also forgot to tell you Mom Mabel is coming by after church on Sunday to see the baby. Aunt Madeline will be coming with her."

"How are they going to get here since neither one of them drives?"

"Lizzie isn't working this weekend, so she's bringing them."

"Wow. That's big for Lizzie."

"I know. Being within inches of either of her aunts shows her counseling dollars have paid off."

"Well, I'll be glad to see them."

David laughed and got up from the couch. "What does my family want for dinner?"

"Hamburgers!" shouted Johnny.

While David started prepping for dinner, I took Eva upstairs to her room and laid her in her crib. I sat in the rocking chair in her room and closed my eyes with the intention to get a little cat nap, but my phone chimed. A text message from Sasha with details about the playdate.

I put the phone down and closed my eyes only for the phone to chime again. More details from Sasha. This time I turned the ringer off. I rocked a little in the chair and felt my body relaxing into sleep mode. Then Eva began to stir and proceeded to cry. I reached for her pacifier and quickly put it in her mouth. That did the trick. This time I succumbed to the relaxation and actually make it to sleep mode.

"Mom," DJ whispered as he tiptoed into the room. I open one eye and glared at him. "Dad wants to know if you want bacon on your burger."

"That's fine," I whispered back. He tiptoed out of the room and then yelled downstairs to his dad about the bacon on the burger. Once again Eva stirred, but she stayed down. I closed my eyes again, determined to catch a few minutes. And I did, but only a few. Dinner was ready, and Eva was done napping.

We closed our evening together with hamburgers, a movie, fun conversations, and expectations for the upcoming school year. After the boys went off to bed, David and I lay in bed and chatted about our kids, our family, and how much we loved each other. I loved our pillow talk moments. No matter how dark some periods of our marriage may have been, despite our personal lows and during glorious highs, we were committed to this marriage and knew that what we did together would be better than anything we would do apart from each other.

It was Friday. I agreed to attend the playdate, and I was lying in bed wondering why I agreed. Eva wasn't even a month old. This was silly. I'd only had two hours of sleep. Eva was up and down all night. David tried to help, but she calmed so much better with the boob, and we just wanted to get back to sleep. Now he was up getting ready for work, and I couldn't go back to sleep. Since my mind wouldn't cooperate with my eyelids and go to sleep, I added my adventures from the week to my video diary. I spent a long time breaking down my theory on playdates.

After the menfolk headed out for the day, I began preparing Eva and myself for the playdate. The thing that bothered me the most about this was that it was similar to a real date. You had to consider what you were going to wear, what you were going to say, and a scenario that would give you an excuse to exit if things went south. Too much pressure.

I picked out our outfits, fixed our hair, topped off Eva so I didn't have to feed her while we were there, and got us out the door.

Today's playdate was at Sasha's house. As I pulled up to the address she sent me, I checked it twice because I'd arrived in one of those posh neighborhoods with ultra-manicured lawns and only foreign cars in the circle driveways. I got Eva out of the car, walked up to the double doors, and rang the bell. A lady I'd never met answered the door. Now I was sure I was at the wrong address.

"I'm sorry. I might have the wrong address. I'm looking for Sasha," I said with reservation. It dawned on me I didn't even know her last name!

"You're at the right home. Come in. Are you Lonnie?"

"Yes, I am."

"You can leave your shoes here. There are slippers there if you don't prefer to be barefoot."

As I looked around this beautiful home, my mind was spinning. Did Sasha only work to support her shopping habit? But in a home like this, how bad was her habit? After I slipped on my complimentary slippers, the lady escorted me to Scarlett's nursery. The room was something out of a magazine. Lavender, silver, flowers (fresh), and toile everywhere.

A beautiful crib was in the center of the room on a faux fur rug (I think it was faux) with a mobile hanging over it that resembled a chandelier. There was a play area in one corner of the room. Sasha and Rachel were sitting on the floor with the babies lying on the rug in that corner. There was a small tea cart with beverages and scones.

"Hey, lady, glad you could make it." Sasha got up, took my free arm, and walked me over to the corner.

"Your home is beautiful," I stammered.

"Thank you. Rachel just got here. You want a snack? You don't have any allergies, do you? I can have Marie get you something."

"Whatever you have is fine."

"Cool. What have you and Eva done today? Scarlett and I went to get her christening dress. Do you want to see it? It's gorgeous!" She took Rachel and me to this walk-in closet that could double as a spare bedroom. She presented this white gown that looked like a mini bride's dress. Ruffles, satin, and chiffon. I didn't think I'd ever seen anything like it.

"There's nothing like this in any store," she said with a certain level of giddiness. "The lady that made my wedding gown made the dress! My mom made the socks and bonnet to match. Scarlett's christening is in two weeks. You should come."

"Wow. I'll look at our schedules."

The dress was gorgeous. I don't think my wedding dress was that nice. We left the closet to sit in the play area. Scarlett's classic oversized bow was hiding her face. Sasha took pictures of her on her phone and posted them to social media. Rachel was playing with Emma's feet. My baby was sleeping and still in her carrier, so I had nothing to do but shove scones in my mouth. Then it began.

"So, Lonnie, how is breastfeeding going?" Rachel asked.

"It's improving. She's still not staying on long enough, and she's not consistent with a bottle."

"Scarlett eats like a champ," said Sasha.

"Emma does pretty good too," Rachel said.

"So, what do you think about the support group, Lonnie? I'd think you would have enough experience that you wouldn't need to go. Don't you have two other kids?" asked Rachel.

"The boys are older. The pediatrician and lactation consultant thought it would be a good idea to attend the group since Eva was having difficulty latching on in the beginning. I'm doing my time."

"But do you think it's helping you?" asked Sasha.

"I like being able to have her checked so I can be sure that she's growing the way she's supposed to. It's been a while since we've had a baby in the house. It gives me peace of mind to know that I'm doing the right things."

"I don't think I could have a baby past thirty-two. I hear once you get to thirty-five your chances of getting pregnant drop like a hot brick. You proved them wrong, didn't you, Lonnie?"

"Sure did," I said and managed a chuckle.

"And what about that chick at the support group. What's her name?"

"Which one?" Rachel asked.

"The one that tried to lead just because she's got a five year old she still breastfeeds," said Sasha.

"I believe her name is Tish," I said. If this turned into a gossip session, I was out. I have a very low tolerance for this kind of meaningless chatter. I quickly redirected the conversation. "Sorry to change the subject, but, Rachel, when are you going back to work? I'll be going back in a few weeks, and I'm starting to get a little anxious about the breastfeeding and daycare."

"We have Emma setup to go to Little Tots. It's close to my job and it's reasonable. We got a good vibe when we visited. I actually go back full time the week after next. I started picking up a few shifts last week."

"You sound pretty confident about it."

"I don't have a choice," said Rachel. "I'm trying to go back to school next semester to finish my degree. Those classes don't pay for themselves. What kind of work do you do?"

"I work for a local advertising company. I was promoted to Assistant Vice President of my branch while I was pregnant, so I'm very anxious about going back."

"Wow. So you're the alpha in your office," said Sasha. "I'm impressed, Lonnie. You've got your stuff together. I'll be staying at home with Scarlett. My paycheck wasn't enough to cover childcare. I either had to get a real job where I work nine to five or stay at home and stop shopping cold turkey. I chose the latter." Sasha leaned in close and whispered, "I may have to let Marie go if it gets too tight."

"If you don't mind me asking, is she here every day and what does she do?" I asked. The better question was what did Sasha do?

"She cooks and cleans. Sometimes she helps out with Scarlett. She's here Monday through Friday."

"Must be nice," Rachel and I both said.

"I keep telling her she has it good," said Rachel. "She doesn't have to cook or clean. She comes to work for fun, just to get out of the house."

"That is not true," Sasha objected. "There was a time where I didn't work, and we got into financial trouble, so holding a small job is part of my agreement to keep us out of that situation. I do have a degree and could work something better than our store, but I like it, and it's just enough to meet my needs."

"My job doesn't meet mine, but I'm limited until I finish school," said Rachel.

"It's best to finish school now while you only have one child. As life goes on, you'll accumulate so many other things that can prolong completing school if you do it later," I told her.

"Do you have a degree, Lonnie?" asked Rachel. I nodded my head yes.

"In what?"

"I have a bachelor degree in Communications and an MBA. I went through my MBA program when my first son was a baby. So, I understand that struggle of working and going to school with a small child."

"Ultimately, I would like to go to law school, but I don't know if I can afford that," Rachel said.

"Make plans to go all the way through and cross the financial bridges when you get there. Don't let money stop you."

Rachel picked up Emma and started to breastfeed her.

"Lonnie, Rachel is another one of those women who don't cover up when she breastfeeds. I told her she can't do that when Terrance is here, no peep shows!" Sasha laughed.

"I am not. The only reason I'm not covering here is because I'm among friends in a baby nursery. I don't use a cover at home. Do you, Sasha?" Rachel snarkily asked.

"For the most part, yes I do. There's almost always somebody here. And it grosses Terrance out to see how hard the baby's sucks. He thinks she's hurting me. Every morning when I'm feeding her I hear him thanking God he's a man and then praying that my breasts aren't damaged in the process. He's a breast man."

We were forty-five minutes into the playdate when Eva decided to join the party. I pulled her out of her car seat and laid her on the rug with Scarlett and Emma. Sasha began snapping pictures of the trio. We chatted for another half hour and took more pictures of the girls, then I pulled out my exit conversation.

"Well, Eva and I have to get ready to go. We have a full day tomorrow, and I need to prep our things today. I had a good time. I hope you'll let me know when the next playdate is," I said.

"We're going out next Thursday to celebrate Rachel's transition from maternity leave. Since she'll be heading back into the workforce, we're going to have a girls night out. No babies though."

"I'll see if my schedule permits," I said as I gathered our things and got Eva bundled into her car seat.

After I said my goodbyes, Marie walked me back to the door where I changed shoes. On the whole, the playdate was better than I anticipated. Eva and I were both relaxed on the drive home. I planned to do a quick entry on my video diary updating my views on playdates based on today's experience.

Old School Opinions

The night was sleepless for me. Eva must've been going through a growth spurt. One look in the mirror the next morning told me I looked rugged. With David's family coming, I was going to need to pull it together. I had the boys doing some cleaning, and I sent David to the store for coffee and tea supplies and pastries. His grandmother was tolerable and pretty easy to please; it was the *aunt* who always gave me the headache.

Their church service would end at noon. It would take them twenty minutes to get here, and it was now a quarter after twelve. Everyone was scurrying around the house to make sure everything was in place. David set out the coffee and tea supplies and a plate of pastries that were looking pretty good to me right about then. We couldn't give his aunt anything to talk about except the weather.

At 12:20 Lizzie's car pulled into the driveway. We sent Johnny out to greet them. Jordan was with his mom. Johnny and DJ love it when he comes over. So, of course, they ran off to do their guy stuff after Jordan greeted David and me with hugs.

"Lizzie!" David exclaimed and embraced his sister. "Your work schedule is brutal. We've been missing you."

"I know. I've been wanting to get here to see this baby! Lonnie, you look awesome. How have you been?" she asked as she hugged me.

"Well, typical newborn shenanigans. Sleepless nights, poopy clothes, and lots of lovin'."

"Show me the way to the baby," Lizzie said with giddy excitement.

I took Lizzie to the family room where Eva was sitting contently in her bouncy seat. I left her there with the baby and went to greet David's grandmother and aunt so I wouldn't be told that I'm rude.

"Mom Mabel," David said as he assisted his grandmother up the steps, "I saw your team lost last week. So sorry about that." I smirked at his words.

"It's still early in the season," she snapped. David helped her to the family room, leaving me with the honors of greeting Aunt Madeline.

"Aunt Madeline, welcome. It's been a while since you've been here. We're so glad to see you," I said as I welcomed her into the house. Thankfully she wasn't a hugger so a verbal greeting sufficed.

"Lonnie." She nodded at me as she stepped inside and looked around.

"Everyone is in the family room," I said and began to walk that direction.

"My throat is parched. Do you have anything to drink?"

"Of course. Would you like water, tea, coffee, or juice?"

"I'll take green tea with honey, thank you."

I showed her to the family room and asked what beverages everyone wanted. I came back with a tray holding their drinks and the pastries. I served everyone and sat down next to David.

"Mom Mabel, how was church today?" I asked.

"Seeing that I'm old, I've heard it before. Never hurts to hear it again."

"Mother is not the appropriate one to ask. She only hears portions of the message as she nods off throughout the service. The teaching was on Mary and Martha," Aunt Madeline said.

I sat up, anticipating she'd elaborate on the teaching,

but nothing. Mom Mabel broke the silence. "Looks like I wasn't the only one nodding."

"So, Lonnie, what are you making your family for dinner today?" Aunt Madeline asked.

"David is making dinner tonight. Babe, what are we having?"

"I found this recipe for a pasta dish with chicken and a red sauce that sounds delicious. I'm looking forward to trying it out," he said proudly.

"When my family was younger, Sundays were *my* day to make a big meal," Aunt Madeline said in a royal tone.

"We typically have a bigger meal on Sundays that *I* cook, but since we have a new addition to our family, we're flexing our roles a little to make sure no one is overwhelmed," I replied.

"Interesting."

"Well, I'll be able to cook more Sunday meals. My work schedule is changing, and I won't be scheduled to do as many weekends and evenings," Lizzie interjected to ease the rising tension.

"That's awesome, sis. Maybe we can start doing Sunday dinner rotations like we did a few years ago," said David.

"That's a good idea. We'll talk to Mom to see if she can plan that out for us."

"She'll be watching Eva for a few days when I start back to work. She and my dad are going to tag team the first few weeks."

"Don't new mothers usually take three months off?" asked guess who.

"Yes, Aunt Madeline, you can take that much time, but most women go back after six weeks. I've heard of women going back a week after giving birth," said Lizzie.

"Lonnie, haven't you worked at your job long enough to be able to take a longer leave? Family comes first," said Aunt Madeline. At this point, my blood was starting to boil, so I needed to find a way out of this conversation. I stood and gave my response on the way to the kitchen.

"I have worked there for quite a while, but I was recently promoted to running our branch, so I will go back to work sooner due to the responsibility of the position. But we have a great support system. Eva will not be lacking in any way. Does anyone want something from the kitchen? We've got some cookies and crackers and more pastries if you're hungry."

"No, thank you. Let me hold this child before we leave," said Aunt Madeline as she retrieved Eva from Mom Mabel. David and Mom Mabel began a feud over sports. Mom Mabel has always been a sports enthusiast. David and his cousins played various sports throughout high school and college with Mom Mabel as their biggest supporter. She's even made it out to the boys' little league games. It baffles me how she raised two hateful women.

We showed David's family the baby's room and had a little more chitchat. By then Mom Mabel was ready to go to lunch.

"Well, Lonnie, I hope to see this little lady again soon. I'm not getting any younger, so you all need to bring her around a little more often."

"Yes, ma'am, we'll do that," David answered.

"Lizzie, I'm ready to go eat," Mom Mable commanded.

"Yes, ma'am. What do you have a taste for?"

"If we go to a buffet, I can choose what I want."

"Buffet it is. Jordan, let's go, bud. Mom Mabel is ready to go eat."

"Where are we going?" You could hear his joyful exclamation and heavy footsteps running up the stairs, followed by DJ and Johnny asking if they could go.

"Not today, gentleman," their dad said. "I've already got dinner planned."

The boys said goodbye with some convoluted handshake and David and I said goodbye to Mom Mabel. Lizzie hung back to chat with me.

"So how did you end up driving these two today?"

"I told Mom Mabel last week I'd take her out to dinner.

She always picks Sundays so I can go to church with her. She says my church isn't good enough and that I could hear the Word clearer without all that loud music they play. She nodded off through most of the service. I doubt she was hearing the Word clearly either." We both laughed. "Since Aunt Madeline goes there as well, it would be rude to take Mom Mabel and not her too," she said.

"Have you been well? You look good."

"I should be asking you that. This is a big transition, new mom all over again."

"I'm adjusting. The closer I get to the six-week mark, the more anxious I get about going back to work. I'm worried about not being able to keep up with the demands of being a leader. My priorities are so backward, I feel guilty."

"That opportunity was something you earned, Lonnie, and you have every right to make the most of it. Don't feel guilty. You are a great mom and a great boss. You don't have to give up one to do the other as long as you balance and give each the attention they need."

The car horn blared. "Mom Mabel is so impatient. I'll talk to you later. Take care of that beautiful girl." She hugged me and ran to the car as Mom Mabel gave the horn another push. David opened the car door for Lizzie, she scooted in, and off they went.

David and I walked back into the house. We stood in the entry way to the family room and watched the boys as they played with the baby in her bouncy seat. He kissed me on the forehead and pulled me close to him. I laid my head on his shoulder. Scenes like this are the ones you want to freeze in time. Everything is all right in these moments. No worries or fears, just peace. A moment where no outside factors invade your thoughts, just the simplicity of what your eyes see and your body feels. I would have loved to stay there a little longer, but life has a way of interrupting little moments and even entire seasons of your life. The interruption this time was my bladder. I was about to pee on myself.

Breastfeeding Detention

I opened my eyes, realized it was Tuesday, and that meant the breastfeeding support group was meeting today. I closed my eyes and began the weekly debate on whether I should go. But this morning the debate ended rather quickly. I wasn't feeling that ball and chain of breastfeeding detention weighing on me. I actually wanted to see the ladies in the group. Not all of them, but definitely LeeAnn, Rachel, and Sasha. They had brought some comic relief to this drastic change of life situation I had found myself in. And I couldn't stop thinking about Grace. Every time I sat down to feed Eva, I wondered if Grace was doing better with her little man.

David got Eva to take a bottle long enough for me to get a few consecutive hours of sleep. What a difference it made. I mentally mapped out my day while I was in the shower. I decided to spend the morning making sure the boys had all of their gear for their annual camping trip with my father-in-law. Next, Eva and I would go to support group. We'd be back in time to send off the boys with their grandfather. David would join them on Thursday and Friday, so Eva and I would have a few days on our own.

I heard Eva whimpering and headed to her room. I picked her up and plopped down in the rocking chair. I presented her my breast, and we got a good latch! Fifteen minutes later, we had a full baby. Today was going to be awesome!

I took a few minutes with the boys to go through their bags. I'm always amazed at their lack of detail. Toothbrushes, underwear, and soap were among the missing items. "I know you all are going to be out in the wild, but it's okay to take a little piece of civilization with you," I told them. Once they were headed in the right direction with their packing, I got Eva ready for support group.

At the pediatrician's office, we went straight to the room with the "Breastfeeding in Progress" sign. Mary was in the corner weighing in a new baby joining the group. Rachel and Sasha were sitting on an area rug in the center of the room, chitchatting. LeeAnn was fully exposed feeding Wind across from the two in the center of the room. I looked around, but I didn't see Grace. Maybe she'd come a little later. I sat a few seats down from LeeAnn and began unpacking Eva from her carrier.

"How's your week starting off?" LeeAnn asked.

"So far, so good. Last night I got the most sleep I've had in a few months. I feel so productive and fresh."

"Sleep has a way of doing that for you. I sleep whenever Wind sleeps for the most part. Neither one of us has a normal sleeping pattern, but as long as we're abnormal together, I stay sane."

"Wow. What are you going to do when you go back to work? Are you working? I never asked you that."

"I work for myself. I make furniture. You should come by and see some of my pieces."

"I'd like that. You are full of surprises."

"Not really, you just don't know me yet. I'm very transparent," she said as she began to undress Wind for his weigh in, totally neglecting to put her breast back in her shirt.

"Lonnie, how are you?" asked Sasha from center stage on the area rug. "Are you going to be available next Thursday for Rachel's back-to-work bash?"

"I think I should be available, but let me get back with you before I commit."

"Is this a private affair or can others come?" asked LeeAnn. "I'm a little overdue for a pump and dump. This is an adult party, right?"

"You are definitely welcome to come and, yes, it's an adult party at my house. My baby will be there, but she'll be supervised."

"Sign me up," said LeeAnn as she walked over to the weigh in station.

"Was she serious about pumping and dumping?" whispered Rachel.

"She's very transparent, so I'm a hundred percent sure she meant what she said," I said.

Mary wrapped up the last weigh in and introduced a guest speaker who talked about SIDS and how we can protect our babies. The speaker offered to answer questions after her talk, and the first hand raised was Tish's.

"Why is she even raising her hand? Her kid is too old to be at risk. He's practically walking," LeeAnn leaned over and commented. Of course Tish took notice and glared at us as she finished up her question. She ended up being the only person with a question. Once her question was answered, Tish approached LeeAnn and me.

"Ladies, is there something you need to say to me? You seemed to be directing your conversation toward me earlier," Tish asked in a pissy tone.

"I was just wondering why you had a question since your child is not at risk for SIDS because of his age," LeeAnn responded.

"I ask questions in case a new mom might be too shy to ask questions. Questions trigger others to think, and we are all the better when we get answers to even a simple question. Anything else you'd like to share?" She looked at me.

"We're all adults here. If someone wants information, they'll get it. These are our children, and we're all moms. We want what's best for our babies, so I'm sure if there were questions, people would speak up."

"That's an assumption. Moms need to get all they can from these sessions and if asking a probing question makes this support group more meaningful, I've done my part in building its significance. If you all don't take this support group seriously, maybe it's not right for you."

"It seems as though you take it too seriously. The main reason we come is to get our babies checked out and to have our questions answered by Mary, not you," said LeeAnn.

"Yes, I do take it seriously. Attending this group helped me through the tough times of breastfeeding, and I'm committed to helping make it a valuable resource for other mothers."

"Tish, I commend you on your loyalty to the group, but the support group is run by the pediatrician's office. They structure the group to meet the needs of new moms, so the group already has value," I said politely.

"Are you insinuating that my participation adds no value," her voice now elevating in volume.

"We all validate the value of the group by showing up each week. There's something here that keeps us coming back. What keeps me coming back is seeing that scale number increase every week. Everything else is a perk," I said.

"It's so much more than a weigh in. You can do that at home. I guess the good thing about women like you is that your time here is relatively short," she snapped.

"Do you run everyone off like this?" LeeAnn said.

Tish walked away in disgust. She made a few comments to her buddy, who always sat with her, and gave us the evil eye. When I looked away from her, I noticed Sasha and Rachel were completely engrossed in the confrontation. I shrugged my shoulders and began packing up Eva.

"Let's grab a bite at Hot Spatula," LeeAnn suggested.

"I think that would be good. I need to process that interaction before I go home."

Sasha handed LeeAnn her contact information and address for Rachel's back-to-work bash and then she and Rachel left.

I hung back because I wanted to ask Mary if she could give me a phone number for Grace. I wanted to make sure she was okay. Mary checked the group contact list and Grace had shared her number with the group. I quickly wrote it down to call her later.

I thanked Mary and left the meeting with LeeAnn.

"LeeAnn, I can't be hanging with you if you're going to get me in trouble."

"You're the one who said I'm full of surprises. You better get to know me so you can decide if you want to walk on the wild side."

We went to our cars, and I followed her to the cafe. We took a little booth and set the babies' car seats next to us on either side of the table. LeeAnn knew what she wanted, so she bypassed the menu and started talking.

"So how much longer *are* you going to come to the group?" she asked

"Until I go back to work, which is coming up in a couple weeks."

"I'll miss you. Who will tag team with me when Tish gets out of hand?"

I laughed. "Sasha will probably still be there."

"She's too soft. Maybe I can recruit the new mom who came today. She's got a tattoo on her neck, so she must be hard core."

We both laughed. "Just because I won't be at the group doesn't mean we can't hang out."

"Really, Lonnie," she said sarcastically. "Once you go back into your corporate dungeon, we'll see each other at kindergarten round up for these two."

"That's not true."

"Take it from someone who knows." She sat back in the booth, and her wild adventurous demeanor shifted. She began to share a story that shifted a coffee chat with an acquaintance to a lunch date with a friend. "I used to be corporate like you."

"That's hard to believe."

"Wind and Rain aren't my only children. I had my first child and went back to work after maternity leave. I was in upper management, so my schedule was crazy busy. I didn't breastfeed because I didn't have the time or patience for the feeding or the pumping. I did my best being a new mom, dropping my child off early at daycare, working until daycare closed, picking her up, and then getting home with enough time to feed her, wash bottles, and get us to bed.

"In the winter, I literally never saw daylight. It was dark when I dropped her off and when I picked her up, and I had an interior office without a window. When my baby was one, she caught the flu. Although I tried to do everything right to care for her and manage work, it wasn't good enough. She died from flu complications.

"That changed me, Lonnie. I couldn't walk back into that office. I spent a year at home battling major depression. I even contemplated suicide. I couldn't forgive myself for not devoting more attention and care to my child. After months of counseling, I finally came out of myself enough to start a hobby.

"I went to a woodworking class a few times a week and fell in love with it. So much so that my husband made me a little shop in our garage. I started making pieces for family and then friends and then local stores started showing interest. I threw myself into my work.

"One day I realized that the pain I felt from the loss of my first child didn't consume me anymore. It still hurt, but it didn't keep me from enjoying life. That's when we decided we'd try again. When Rain was born, I vowed to give my all to her. I breastfed, I stayed at home, I put her needs first, and it worked out. It worked so well, we decided to have Wind.

"I know people are put off by me and how open I am about breastfeeding and how brash I can be. But I'm grateful to be alive and even more grateful to have my children. I live everyday free and open. Each day is a gift and I'm not letting anyone take that from me or my babies."

I was stunned. "Wow, I . . . I'm amazed at your resilience. I couldn't even imagine going through that or finding the courage to try again."

"Those were the darkest days of my life, and now, I live for the light." She looked over at Wind and smiled.

The waitress came to take our order. LeeAnn spouted off her choices, but I was stuck in her backstory and asked for a few more minutes to look at the menu. Of course, her story hit home. It scared me. It inspired me. It made me see her in a different light. I ordered a muffin and started sharing some of my anxieties about returning to work.

"I'd never suggest that you not go back to work. Just make sure you put first things first. It sounds like you've got a good man and a very supportive family, so you should be fine," LeeAnn said.

I looked at my watch. I needed to get back to the boys. It was different when we said goodbye this time. We were now friends.

When Eva and I were tucked in our car, I called the number Mary had given me for Grace. I got her voicemail, so I left my name and number. I really did want to hear from her.

I got the boys and all their camping gear together once Eva and I got home. Everyone piled in the car. The boys were full of excitement as we drove to David's dad's.

When we arrived, Jerry and Jordan were hooking the camper up to Jerry's truck. Sheryl came out and quickly kissed each boy on her way to the backseat of my car.

"Where's that beautiful baby? Ohhh, Lonnie she's getting so big!" She took Eva from her car seat and held her across her chest. "I can't wait for our Nanna-Eva days," she said as she carried her into the house. "I picked up a few things for us to have here when Eva comes." She pointed out the portable play yard and bouncy seat.

This didn't surprise me. Sheryl lived to be a grandma. Eva would be in good hands. I offered my help to Jerry, but he shooed me away. He's one of those DIY types, with heavy emphasis on the "Y." I went inside and helped Lizzie. When Lizzie, Joanna, and David were young, they would go camping as a family. Then when the grandkids came along, Jerry and my husband started going with the grandkids and left the women at home.

Lizzie and I packed up meals for the guys and double-checked all their gear.

"Have fun, guys! When you come back, it'll be time for school."

"Mom, don't remind us!" said DJ.

"I can't wait. You'll be going to high school. That's a big deal. I'm going to stand outside the school and wave goodbye and blow you kisses on the first day. And then I'm going to cry because my baby is going to high school." I leaned over and pretended to cry on DJ's chest.

"Mom!" He was mortified.

"Dad will be there tomorrow evening, so you guys help Grandpa. He's going to try to do everything himself, but don't let him, you understand?"

"Yes, Mom."

"Yes, Aunt Lonnie."

"All right. I'm going home with Eva. I'll see you all this weekend. Love you!"

"We love you too," they all chimed in.

"Now, Dad, you make sure those boys are doing most of the work. You need to start handing some of the responsibilities over to them," said Lizzie.

"Don't worry, they'll have their work cut out for them," Jerry assured us.

"Lizzie's right, Jerry. You always try to do everything on your own. You are not so young anymore. Let those boys do the strenuous tasks," said Sheryl.

"Sheryl, I know what I'm doing. You all haven't been the last few years. The boys do a lot."

"I'm just saying, Jerry." Sheryl walked into the other room and made sure I had all of Eva's things.

"Be careful, Dad." I gave hugs to him, Sheryl, and Lizzie and headed home with Eva.

That evening I helped David locate and pack everything he needed for the trip. Before bed I added another recording to my ongoing documentary of this strange new time in my life. There definitely was a mix of strange and heartwarming moments today.

My body was beginning to get into the rhythm of less sleep at night, so when Eva roused at three, it was no struggle to tend to her needs. David got up shortly after that and got himself prepared to join his dad and the boys at the camping spot. I made him a cup of coffee for the trip and stood at the door as he collected his things.

"Have a great time, babe."

"I can't wait to get there. But I can't wait to come back to you. Six weeks is almost over." He started to do a little dance. I gave him a tap on the backside and pushed him out the door. I waved once as he was backing out of the driveway, then I happily went back to bed to get in a few hours before Eva's morning feeding. As I was drifting off, I decided I would sleep whenever she sleeps since it would be just the two of us for the next few days.

After her morning feeding, I let Eva play a little, then we both went back to sleep. About an hour into our morning nap, my phone rang. Unknown number. My first instinct was to ignore the call and roll back over, but I answered it.

"Hi, is this Lonnie?" asked the timid voice on the other end.

"It is. May I ask who's calling?"

"This is Grace from the breastfeeding support group. You left me a message yesterday."

"Oh, Grace! Hi, yes, this is Lonnie. I saw you weren't in group this week, and I wanted to check on you. How is everything going?"

"I'm okay." Awkward silence.

"How is breastfeeding going? Is Jackson tolerating it better?"

"He's doing better, but he still will choke every now and then."

"I'm glad to hear he's doing better. Will you come back to the group next week or are you heading back to work?"

"I'm hoping to be working next week. I've had a few interviews but no call backs yet."

"What are you doing for childcare?"

"My mom is helping me out."

"That's awesome your mom is available to help out. Where have you interviewed?"

"Just a few restaurants and temp agencies."

"I can check with my Human Resources department to see if we have anything open. What type of work have you done?"

"I've waited tables and done some receptionist positions."

"Is it okay if I check to see if we have any reception positions open and call you back? I'd love to help you out if I can."

"Sure." More awkward silence.

"Well, I'll be in touch. I'm glad to hear things are getting better with the breastfeeding. Call me if you need anything."

I immediately checked our website for openings and found we had one at Main Branch that might work for her. I sent Grace a text telling her where to find the position online and encouraged her to send her resume to our Human Resources secretary. I provided the email and told her to put me down as a reference. She texted back with a simple "thank you." I hoped she followed through.

I rolled over thinking I was going to get some sleep but then my dad called. We chatted for a while. He was trying to get all of his ducks in a row for the two weeks he'd be keeping Eva. I could hear the anxiety in his voice between all the questions.

"Dad, why don't you come over tomorrow and see our routine and then next week you can come over on a day when the boys are back in school, and I'll let you do everything, but I'll be here to coach you." He agreed to that plan. "Thank you, Dad, for doing this."

"You know I've always got your back, Lonnie."

We finished our call with a few updates on family and friends, and then I quickly fell sleep.

The entire day was filled with sleep, changing diapers, breastfeeding, eating, and a few phone calls and text conversations. It was glorious. Why did I wait four weeks into this leave to have this type of day? Dad will be coming tomorrow, but Friday will be a repeat of this day.

I had coffee ready for Dad the next morning. He has worked a 3 p.m. to 11 p.m. shift for as long as I can remember. When my mom died, he would drop me off at my aunt's house every afternoon before he went to work until I was old enough to stay home on my own. He's getting pretty close to retirement. Whenever I bring it up, he just grunts and changes the subject. I think retirement scares him because all he's done in life is raise me and work. Since he's done raising me and will no longer work, what will he do?

He knocked lightly on the door, and I opened it for him. We embraced and walked into the kitchen.

"I made you coffee."

"Thank you. Where's the creamer?" he asked as he peered into the fridge.

"Left hand door."

"What's this with the yellow top?"

"Breastmilk. It's pretty creamy if you want to use some in your coffee."

"I'll pretend I didn't hear you say that."

"Eva will sleep for probably another thirty minutes, so relax and enjoy your coffee."

"David and the boys enjoying their camping trip?"

"They are. I talked with them last night."

"I love taking the boys fishing, so I know Jerry is having a good time with them."

"Do you think you'll do more fishing once you retire?"

He grunted. "They coming back on Saturday?"

"Yes, they are. You didn't answer my question."

"We'll see when that time comes. So, will I have to wash bottles and do laundry?"

"No, I wouldn't do that to you. I'll have all of her bottles prepared. When she wakes, I'll show you where all of her things are. Watch me closely. This will be you for a few weeks."

"I may be a little rusty, but my Papa powers will kick in once it's just her and me."

"Okay, Super Papa."

He enjoyed his coffee, and I drank good ol' water. When Eva woke, we started our daily routine. I showed him where I kept all of her things. I let him take a test drive in the rocking chair to feed Eva. We had a refresher course on burping and the importance of positioning the baby when she's in the crib to prevent any hazardous situations. He rebutted a time or two with, "Well, when you were a baby . . ." and I gently redirected the discussion back to the present and had him repeat what I said to ensure he heard me.

After the second round of Eva's routine, he was sitting on the couch with the milk intoxicated infant on his chest. "Wow, I never imagined that we'd be doing this again. I love the boys so much, I couldn't imagine having another inch of space for another, but she's made a place in my heart."

"I feel the same way, Dad. I feel guilty for going back to work and having work compete with her, David, and the boys. I'm nervous about being able to manage it all."

"You've met every challenge in your life with a good plan and perseverance. I expect nothing less this time."

"Thanks, Dad." I looked at the clock and noticed he needed to get going soon to prepare for work. "It's almost two, Dad. Do you need to get ready to leave for work?"

"Yeah, I'll head out in a few." He was enjoying his Papa moment. He eventually motioned for me to take Eva, and I situated her in her bouncy seat. I walked him to the door and gave him a hug. "See you next week. Do you want to come over on Thursday?"

"That should work. I'll see you then."

I had the rest of the afternoon and evening ahead of me. Time for a little more napping with Eva. A perfect setup for a repeat of yesterday to carry over to tomorrow.

The weekend was filled with cleaning up from the camping trip and prepping for the first day of school, which would be Wednesday. I had successfully let go of work and fully participated in my maternity leave. That time had come to an end. Monday I started reading through the work emails and painted a mental picture of what the office would be like when I got back.

One of the newer emails was a reference request. I opened the email, and it was for Grace! I skipped the instructions in the email and got on the phone with the contact person in HR. I gave her my recommendation, hoping that this wouldn't blow up in my face. I knew nothing about Grace's work history, but I really wanted to help her. The HR contact let me know that they'd move forward with the interview process. I was nervous yet excited for Grace.

Julia, who opposed me in the interview process, was next in line to run the office while I was on leave after Mike, the person I left in charge, resigned. To my knowledge everything had been running smoothly, but the anxiety associated with being immersed in work with milk-filled breasts was creeping up inside of me. How do I prioritize Eva, my job, David, and the boys? And where do *I* fit in this equation?

I took a minute to record the thoughts swirling in my head in my video documentary.

> **Things start to heat up this week. I've got a back-to-work party for Rachel, the boys start school, Dad is coming over for more nanny coaching, and I will start sliding back into my work role. Next week is my last week at home with Eva.**

I fought back tears at that thought. And just a few months ago I was more concerned about my recent promotion and how a baby was going to impact my performance and interfere with all that I'd worked so hard for. The tears started rolling down my cheeks. How could my priorities have been so backward? One day I'd be too old to work that job, but my daughter would still be with me. Now I was sobbing. I stopped the video. Ugly crying isn't cute.

Do Not *Try To Do This in the Bathroom*

Today was support group day. I hoped Grace would be there and I was looking forward to the post session with LeeAnn. What type of ridiculous hair accessory would Sasha put on that poor baby this week? But most importantly, was Eva getting bigger from the life giving substance that only I could provide?

When I got up that morning, David was the only one up. The boys were getting in their last bit of summer sleep. I fixed David's breakfast, saw him off to work, and turned my attention to getting Eva and myself ready for our outing.

The boys were still sleeping when I was ready to leave, so I left them a note in the kitchen with honey dos. When I got to the group room, the gang was all there. I waved at Sasha and Rachel, set the baby down next to LeeAnn, and zeroed in on Grace.

"I got a call yesterday for a reference! Which job did you apply for?"

Grace was wearing a smile, one of the few that I had seen on her face. "I applied for a receptionist position at the main office. I have an interview tomorrow!"

"I'm so excited for you, Grace. I've been with our company for over 15 years, and it's been wonderful. I hope your interview goes well. Call me and let me know how it goes."

"I will. Thank you, Lonnie."

"You're welcome."

There was nothing special going on this week at the group.

A few new faces and Tish's old face. When it was my turn at the changing table with Mary, we talked about Eva while she got weighed and her diaper contents checked.

"She's gaining every week, Lonnie. Looks like she's getting enough milk. Will you be going back to work?"

"Funny you should ask. I am going back to work the week after next. I'm nervous about maintaining this. I'm in a leadership role at work, and I don't know how I'm going to manage pumping and working and bottles and schedules. To be honest, I'm a little overwhelmed."

"That's normal to feel overwhelmed. I would take advantage of your leadership position and block out two to three fifteen-minute intervals throughout your work day to pump. That should be consistent enough to keep your milk supply up. You want to make sure you are breastfeeding in the morning before you head out and as often as Eva wants to eat in the evenings. You have family at home, right?" I nodded. "Great, have them wash and prep the bottles. Teach them proper handling of the milk and how much to put in the bottles. Is Eva going to daycare or staying home with a family member?"

"She'll be home with a family member the first two weeks, but then she'll go to daycare."

"That's when the fun starts. It's important that you keep breastfeeding to help guard her from the exposure to germs. Breastmilk doesn't make her immune, but it does boost her immune system, so be prepared for that. We are always here if you need to pop in after you go back to work or you can email me."

"Thanks, Mary." That interaction was worth coming to this group. The transition into real life while nourishing this little human was a pivotal time. Mary got everyone's attention to start group.

"I think I've had a chance to speak to everyone one-on-one. Lonnie brought up a very important topic. Going back to work. How many of you are on maternity leave and will be going back to work?" Seventy-five to eighty percent of the hands went up in the room.

"First things first, you need a breast pump. Is there anyone here who does not have a breast pump?" One mom raised her hand. "See me after group. Second, before you return to work, make sure there is a place where you can pump milk. *Do not* try to do this in the bathroom, trust me! You want to make sure your HR department is aware of your intent to provide your child with breastmilk. This is important because you'll need to take breaks throughout the day to pump. I know some women get away with pumping over their lunch break. Pumping once during your workday could lead to a drop in your supply and, over a period of time, you may not be able to recover from a prolonged drop in your supply.

"*Do not* wait until a few days before you go back to introduce your sweet baby to the bottle. If you exclusively breastfeed, it may take a while to find the right nipple that your child will accept. Once you are back to work and have a schedule for pumping, you want to pump both sides together if your machine has that capability. It sends signals to your brain that milk is in high demand.

"The biggest key to successful breastfeeding when returning back to work is support. Support from your family, support from your job, and support from places like this. Get your family involved in helping with preparing and cleaning bottles. You don't have to do it alone. And if you are alone, make some friends, rekindle some relationships, hire somebody. Are there any questions?"

Hands flew up all over the room. One mom had two hands up. Question after question, Mary broke down how to be successful when we go back to work. I was expecting to get out early since there was no speaker today, but today's group went longer than usual.

"Wow, ladies," Mary exclaimed, "this has been one of *the* most interactive sessions we've had. Thanks, Lonnie, for opening up that conversation." The whole room applauded. Many moms lingered afterward, sharing past experiences and resources they had found helpful.

"Way to captivate the room, Lonnie," said Tish on her way out, "Too bad you'll be returning to work soon. We'll miss you." Her words dripped with sarcasm as she moved past.

"Lonnie, hold me back. She's got it coming to her!" said LeeAnn.

"She's not worth your energy. If this is the only place she feels validated, let her have it."

"You're better than I am. I have no patience for that pettiness. If she needs validation, she needs to go get a life and validate somewhere else."

I shrugged and put Eva in her car seat. "You have time for Hot Spatula today?"

"I don't today, Lonnie. I have a meeting with a local store that wants to feature my furniture."

"Congrats, LeeAnn! That's exciting."

LeeAnn saw Rachel and Sasha heading for the door and called out to them. "We still on for Thursday? What should I bring?"

"Just yourself! Everything is covered. Gotta send my girl off right."

While LeeAnn was insisting on bringing something, I looked for Grace. A night out might be good for her, so I decided to invite her. I was confident Sasha would be okay with this.

Grace said she needed to check her mom's availability to babysit and asked if she could call or text me when she knew. I went ahead and gave her the address. I let Sasha know there might be one more and, unsurprisingly, she said the more the merrier.

It was probably best LeeAnn and I didn't go to Hot Spatula. With the first day of school tomorrow for the boys, I needed to think through this new routine and start assigning people roles. I also needed some items for Johnny to put in his lunch, so a supermarket stop was necessary.

I pulled into the parking lot and parked in the space

allotted for new moms. The cars on either side parked right on the line.

I carefully opened my door and gently rested it against the car in the handicap parking spot. I tried to slide out of the driver's seat but my hips lodged in between the door and car frame. I felt entitled to this parking spot, so I tried getting out on the passenger side, which also failed. I gave the driver's side one more try and was able to get out. Success! Then I realized I'd have the same problem getting that car seat out of the back. I reversed the process and found another parking spot.

The walk from the backside of the parking lot with this heavy car seat had me agitated. By the time I picked up my groceries and got in the checkout line, Eva was beginning to get upset. We were past her feeding time. The lady in front of me was paying for items using coupons and taking forever. Eva began that shrill infant cry that made everyone look at you like you're committing a crime. At this point, all of my items were on the conveyor belt and I was trapped between the coupon queen in front and an irritated man behind me. The shrill cries intensified, and my patience was bankrupt.

"Excuse me," I interjected into coupon lady's checkout session, "I need to tend to my child. Can you ring up my items, and I will come back and pay for them?"

"Umm. Let me check with my manager."

She put on her light and continued with the coupons. The manager quickly came and assessed the situation. She agreed to ringing up my items, and I hurried out to my car, on the back side of the parking lot. I pulled Eva out of her car seat and jumped into the backseat of the car. I threw on the nursing cover and fumbled around with the snaps on this nursing bra and finally got the boob to the child, and she sucked away.

As Eva chugged, she took in a little too much and regurgitated milk all over my top. I tried to clean myself up, and she resumed screaming, so I put her back on the boob. We were both overstimulated. I chose to do what anyone in my situation would do.

Cry.

I don't know how I'm going to do this. What am I thinking, trying to go back to work and run a company when I can't even make a successful run to the grocery store with an infant? I was seriously starting to doubt myself. I knew my hormones were behind this foolish thinking, but maybe there was some truth to my thoughts. Now I was the crying baby. After Eva finished eating, I changed her diaper, and we headed back into the store.

I went to the customer service desk and explained my situation. The woman eyed the milk stain on my shirt and had trouble maintaining her gaze on my tear stained face.

"Yes, ma'am. I have them over here. The total is $34.23," she said.

I paid for the groceries and trekked back to my car. I thought about the night LeeAnn was breastfeeding in the store and how her frustrations weren't about a crying child but about offended people. What if I had just sat down, *with* my nursing cover, and fed the baby in the store, would my stress level have been different? Who knows. For now, I'd avoid grocery shopping with Eva, especially if I didn't have a bottle. I'd rather avoid the stress than confront it with new methods. I wouldn't do that in any other area of my life, but in this area, I was vulnerable and would rather tuck and run. Don't judge me.

When Eva and I got home, she was napping. I decided that might do me some good as well. I instructed the boys to listen for her, and I headed to my room and quickly fell into R.E.M.

I dreamed that Will put me on probation because I was underperforming at work and then Eva was talking to me from a bassinet in my office.

My eyes flew open. I looked around my room, and I heard the boys in the kitchen. The sun was setting. How long had I been sleep? I got myself out of bed and headed downstairs. Eva was sitting in her bouncy seat being entertained by Johnny, and DJ was in the kitchen taking something out of the oven.

"Hey, Mom, you're up. You were sleeping, so I threw some chicken tenders in the oven for dinner. Eva woke up, so we gave her a bottle and kept her down here." I was impressed with his status report.

"I'm sorry, guys. You have your first day of school tomorrow, and I should be helping you."

"No way, Mom. You need our help with Eva. It gives me the chance to show how responsible I am. I'm a high schooler now, so I should have more responsibilities."

"You're not a high schooler until tomorrow," Johnny piped in.

"Nobody was talking to you, Johnny. I became a high schooler the day I graduated from middle school."

Johnny quietly mocked him and resumed entertaining Eva.

"Thank you, boys. You are so good to me." I gave each of them a big hug. "What time did you feed Eva?"

"Maybe an hour ago."

I sat on the couch and watched my children. Shortly after this exchange, David came in from work. Johnny had just finished setting the table, so we all came around for dinner.

"Bon appétit! Dinner is served," said DJ. He placed a plate of chicken tenders and broccoli in front of each of us.

When I got in bed after my "therapy" video session, I was scared to close my eyes and go to sleep, fearing the dream would continue.

Eva woke at her usual time. I stayed up to begin prepping breakfast and lunch for the boys. Well, Johnny's lunch. DJ was too *mature* for a lunchbox. He planned to buy lunch. When their alarms went off, I waited for the snooze alarm to come on and then I went and woke the boys. I had to literally drag Johnny out of the bed. DJ popped right up and headed for the bathroom.

"Good morning. Is my high schooler ready for his first day of school?"

"Mom, it's just school, no big deal."

"Of course it's a big deal. Today marks the beginning of a four-year journey that will take you off to real life, without Mom and Dad caring for you. It's the beginning of my last four years being in your presence every day."

"Mom, that's four years from now. And what if I decide to stay home and go to college? Then you'd still see me every day."

"But you'd be an adult, and you wouldn't need me like you do now." I walked over to give him a hug from behind.

"I'll always need you, Mom." My mommy heart melted with the warmth of his words. I kissed his cheek and headed upstairs to check on Johnny. His head was on the bathroom counter, and he was still in his pjs.

"Johnny! Let's go."

"Huh? Mom, I'm too tired. Can I go back to bed for a few minutes. School doesn't start till eight."

"The first day of school is always busy. It's good to be early." I attempted to pull him into standing, but he resisted me. So, I tickled him. Soon he was curled up on the floor, laughing, trying to block tickles.

"Okay, okay! I'm up!"

"Get busy, breakfast is waiting." I headed into the bedroom to check on David.

"Good morning, Mr. Peterson."

"Good morning, Mrs. Peterson," he leaned over to kiss me. He smelled fantastic.

"I'd like to take you out next week before you head back to work."

"Well, that's thoughtful. I'd love that."

"How are you feeling about going back?"

Those words made me sick to my stomach. Pictures from that dream flashed in my head.

"Truthfully, I'm nervous. I'm so glad our parents are going to help for a few weeks. It calms my anxiety some. I'm afraid I won't be able to balance it all."

"You don't have to. You have me and the boys and

our families to help." He stopped his grooming routine to embrace me.

It was amazing how that embrace melted the anxiety away. I could have stayed in his arms for hours. I felt safe and carefree. I didn't want to go back out to the world, but the sound of a crying infant caused my carefree zone to collapse.

David released me and grabbed my hand. "You can do this. We can do this," he said, looking directly into my eyes, speaking to my soul. I kissed his hand, and he pulled me in for one more embrace. Then I headed to Eva.

"Okay, boys, we've got to get our first day of school pic on the porch."

"Mom, really. That's for elementary school kids."

"It is not, sir. I need to remember this day so when we get to the last day of school I can look back and see how much you've grown. Who knows, you may be three feet taller and have a beard by the end of school year. I'll only know it's you by looking back at that picture."

DJ rolled his eyes. David came down, and I herded everyone to the front porch for the pic. I got pics of each of the boys individually and then all three kids together. DJ and David gathered their things and were off to drop DJ at school.

"Babe, make sure you walk him in and give him a big kiss for me in front of the whole school," I said as they got into the car.

"Mom!"

I blew them kisses as they pulled out of the driveway. I could hear Eva getting agitated. I went to her room to feed her while Johnny caught his last opportunity to play video games on a school day. Eva and I finished up in time to walk Johnny to the bus stop.

"Are you excited? We've been making such a big deal about DJ going to high school, but this is your last year in elementary school. You're going to be an elementary school senior this year. Big sixth grader."

"It doesn't feel any different. The same people will be there."

"I guess you're right. Anyway, I'm proud of you, and I hope your first day is awesome."

He gave me a hug, "I hope you and Eva have an awesome day too, Mom." He gave Eva a kiss. "Be good, baby girl."

The bus pulled up, and Johnny confidently boarded. I waved at him when he got seated, he waved back, and off the bus went. I have always gotten sentimental on the first day of school, and this day was no exception. I took a walk around the block, hoping to settle my emotions.

When I got back home to an otherwise empty house, I put Eva in her bouncy seat in the office and started to go through work emails. I got a calendar reminder that I was meeting with Will next Thursday to prep for my return to work the following week. After I skimmed through the emails, I decided to have a do nothing day. The last time Eva and I did that, I felt great. Plus, it would only last until the boys got out of school. I needed to maximize my maternity leave and actually *leave* all the cares of real life alone until I went back. With that decided, I took a nap.

When the afternoon rolled around, the boys came home full of energy. It felt good to ask about their day and listen to their stories. Dinner was ready and homework was done by the time David came home. It was an evening for sharing and listening until bedtime. Just what I needed, and I think David did too. All in all a perfect do nothing day.

The morning routine went a little smoother on Thursday. Shortly after I got Johnny on the bus, my dad pulled in the driveway for day two of his training. I got him a cup of coffee, and we sat at the table.

"I've been meaning to tell you something," he said. Of course my heart started racing, and the adrenaline caused my breasts to start leaking. Good thing I had those breast pads in place. "You keep asking me about when I'm going to retire. Well, my last day is next Friday."

"Dad! How long have you known this?"

"About a month now."

"Why didn't you tell me? We could have planned a party or something. This is a milestone in your life. The capstone to your career."

"Capstone of my career or gravestone of the good years of my life."

"What do you mean?"

"I've worked all my life, Lonnie. I provided for you and your mom and then just for you and me. I worked hard to make sure I had enough to live on for the rest of my life, but for what? So I can spend it on some swanky nursing home?"

"Dad, first of all you're not old enough and you're too healthy to be thinking about a nursing home. There's life after retirement."

"What am I going to do all day? I spent all these years planning for my financial security, but now I don't know what to do with it. I thought retirement would be something to look forward to, but the closer it gets, the more afraid I am."

"You're overreacting, Dad. You can't be afraid of it if you've never experienced it. And just because you're leaving this job doesn't mean you can't get another small job that keeps you busy. Like checking people out at the store or being a crossing guard."

"Come on, Lonnie. Can you see me doing those things?"

"No, not really, but we have to start somewhere. I think you should take a few months to think about what interests you. I can't believe you didn't talk to me about this. Every time I brought up the topic, you changed the subject. Give me a few weeks, and I'll have a huge bash planned for you."

"No, Lonnie. I don't want anything like that. I don't feel celebratory."

"Dad, you deserve to be celebrated for all the years you gave to that company and for your dedication to our family as a breadwinner. No, Dad, you will be celebrated. Can we do a small get together at a restaurant, just close family and friends?"

"Let me think about it. So, what am I learning today?"

"Today we're learning about the car seat and stroller, and we'll recap her schedule, bottle preparation, and diaper changing."

Training day two went well. I encouraged Dad to consider that retirement would be sweet for him and not to fear this new season in life. I think I needed that same pep talk about not fearing the new season in my own life. Dad hung around with me until the boys got home from school, so we had some dad, daughter, granddaughter time.

David came home a little early to relieve me for the back-to-work party for Rachel. I took some time to pump. While I was pumping, I remembered that Grace was supposed to get back with me to let me know if she was going to make it tonight. I texted her, but got no response. Thinking of Grace made me think about LeeAnn and her anticipation to pump and dump. She might need a designated driver, so I texted her, asking if she wanted to carpool.

"LOL. You're a good friend. I'll take you up on that," she texted back along with her address.

I sent her a pickup time when I was ready to leave.

"Don't get too crazy," David warned from the living room where he and the kids were watching TV.

"You boys are not supposed to be watching TV on a school night," I scolded on my way out.

I'm actually excited about this party. I didn't get to do things like this as often as I'd like with my long-time friends. We let our busy lives eat up our social time, or we just can't sync our calendars. I pulled up to LeeAnn's house, and her husband came to the car with her.

"Hi, Lonnie, I'm Chris. I've heard great things about you. Keep this girl in line tonight." He kissed her and opened the passenger door for her.

"It's nice to meet you, Chris. I'll bring her home in one piece. But you know what goes on at a girl's party stays at the party."

"That's cool. As long as she still loves me when she comes

home." She shooed him back toward the house. When we pulled up at Sasha's, LeeAnn sat forward in her seat.

"This is her house?"

"Yes. Wait till you see the inside."

We rang the doorbell, and there was Marie.

"Hi there, Lonnie. And you must be LeeAnn," Marie greeted us and invited us into the foyer. We stopped by the shoe depository and got slippers. LeeAnn sent me an inquiring *what the heck* look.

We followed behind Marie, who led us to the kitchen. LeeAnn whispered, "What does her husband do anyway?"

Sasha greeted us and so did Rachel. Much to my surprise, Grace was there.

"Welcome, ladies! What can I get for you? We've got a variety of hors d'oeuvres and drinks for the evening."

"Your home is exquisite. You should come by my studio and look at some of my pieces. I can totally see one of them in your space."

"Pieces as in furniture?"

"Yes. Can I look at the other rooms?" LeeAnn asked, checking out Sasha's living room. She, Sasha, and Rachel begin walking through the main level of the home. I took a few hors d'oeuvres and greeted Grace.

"Hey there. I sent you a text. I didn't know if you were going to come or not."

"I did get it, but I was already on my way, so I figured I'd see you here. Guess what? I got the job at Mendallmen!"

"Grace, I'm so excited for you! When do you start?"

"I actually go in on Monday for general orientation. Do you work at the main office?"

"I'm at South Branch, so I won't get to see you often. Maybe I will when I have a meeting there. Will your mom keep Jackson?"

"Yes, that's the plan. I don't think I would be able to afford daycare. Not decent daycare. Lonnie, thank you so much. I really needed this job."

"I'm glad I was able to help."

The other ladies joined us in the living room. Sasha took center stage. "Ladies, I'm so glad you all could come tonight. We want to give our fellow BSG—breastfeeding support group—member a proper send-off back to work."

"Grace is heading back next week too," I chimed in.

"Aww, Grace. Where are you working?"

"I actually just got a job at Lonnie's company as a receptionist. My first day is Monday," she said with a nervous smile.

"That's exciting, congrats. Well, for our ladies returning to work, we've got a special treat." Sasha opened a cabinet and pulled out two glittery crowns. "Good thing I brought both of them. I didn't know which color Rachel would want. Ladies, tonight we honor you." Sasha crowned both of the ladies. "We'll commence our evening with a send-off toast. What will everyone have to drink?"

LeeAnn held true to pump and dump plans and requested an alcoholic beverage. The rest of us weren't that brave and chose a non-alcoholic cocktail creation that Marie had prepared. We raised our glasses and toasted to returning to real life.

The evening was full of laughter. The conversation was a little wild. LeeAnn gave a tutorial on how to clear a clogged duct with your husband's help, as if an infant's suck wasn't hard enough.

"Don't knock it. If you give him good instructions, he'll have you unblocked in under a minute. Don't suffer ladies, I'm telling you."

"This night has been fun and educational. We can do it again when these working mommas have a break in their schedules," Sasha said.

"Let's do it again next Thursday. Lonnie is going back to work in a week," LeeAnn said.

"Yeah, but let's go out this time," Rachel said.

"I've got the perfect place! Let's do it. Next Thursday at eight. I'll text the address," Sasha said.

"Let's do seven. Some of us have to get up in the morning and go to work," Rachel said. Sasha cut her eyes at Rachel.

"Seven work for everyone?" We agreed, gathered our things, and Marie appeared to walk us to the door.

"Thanks again, Sasha," said Grace.

"Don't forget to text me a time when you can come by, Sasha. Just looking at your home, I think you and your husband would like my work. Thank you again for this evening. See you next week," LeeAnn said.

When I pulled up to LeeAnn's house she invited me to see some of her work in her garage-converted-workshop. When I stepped in I could see how this space brought her out of a dark season in her life. As she explained her creative process and showed off her work, I was amazed at the creativity and level of craftsmanship. The style of her work was unique. And not in a weird, abstract way, but truly works of art. LeeAnn intrigued me. She was edgy, tender, free, passionate, outspoken, and just real.

"So, what do think about this one?" LeeAnn asked.

"It is stunning. What was your inspiration?"

"Rose, my first daughter. On every one of my pieces, I carve a small rose into the wood. Just like she's etched in my heart, I etch a rose on each piece of furniture I make."

"Your passion shows in your work, LeeAnn."

"Thanks, Lonnie. Well, you better get home so your husband will let you hang out again." We both laughed.

I stopped for gas and decided to recap my day in my video diary while I waited at the pump. I would never have thought to have my husband suck my breast to remove a clogged duct. Who does that? LeeAnn!

Pumping and Dumping with Sober Sally

David's family was here for Sunday dinner. Just his parents and sisters. My husband and father-in-law were in the living room, watching whatever sport was available at that time of day. All the ladies were buzzing around in the kitchen and dining room, getting dinner ready and setting the table. Sheryl, with Eva in her arms, called for everyone to come to the table, and a herd of males came rushing in.

"The last time we sat at this table, this little princess was still in her momma's belly," Sheryl said. "After dinner, Lonnie, you need to show me where all her things are and tell me her routine."

My sisters-in-law cleaned up after dinner while Sheryl and I went over everything Eva. I had Sheryl change a diaper, oriented her to the supplies on the changing table, and went over Eva's usual sleep and feeding patterns. We went to the kitchen to check out the bottles. My sisters-in-law were on the other side of the kitchen giggling as I explained the different pieces of the bottle and how to assemble it.

"Laugh now. See if I feed any of your future babies," said Sheryl.

"Mom, you're going to let our babies starve?" Joanna snickered.

"It takes three days to starve. I'm sure you'll be back before then. I'm listening, Lonnie."

After we finished up with the bottles, I showed her how to buckle Eva into the car seat and how the stroller unfolded.

By this time, the whole family had come to watch the tutorial. Jerry insisted on trying to open the stroller without instruction. Lizzie and David made wagers on how long it would take him to get it open and whether he'd break it in the process. He defied all their low expectations and got it open in one motion, just as it was intended.

"You got lucky, Dad. They engineer these things now to accommodate grandparents," said Joanna.

"No luck, baby girl, all skill," Jerry said proudly.

After dessert we ushered everyone to the door. We gave hugs all around and waved as they pulled out of the driveway.

While David and the boys got prepared for Monday, I rocked in the chair with Eva while trying to decide whether this week was going to be a rev up week or a do nothing week. If I revved up, I'd be more prepared when I went back to work, but I'd cheat myself out of a week of an already truncated maternity leave. I decided to go with the do nothing week. Come next week, I'll have the world on my shoulders. It's a good plan to rest up before I take that on. I'll rev up on Thursday.

Tuesday was my last breastfeeding support group. I was kinda bummed about it. The ladies I'd met had really made this life change enjoyable. I hadn't realized a new child at this age would also bring new friends. When Eva and I walked through the door of our meeting room, there were balloons and everyone began clapping as Eva and I entered the room.

"What's going on? Am I the 100th customer?"

"We had so much fun celebrating last week, we talked to Mary about celebrating in the group," Sasha said.

"I thought it was a great idea. Going back to work is a big transition and celebrating among those going through the same experience can be encouraging," Mary said.

"This is amazing. Thank you!"

"And I'd like to drink to Rachel and Grace who are not here today because they have already returned to work." LeeAnn raised her bottled water to the sky and then took a big gulp.

"I'll drink to that," said Sasha, and others in the room chimed in and raised their bottled water to drink in honor our moms who have returned to work. All except Tish and her sidekick Bobbi, who were sitting in the corner with sour faces.

"Last week's discussion on breastfeeding when returning to work really inspired me. I am so focused on a mom and baby becoming successful with breastfeeding that I haven't spent any time on preparing moms for the transitions like returning to work and weaning," Mary said.

LeeAnn leaned over and whispered, "Tish needs that lesson on weaning."

"Some of that is because most moms are only here during the beginning stages of their baby's infancy. But I'd love it if they could come back and continue with us through the first year of their baby's life."

"You could have the group in the evening once a month so working moms can come," suggested a newer mom to the group. "I know I'd come. This is all new to me, and I'll be back to work in a few months." Others in the room agreed.

"Well, I never thought to hold the group in the evening. I love that idea. I'll talk to the office manager to see if we can make that happen. Well, Sasha brought cupcakes, so everyone enjoy, and I'll start weighing babies," Mary said as she grabbed the first cupcake on her way to the weigh station.

Sasha sat down beside me. "Lonnie, I'm going to miss you being in the group with us."

"Sasha, we're going out on Thursday. You'll see me then."

"I know, but who's going to start insightful discussions?"

"I can start insightful discussions," said LeeAnn.

"I said insightful, not controversial," Sasha countered. We all chuckled, not aware that our conversation was being tapped by none other than Tish. She walked over to us, giving a slow clap, acknowledging her displeasure with the honor that I was being shown.

"You will be missed, Lonnie." Tish said and turned to walk away. I had no intention of responding, but LeeAnn never backed down from a potential fight.

"Jealous much," LeeAnn said.

Tish spun around and snapped, "I have no reason to be jealous."

"Then why the sarcasm? We're all excited for Lonnie's transition. Why are you and Butt Buddy Bobbi sitting in the corner with the prune faces?"

"At least I don't have a pit bull doing all the barking for me." She directed her gaze toward me. "This group was harmonious and very impactful before you showed up."

"There's nothing wrong with change, Tish."

"I don't have a problem with change."

"You do when you're not initiating it," LeeAnn retorted.

Tish glared at LeeAnn, "Take your flunkies with you when you leave." She walked away. LeeAnn was ready to go after her, but I motioned for her to sit.

"She's talking to the wrong person. I'm nobody's flunkie."

"We all know you're no flunkie, LeeAnn. Let her have her moment. I'm getting a cupcake. You want one?"

Sasha returned from the weigh station and LeeAnn, with a mouthful of cupcake, asked, "So, where are we going on Thursday?"

"It's this new spot south of downtown. I'll text you the address. They recommend being there no later than eight as it gets crowded around then. Good thing we will be arriving at seven."

"Do they serve adult beverages?" LeeAnn asked.

"They do. And since you educated us on the pump and dump, I'm going to join you this time," said Sasha.

"Did you check in with Grace to see how her first day was, Lonnie?" asked Sasha.

"I didn't, but I will today. I'm so excited for her."

LeeAnn came back from the weigh station and said, "Tag, you're up next."

I took Eva for our turn and waited as Mary finished up a conversation with another mom.

"Lonnie, I'm so proud of you and Eva. You have done beautifully over these six weeks."

"Thanks, Mary. I dreaded coming here, but it's been so valuable. Thank you for all your help."

"Thank *you*. You've been an asset to the group. I hope everything goes well with your return to work. I'm going to send out an email by the end of the week to let everyone know the verdict on the night meeting once month. I love that idea!"

"I would definitely come."

Mary did her usual checkup and recorded how Eva was doing. We went over last week's numbers to show how well Eva was developing compared to the norms. We quickly recapped pumping at work and ended our visit with a hug.

LeeAnn and I decided to get in one more lunch date at Hot Spatula. When we arrived, the waitress who usually served us asked if we wanted our usual drinks. We both agreed that sounded good.

"One check today," LeeAnn said. "We're celebrating her return to work next week. My treat."

"You don't have to do that."

"I know, but I want to. Meeting you has been a breath of fresh air for me. At this age, meeting someone who's a new mom again is rare. And you're just a great person. I've made a new friend."

"I feel the same way. I told Mary that I had dreaded going to the support group, but I was glad I did. I got more than what I expected—new friends."

We lingered longer than usual. We talked about an exhibition she was participating in the next month that she wanted me to attend. I put it on my calendar. She encouraged me again to maintain balance and call if I needed a pick-me-up. Our leave-taking included a hug preceding our goodbye.

Thursday I joined in the morning routine and pulled Eva into the mix. We got ourselves together and the guys headed out for their day. My mother-in-law arrived in good spirits, and I left for work.

This was it. I was only a few days away from fully embracing the opportunity I had worked so hard for. As I drove to the office, a feeling started building inside of me. It was anticipation. I'd made my way through my detour, and now the thing I set out for in the first place was in view. I pulled into my parking spot, grabbed my briefcase loaded with an agenda in case one hadn't been prepared for this meeting. When I stepped into the office, there was fanfare.

Everyone was excited to see me. They asked for pictures of Eva and wanted to know when I was coming back. I addressed all the attention and made my way to my office. I took a few minutes to sit in my chair and reacclimate myself to my space, then I walked to the conference room for the meeting.

Danielle, my secretary, greeted me along with Julia and Will. I was ready to get down to business. They updated me on personnel changes including Mike's replacement who started this week. They got me up to speed on every department, account, and the financial status of our branch. They addressed all the questions that I had prepared based on my emails. It went slick as glass.

"I just want to thank you all for covering me during my maternity leave and making this transition successful despite the unexpected. Julia, thank you. It sounds like you have done an amazing job sitting in for me and filling the void that Mike left."

"My pleasure. You deserve this position, Lonnie, and having a taste of it let me know that you were the right person for the job. So, get in here and take your place."

"Lonnie, is there anything we need to do for you to help with your transition back to work?" Will asked.

"I'm breastfeeding, so I'll need to block out half an hour or so twice a day to take care of that obligation."

"Do you want that to be a standing block of time on your calendar or is this a floating block of time?" Danielle asked.

"Let's start with a fixed time. Also I'll be out of the office early next Thursday for a doctor's appointment."

After the meeting, Will introduced me to Rob, the new Director of Creative Services, then we did a post meeting back in my office. Luckily, except for the Mike incident, the branch had done well in my absence. Will was able to smooth things over with the client who was threatening to leave.

"Lonnie, if you need help, you know you can reach out to me."

"Thanks, Will."

"I'm serious. Coming back to work is going to be a big change. I want to make sure you don't crash and burn."

"I know when I'm at my limit, Will. I will ask for help as needed."

"We have our weekly conference call, but I'm open to meeting in person or meeting more than once a week if you need that."

"I'll make use of that offer if the need arises."

"All right. I'm confident you'll do great, Lonnie. I've got a few other meetings at my office, so I'm going to get going. I'll chat with you next week." Not two seconds after Will was out the door, in came Leonard with his pleasantries.

"Lonnie, how are you? How is Eva?" he asked.

"We are both doing great, Leonard. I was just in the process of sending out calendar invites with all the department heads for next week. What day and time works for you?" I tried to stay ahead of his meaningless chatter.

"Tuesday around ten would be good for me."

"Perfect. I'm sending you the invite now. I've got quite a bit to catch up on. Can I follow up with you next week in our meeting?"

"Oh sure. I just wanted to stop by and say welcome back."

"Thank you, Leonard. It's good to see you."

After I sent my calendar invites, I recalled that I

hadn't followed up with Grace. She may still be in orientation. I looked for her name in the directory, and it was there. I sent her an email asking how her first week was going, and I gave her my office number in case she needed anything. After I sent the email, I remembered I was going to see her tonight anyway, which triggered me to look at the clock.

My time had gotten away from me. Of course, as soon as I needed to leave, people began stopping by, one after the other. Before I knew it, another hour had gone by, and my breasts were screaming at me. I rushed out of the building, but my breasts reached their spill point and began leaking. I hadn't brought my breast pump, because I didn't think I would be at the office this long. I called Sheryl and asked when Eva had last eaten. She said Eva was napping but due to get up and eat soon. I told her to hold off on that feeding because a fresh meal was on the way.

I flew into the house and found Sheryl with a very unhappy baby. I swooped her up and ran up to her room. We got settled in the rocking chair. We both found relief in a common denominator, my breast. I watched this little baby happily chug away and relaxed in that moment. I'll look forward to this in the evenings. Our moment together. Sheryl knocked on the door. I grabbed a receiving blanket that was close by and covered up.

"You can come in."

"Is she a happy baby now?" Sheryl asked as she peeked into the room.

"She is. Thank you for tolerating her hangry cries."

"I remember those days."

"How long did you breastfeed?"

"It was regaining popularity at the time, but most people were using baby formula. When your money is small, you can't afford to be popular. I breastfed until they could eat cereal, so no more than six months. You all have it good. You can feed your babies anywhere, pump milk at work, and you have enough money to choose what you want to do."

"It's hard to imagine how women were able to function without some of the necessities we have now."

"I don't know how we did it, or how my mother did it. But we're all here today, so I guess whatever we did worked."

"Thank you for being willing to help me these next two weeks. I know I'm fortunate to have a supportive family."

"We're lucky to have such a wonderful daughter-in-law to help our son raise wonderful grandchildren. Well, is there anything I can do before I go?"

"There's some chicken in the freezer. Will you put it in the microwave to defrost it? Tell DJ to turn it over when it beeps."

"Will do. What time do I need to be here Monday, Tuesday, and Wednesday?"

"Eight-thirty would be perfect."

"Got it. See you at eight thirty on Monday. I'll get that chicken started for you before I leave."

"Thanks, Sheryl."

I peacefully rocked, in no hurry to finish, but I needed to get ready for my outing. I put Eva down and texted LeeAnn to see if she needed a ride.

"YES! Sasha does too," LeeAnn responded.

A text to Sasha revealed Rachel's husband was dropping her off and picking her up from Sasha's, so they both needed a ride.

Noticing a trend, I texted Grace and got back a yes. A quick group text with pickup times handled details.

David took over in the kitchen. I squeezed in a pump session. I told everyone goodbye and was out the door to pick up the ladies. Grace and LeeAnn were first. When we got to Sasha's, Rachel was ready to go, but Sasha was still putting the finishing touches on her look.

"Okay, LeeAnn, we're taking your word on this pumping and dumping. If my baby is chill and sleeping extra-long, I know where you live," Grace said.

"I actually did some more research on consuming alcohol while breastfeeding. As long as you're not silly drunk, you're cool. You don't even have to pump and dump. Just wait two hours after you consume the alcohol or until you're sober. So, we should be free and clear by time we get home," Rachel said.

"You all are funny," I said.

"Thank you, Lonnie, for being the good girl. Everything is on us tonight," said LeeAnn.

"If anyone throws up on me or spills a drink on me, I'll leave you there," I said.

We were greeted with a neon sign across the entrance reading The Hole. I looked at the people filing into this place, and started to have second thoughts. I looked at LeeAnn.

"Don't go geriatric on us. We are out to celebrate you, and you're going to have fun."

We piled out of the car. The closer we get, the louder the music was thumping. The Hole turned out to be a club. A high end one, but a club nonetheless. I haven't been to a club since I was in college. The other ladies started dancing toward an open high top table along the wall.

"What do you think, Lonnie? You ready to celebrate?" Sasha asked over the music.

"I think I was expecting a fun evening at a chain restaurant."

"Boring! You only live once. When will we ever do this again, Lonnie?" asked LeeAnn.

Grace was on the other side of the dance floor chatting with another group of women. Sasha and Rachel were on the dance floor with drinks already in hand. And LeeAnn placed an order with the waitress who came to the table.

"Can I get something for you?" she asked.

"Uh, a lemonade please."

"She's the designated driver for us," LeeAnn blurted. "Let's dance, Lonnie!"

She grabbed my hand and pulled me to the dance floor. I must admit, it's been a while since I've danced, so it took me a minute to warm up. LeeAnn was right, when will I do this again? I shouldn't be doing it now, but I'm here. I loosened up a little and began to let my body flow with the music.

We danced a while and returned to our table.

"Here's a real toast," said LeeAnn, "to working moms!"

"To working moms!" we all shouted. We shared happy hour appetizers while Rachel and Grace gave their accounts of pumping at work.

"I had to borrow a sweater from one of my coworkers because I forgot to wear my breast pads, and I started leaking!" Rachel said.

"You were in the store, why didn't you just buy some?" Sasha asked.

"It was the end of the shift, and I didn't want to spend the money."

"I was too shy to ask where the nursing room was, so I did exactly what Mary said not to do. I tried pumping in the bathroom," Grace shared. The table erupted with laughter.

"No, Grace!"

"Trust me, I didn't make that same mistake the next day."

"You could have asked me, Grace. I could have told you where it is," I said.

"I know now."

"So tell me how that worked. Did you use the handicap stall and sit on the stool lined with toilet paper with your pump on the sink. I bet it took you forever to let down," said none other than LeeAnn.

"Well, Queen NIP, it went something like that," Grace said flippantly. We laughed some more. "Take Mary's advice and don't do that."

"So, boss lady Lonnie, do you know where your pumping room is?" asked Rachel.

"I not only know where it is, I've got reservations." Everyone laughed.

"I've got reservations too," Sasha said, "in my nursery." LeeAnn high fived.

"Another drink to working moms," LeeAnn said and held

her glass to the sky. I raised my lemonade, and we saluted working moms. The waitress asked if our table would like another round of drinks. I had to practically yell over the ladies not to bring anymore as they all protested.

"No more drinks! How about you all go dance that alcohol out of your system and act like you have babies to go home to," I said.

"Boooo, Debbie Downer," Grace said.

"Sober Sally is more like it. I'm your voice of reason," I retorted.

We all danced again before we ended our outing. It felt reminiscent of days before children when plans could be made on the fly, staying out all night and just having fun. I gave myself to the moment, knowing that within the next two hours reality was going to hit me like hangovers were going to hit them.

We piled in my car with all kinds of chatter going on. I gave thanks to God that no one got drunk. I wouldn't have to explain anything to anyone's husband.

"You guys are my breast friends," Rachel said. Everyone looked at the others in car and burst out in laughter. I guess I spoke too soon.

I dropped off Rachel and Sasha first, then Queen NIP. Grace and I chatted on our way to her house. She shared how she ended up being a single mom and her challenges with having to be a caregiver for her mom on and off. She was too young to have this story. I felt bad for every time I thought my life was hard.

"Well, I'm glad I was able to help you out. If you ever need anything, please don't hesitate to ask. I really enjoyed hanging out with everyone tonight," I said.

"I did too. Between caring for my mom, the situation with Jackson's dad, and trying to work, I never went out with friends. Being pregnant didn't help."

We pulled up to her house.

"Back to life," she said as she got out of the car. I waited for her to get in the house safely. She waved before closing the door.

The drive home was bittersweet. The memories of our evening were sweet, but I only had three days left before I had to prove to myself and everyone that I really could be a working mom with an infant. Sure, I've been a working mom for years, but a breastfeeding executive, knocking on the door of midlife, is a whole 'nother level.

I sat in the car and completed my video diary entry. I didn't know why I tried to maintain people's privacy on my personal diary videos, but I did. I ended with

You guys are my breast friends.

"So how was your outing," David asked. "You smell like you had a good time. You didn't pick up a new man while you were out did you?"

"I've already picked up the only man I'll ever need." I kissed him and pulled the sleeping baby from his arms. "When was the last time she ate?"

"About an hour ago."

"Can you grab my pump? I'll need to do that before I can go to bed." I put Eva in her crib and changed my clothes while he was getting the pump. While I used it, we chatted about our day and about me returning to work.

"I was thinking about going by to pick up Dad in a limo and taking him to dinner on Saturday to celebrate his retirement. What do you think?"

"As long as you keep it small. He's really bummed about not working."

"I hate that he won't let me do something big for him. He's worked that job for as long as I can remember."

"I can empathize with him. If I couldn't do what I do, I wouldn't feel like myself. And the thought of living on a fixed income . . ." David shuddered.

"He can always get another job if he doesn't want to be

restricted financially. It's not the end of the world. He's not even that old."

"You'd have to be a man to understand, babe."

"I don't want to think like y'all. You are grim, glass half empty."

"That's why we need women. We're half empty, women are half full, together we overflow." He took my bottles filled to the brim with breastmilk to the kitchen. I got my pump cleaned up and put away. When we got to bed, he started stroking my back.

"Three more days and the wait is over," he said.

"The wait is over after I go back for my six-week appointment."

"You do have that scheduled, right?"

"I do, but it's not until Thursday."

"You gonna make me wait till Thursday? It's cool. You're worth waiting for. It's gonna be like our wedding night all over again." We both laughed uncontrollably.

"Goodnight. Your daughter will have me up soon."

In the morning after everyone got off to work and school, Lisa called me. She scheduled a return-to-work outing. It would be her, Jackie, and me for Sunday. Her outing plan was more my speed—lunch and the spa!

"Lisa, thank you. I'm so excited!"

"You deserve it, girl. You need to get those nails done and have those muscles soothed before you go back into that office."

"What time are we meeting?"

"I'm going to come get you around noon. There's this little restaurant I went to last week with some coworkers that I think you'll like."

"I trust you."

I was too excited! Who doesn't love a spa day with the girls? The company I'd kept for the last six weeks had been a breath of fresh air too. There weren't any spa days involved, but every encounter awakened something new in me. I opened myself to others in a way I hadn't in a long time. I was going to miss seeing the BSG ladies every week. I knew I'd get to see Grace occasionally, and LeeAnn and I would definitely see each other. Maybe I'd run into Rachel at the store. Knowing Sasha, she'd schedule regular playdates to keep us together. Sasha had already sent a text message with a picture of us from last night. A night to remember.

And the Story Continues

I needed to get something together for dinner, but I'd have to go to the store and I was still traumatized from the last grocery outing. David would just have to pick up something. I was not going out today. Staying out late and being able to function the next day had been an epic fail for me today, and I didn't even drink.

When the boys got in, I informed them that today was Papa's last day working and that we were going to take him to dinner tomorrow to celebrate.

"You mean he'll just be at home?" Johnny asked.

"Not for the first few weeks. He'll be here watching Eva. I'm sure he'll get a different job later. He'll be like Grandpa and Nanna. They're retired, so they don't go to work every day like your dad and I do."

"Sounds boring," DJ said.

"Once he finds something he likes to do, it will be the best time of his life. So where should we take him to celebrate this new adventure?"

"He likes Mexican," Johnny piped in.

"You're right, he does. There's a place downtown I think he'll like. I'll make a reservation."

"Why is Papa coming to watch Eva?" Johnny asked.

"I go back to work next week, and Eva can't go to daycare for a few more weeks."

"Back to work! Already? You should stay at home with

Eva. I like it when I come home from school and you're here," Johnny protested.

"Yeah, Mom, one day you're going to look up and we'll be grown men, living in our own houses," DJ said.

Now, that one hurt. Thoughts flooded my mind, and my eyes started to water. The memories of the boys as babies and all their milestones and the imagination of the kind of men they would be overwhelmed me with emotion. "Boys, I'm going to lay Eva down and do a few things upstairs. Dad should be home soon with dinner."

I turned my face away from them and went upstairs. I closed the door to Eva's room and sat in the rocking chair with her and began to cry. We were happy before Eva came. No one was discontent with me working. I was a great mom and a great wife. I received this opportunity at work but everything was fighting against it. I had given everything to my family, but still they wanted more. More of me, which left less for me. I knew this was stinkin' thinkin' and that they were just speaking through a kid's perspective, but there was truth in what they said. One day they would be out in the world, and I'd be parenting sporadically from afar. But should I spend my years fully devoting myself to them and never pursuing my own desires? My family was my top priority, but they were not my *only* desire.

I was messed up emotionally. I tried to think who I could talk to about this. I couldn't fight these thoughts on my own. I put Eva down to sleep and wiped the tears from my face and went to my room to call LeeAnn.

"Well, hello, working mom. Just to let you know, Wind did not have any signs of alcohol consumption from our outing last night," LeeAnn said.

I chuckled. "Funny you call me that. I'm having a meltdown about going back. My kids are putting a guilt trip on me, saying I should stay home because one day they'll be grown men."

"That's true. They will be grown one day. But whether

you work or not won't determine the kind of men they will be. How you spend every moment you do have with them is the secret to success. Stop worrying. Live your life. Don't get hung up in this moment."

"Thanks. I needed to hear that."

"You good now?"

"I'm good."

"Okay, I gotta go. We're taking family pictures tomorrow morning and I've got to get everyone's clothes laid out and both kids need a bath. Wind's got that nasty milk neck going on. You lean in to kiss his little neck and there's curdled milk all stuck in there. In a few minutes, he'll be baby fresh. You can call anytime if you need to."

We ended our call and I felt better. I made reservations for dinner tomorrow at six at the Mexican restaurant I mentioned to DJ and Johnny and then called Dad to tell him we're taking him to dinner tomorrow night and to be ready by five. I called a friend of ours who has a transportation company and scheduled limo service to pick us up here at four-thirty. I heard David come in. I thought I'd need him to manage Eva tonight. I wanted to sleep off these emotions.

On Saturday morning, my eyes popped open and thoughts flashed across my mind. *Did I sleep all night? Did Eva wake up to eat?* I jumped out of bed and rushed over to her room. She wasn't there. I ran back to my room. David wasn't there. I nearly fell down the steps in my mad dash to find my child, only to find her sleeping, laid across David's chest. I went to the kitchen and counted the bottles I had left for the night. He did feed her. Well, that was a first, and it went well. So he could be trusted overnight. I was gonna need that. I thought, we'll make a schedule, maybe we can alternate nights.

I went into panic mode again. I couldn't take my dad out to celebrate retirement and not have a gift! He isn't a jewelry person. He's kind of a homebody, so I didn't know if he'd like to travel. He's not a sportsman or a handyman. He's not techie.

And a gift card or cash was just not special enough. I was at a loss. I could throw on some clothes and go to the mall and hope to find something, but that could turn out to be a total waste of time.

LeeAnn! Maybe she had something that would be unique for Dad. I sent her a text and asked what time her studio opened. She responded with the time and asked what I was looking for. I shared that my dad had retired and I wanted something special for the occasion. She said that she'd see me in a few hours. I pumped, showered, and got dressed. Most of the family had roused and was moving about. I let David know my mission and took off to LeeAnn's studio. Since I was out by myself, I treated myself to a drive-through breakfast. The little things in life.

The studio was located in a small industrial area that had taken on a boutique feel with lots of little shops. LeeAnn's shop didn't disappoint. It was just as unique as she is and so well put together with all kinds of furniture and accessories she had constructed.

"Welcome. I didn't think I'd get you in here," LeeAnn greeted me.

"I told you I'd come see it."

"People say that all the time. I'm glad you're here. Let me tell you how I typically help my customers pick a piece. Think about who the piece is for and what the occasion is. And once you have those thoughts in your mind, look at the pieces that are here and see which one tells your story."

"Wow. That's an interesting approach. Okay, I'll give it a try."

"It's not really any different than when you shop for anything else. It's just that most people don't think of how a gift tells a story of the person they are gifting. They only consider the occasion, but not the story behind their loved one. I'll give you some time and come back to check on you."

She walked to the back, and I began to explore the studio, taking my time to see if I could find a story. I stopped by one chair that looked interesting. I stood for a while looking at it. Then I sat in it. I reached to set my purse on a nearby table and the table itself caught my attention. I began to study its structure. It was tiered with a wide base and the top of the table was beautiful marquetry. And the story began to unfold. The base represented my father, broad and wide with love. That base supported the two tiers, which represented me and my mom. The marquetry top was composed of many shapes and grains of the same material. It reminded me of the many experiences we've had as a family and how those life experiences made a beautiful pattern.

I sat in the chair, enthralled by this story that just sprang into my mind from looking at a piece of furniture! I called to LeeAnn and said, "I'll take this table."

"Nice choice. Tell me the story that came to mind when you saw this piece." I walked her through my thoughts.

"That's amazing, Lonnie. Would you like anything inscribed on it?"

Now I was stumped. How do you put in a few words the importance of the most influential man in your life?

"And the story continues," I said. "That's what it should say."

"Where should I inscribe that?"

"On the base at the front."

"I love it. Come back this afternoon, and I'll have it ready for you."

"We're taking him to dinner at five. Could I come at three?"

"It'll be ready for you."

"Thanks, LeeAnn. This is truly special."

I drove home very happy with this gift for Dad. I looked forward to giving it to him and telling him the story. David went to get the table while I finished getting everyone together.

David maneuvered his car in Dad's driveway and the limo parked behind him. I could see Dad peeking out the front window. His neighbors sitting on their porches stood up to see what was going on.

Dad stepped out the front door. "What is this?"

"It's a celebration!" the boys hollered from the window of the limo. "Congrats, Papa!"

"Before we go to dinner, Dad, we have something special for you to celebrate your retirement and this new stage in your life. Let's go inside for a minute. David will bring it in."

David carried the table in and set it next to my dad's favorite chair where he had a little TV dinner table. I shared with him the story that the table told me and said that the inscription was to remind him that even though he has retired, his story continues. Dad was in tears, and he gave us all hugs.

"Who would have thought a table could talk," he laughed through his tears. "Thank you for such a thoughtful gift."

The driver took us downtown to dinner. Dad was super excited about the restaurant when he saw it was Mexican. Once our bellies were filled to the brim, we left the restaurant and the driver drove us all over downtown. It's so beautiful at night when it's all lit up. I glanced at Dad a few times. I could see his heart was as full as his belly. That was priceless, something that I will always remember. I'm glad I semi-listened to him about celebrating his retirement. I kept it small, so he was happy and so was I.

We pulled back into Dad's driveway and David got the kids in our vehicle while I walked Dad to the door.

"Lonnie, this was special."

"You're special, Dad, and this is a very special achievement and deserves to be celebrated. You deserve to be celebrated."

He hugged me. "I love you."

"I love you too, Dad."

"Thank you for the table. When I sit in my chair to watch TV tonight, it'll hold my tea and remind me how strong I am and that tomorrow will bring something new."

David helped me into the car, and we all did our usual wave as we pulled out of the driveway.

The boys and David happily shared their highlights from the evening on the drive home, but I stared out the window with a full heart, internalizing the joy I felt.

When we got everyone to bed, David and I sat on the couch, not saying much at first, but simply enjoying each other's company.

"Your dad was really happy tonight."

"I know. I got so much joy out of doing that for him. And the gift! I don't think I would have ever come up with a table as a retirement gift." We both laughed because it did sound kind of silly. But LeeAnn was right. We stop at the person and the occasion and don't consider the story that could wrap around the gift. That had made the difference today.

"You ready for your girls' outing tomorrow? There's been a lot of celebrating going on this week!"

"Yes, I am excited. We haven't hung out since the baby was born. And I haven't had a massage in ages."

"You deserve it, babe. I'll hold down the fort for you."

"Thanks, you're the best," I wrapped my arms around him and squeezed.

"How about we celebrate once more tomorrow evening, and I make you something special for dinner."

"How about we just do a special dessert. I think I may still be stuffed."

"Deal."

We talked about the nightly feeding schedule and agreed on alternating days during the week. We chatted for a little while longer before he fell asleep. I took that opportunity to add to my video diary. I wanted to look back on how I felt today. I roused David from his sleep, and we headed to bed where I fell asleep in his embrace. What a perfect day.

Sunday morning I was surprised with breakfast and a card from the boys. After breakfast I started getting myself together for my outing. The ladies showed up right at noon. Let the fun begin!

We went to the restaurant and the food and conversation were amazing. After lunch we were ready for the spa. Hot tub time came before our massages. Our conversation never lagged.

"Lonnie, what has been your happiest moment of having a new baby and what is your greatest fear about going back to work?" Lisa asked.

"That's a loaded double question, Lisa. Honestly, the brightest spot of Eva coming has been the friends that have come along with her. And my biggest fear is not being able to balance it all."

"Tell me more about the friends," Jackie said.

"You know in the beginning breastfeeding was a struggle, so I was sentenced to a breastfeeding support group. Well, the moms I met there have been a breath of fresh air."

"And why do you think you won't be able to balance life? You balance it better than any of us," Lisa said.

"I usually plan the events in my life and prepare contingencies for the ones that aren't planned. Eva was unplanned, and we weren't prepared. Whatever I thought my life would look like in the future, well, that has changed. Everything has and will change because of this little person. The boys told me the other day that I should stay home."

"They really said that?"

"They really said that. I was messed up for a few hours. I was really upset because the promotion at work is something I have really wanted for myself, and they can't see the value in that. I know they're kids, but their desire for me to be with them more often is real. I just want to be able to maintain a piece of me. Is that selfish?"

"NO!" they both exclaimed.

"This is your life, and if you want to work and get fulfillment from that, then do that. If you were to stay home and not be fulfilled, you'd regret it, and everyone in that house would regret it as well," Lisa said.

"She's right. If that's not something you want to do, you're not going to do it well. Some women want that and love being a domestic engineer. But if that's not your passion, you will suck at it, and the boys will be begging you to go back to work," Jackie said. We laughed at the truth of that.

When our masseuses were ready for us, we split up. This would have been the most amazing massage if my breasts weren't leaking. I put a rolled up towel under them to prevent a flood on the table. I ended my session a little early and pumped. I knew I'd be out longer than my breasts' capacity, so yes, I brought the pump. I finished up in time to join the ladies for mani-pedis.

Around five they dropped me off at my house and wished me well for my first week back to work. David was making dinner and Johnny was sitting on the couch feeding Eva when I came in the house.

"Well, family, tomorrow Mom is back to work. We have to make sure as much as possible is done at night so our mornings go smoothly."

"We're already ahead of you, Mom. We pulled out our outfits for the whole week. I'm getting ready to iron our clothes, and Eva's bottles are all clean," DJ announced.

"I'm Impressed, guys."

"Lonnie," David called from the kitchen, "if you want to get your things ready for tomorrow, we've got a few more minutes until dinner."

I took his advice and got my outfit ready for the big day. I'm still wearing my maternity clothes. It'll be a while before I can get back into my pre-pregnancy clothing. I chose an outfit that had the best fit and got it ironed for tomorrow. I took a little more time and wrote down Eva's schedule and where to find all of her things for my mother-in-law. Then it seemed a good time to video the highlights for my last day of maternity leave. Tomorrow would start yet another chapter of this journey.

Daddy Daycare

Eva chose the worst night to be fussy. David and I had taken turns with her. When I finished her five a.m. feeding, I just wanted to go back to sleep even though I knew I had to get up soon. Fatigue weighed down my eyelids, so I decided not to fight it. I set the alarm for six and hoped to get in another 20 minutes of sleep. Twenty minutes later, I hit the snooze button. Fifteen minutes later I hit the snooze button again. Fifteen minutes after that when Johnny came in and woke me up, my heart skipped when I looked at the clock.

Eva was crying and Johnny was trying to comfort her. I grabbed a quick shower and relieved Johnny so he could eat breakfast. After a short feeding, I put her down and managed to deal with my hair and makeup and get myself dressed. I rushed to get Eva's bottles prepped. It had not been a smooth morning when I finally rushed out the door.

I was flustered and my palms were sweaty on the steering wheel. I needed some morning motivation for this commute. A quick skim through recent shows from my favorite podcaster landed on one about transitions. Yeah, that sounded good.

By the time I pulled into my parking space, I was calm and ready for the day.

I walked into the office, head held high, waving like a celebrity. One glance at the number of emails in my inbox deflated my good spirits. My first meeting was in forty minutes. I put on my game face, big girl panties, and whole armor of God in order not to have a mini breakdown before my day even got started.

The forty minutes flew by. I didn't make it through every email but got through enough to get me out of pre-breakdown mode. The first meeting went well, then it was pump time. Our pump room is a small office that was converted to a lactating mothers' room. It has low lighting and easy listening music playing. There's a comfy, oversized chair with a table next to it. There's a small fridge to store milk. I got myself hooked up and broke out my laptop to finish going through the last of this morning's emails. One of my best shower gifts was this pumping bra—hands free pumping!

With the plan to leave on time and feed Eva as soon as I got home, I skipped my second pump session. As the afternoon went on, one person after the next popped in my office, and my soaking wet nursing pads were evidence of the flaw in my plan. I couldn't leave the office soggy every day.

The sound of Eva crying greeted me when I walked in the door. I scooped her up and went upstairs to feed her. David stepped away from meal prep to check on me.

"How was the first day back?"

"It went well. I had to get my head back in the game. It felt a bit overwhelming at first, but I pulled myself together."

"Good girl. Well, my day was interesting. An upper management position became available over the weekend, and my boss recommended that I apply for it."

"Babe! That's awesome!"

"I know! I went back to my desk and wrote a letter to the powers that be with my resume attached and emailed it to HR and my boss. The time commitment and travel concern me, considering we're in a major life change right now."

"Hey, we do not pass up opportunities. We'll make it work. Go for it."

After dinner, even though bed was calling me and tonight was my night with Eva, I recorded a short recap of my first day back to work.

Tuesday and Wednesday were very similar to Monday minus the oversleeping. That wouldn't be happening again seeing as how I set three alarms to go off weekday mornings on my phone. Since today was Dad's first day on the j-o-b with Eva, I didn't rush out when he came in. I wanted to make sure he was comfortable. Lucky for him I had my six-week doctor's appointment today, and Eva would be attending that with me, so I'd be home a little early to get her.

Work was exceptionally intense. I shortened my first pump time and skipped the second session with the intention of feeding Eva when I got to the doctor's office. I barely got out of the office in time to pick her up.

Once we checked in at the OB/GYN's office, I pulled out my handy nursing cover and gave her a quick shot at both sides before we were called back. While we waited for the doc, Eva and I finished our feeding session.

"Well, well. It's the surprise baby. Let me take a look at her!" Dr. Branch held Eva while we discussed labor and delivery, breastfeeding, and return to work. "It sounds like you both have been successful thus far. Let's check out your goods to see if they are faring as well."

She laid Eva in her car seat, and I assumed the position. I had a little discomfort with the exam. She said that I needed an additional two weeks of healing time. No reason for concern. I was just older and needed more time to heal. I made an appointment for two weeks from today. David wasn't going to like that. But I needed my aged vagina to heal properly before he went to work. After the appointment, I took myself to have ice cream before going home. It was the best thing I'd had all day.

During my second pump session of the day, I got an email from Mary at the breastfeeding support group notifying me that they were now offering an evening session once a month. I was happy to see this and immediately put the date in my calendar. I texted the ladies from the group to make sure they were aware, especially Grace and Rachel. I'd been so busy I hadn't even checked in on Grace, so I took a moment to send her an email. Her response that she loved her new job and that she would try to make it to the group made me smile.

The next email made me frown. At the end of the month, every department had reports they submitted for review. I reviewed them to determine if action plans were necessary and then reported these outcomes to upper management. Although I was frowning, I wasn't complaining. This position was perfect for me, and I was happy to have it. I put away all my pumping supplies and milk with a few minutes to spare before my last meeting of the day. I had taken work home the past two days. I didn't see that changing any time soon since it was the end of the month.

I came dragging into the house from work on Friday. Dad was sitting on the couch feeding Eva.

"Hey, Lonnie. Come sit with me."

"Sure, Dad. What's up? Did something happen with Eva today?"

"No. Well, maybe." Now I'm concerned. "I was thinking that you don't have to send her to daycare. I'm not doing anything. I can keep her."

"Dad! You just retired. You should be enjoying your time, not changing poopy diapers. I don't think it's a good idea. Plus, I'd lose my spot at the daycare."

"Lonnie, we both know that her staying home is a better option, especially the first year."

"What's bringing on this conversation, Dad?"

"Well, when I agreed to do this for you, I started reading up on babies since it's been so long ago that the boys were little. I read this article last week about the health benefits of keeping them home their first year. Those daycares are full of germs. It'll cut down on days you would need to take off for having a sick child."

"Dad." I dropped my head and rubbed my temples.

"Think about it over the weekend and let me know on Sunday what your decision is. I'm ready to do it. I've enjoyed being with her these past two weeks."

"You've only been with her Thursdays and Fridays, not the whole week."

"Talk to David about it. What's for dinner tonight?" he said, deflecting my disapproval of his idea.

"I'm not sure. It's David's night to cook. Don't change the subject, Dad. I don't think this is a good idea."

"Talk to David and then get back with me. Do you want me to drop DJ at the football game since I'm heading out?"

"Now *that* is a good idea I'll take you up on." I called for DJ and let him know that Papa was taking him to the game and that his dad would pick him up.

"I'll take him to get something to eat before the game. DJ, let's go. We'll get you something to eat before your game."

That night David and I discussed my dad's offer. I expected David to dismiss the idea like I had, but we spent time debating the pros and cons.

"What if he comes to his senses one day and says he doesn't want to keep her anymore? We'd have to wait forever on some daycare waitlist to get her in. That's too risky."

"I hear you, but the money we would save and the PTO days we wouldn't burn on a sick kid needs to be considered. And I trust your dad over a daycare provider."

"Those are valid points, but he just retired. I felt bad for asking for the two weeks."

"Lonnie, this is your dad we're talking about, not a friend. He'd do anything for his family, and he always puts family first. What if I asked my mom to do one day a week and he can do four days. Would that make you comfortable?"

"This isn't what we planned."

"Are we talking about daycare or having another child?"

"Either."

"Okay. Sleep on it tonight. Let's talk again tomorrow.

We can have them over for dinner on Sunday to discuss it."

I reluctantly agreed. This idea didn't compute with me. I knew Dad was struggling with being retired, but caring for an infant wasn't a logical replacement for work. This conversation messed up my night to sleep in. I kept thinking about this proposal from every possible angle. I hated the idea of putting my dad to work so soon after he retired. I decided to oppose this as the person with the final say.

I finally dozed off, but my sleep was not good. My thoughts kept waking me. When Eva woke for her early morning feeding, I got up to feed her and let David sleep. As we peacefully rocked, I wondered if this was what Dad felt. Not the vigorous sucking of a baby on your breast, but the calming assurance that at that moment, you are giving another human being what they need to thrive. The pride you feel supersedes fatigue and selfish thoughts. In that moment you are operating at the highest calling of the human experience. Pouring yourself into someone else.

If I were to guess what Dad was thinking, I'd guess he was feeling that pinnacle of the human experience. He could look at me and my family and know that he poured himself into me to help all this happen. If holding a baby girl again gave him hope that retirement wasn't giving him, that would be a good thing. I didn't want to rob him of an opportunity that he would never experience again. Eva would only be a baby for a short time. So, why not fill Dad's days with something that would give meaning to his life? And, besides, we could save money. Was I talking myself into this? We'd see what everyone had to say on Sunday.

I took a walk Sunday morning. My thoughts were churning, and I couldn't refrain from taking a position of defense. In my mind, I already had two against me and there were only two others who could be persuaded to my position. David's parents were reasonable people. Surely they'll see my point of view.

My mother-in-law brought a dessert that my husband absolutely loves. I couldn't help but think this was a sign that she'd choose her own flesh and blood over me. I shook that thought off. This wasn't David versus me. We enjoyed dinner and then sent the boys outside to play, and David initiated the discussion.

"So, we had you all come over because Evan has asked to take care of Eva while we're at work. This means Eva wouldn't have to go to daycare. We wanted to have you all here so we can make a sensible decision. I'm in favor of Evan keeping Eva. We know she'll be well taken care of, and the money we would have spent on childcare can go into a college fund."

"And I am opposed," I quickly said. "Dad retired a few weeks ago and now has an opportunity to spend his time focusing on himself and not working or caring for someone. Retirement is a special time for an adult and shouldn't be consumed with responsibilities. Dad should be doing something he enjoys, not changing dirty diapers."

"Lonnie," Sheryl said, "retirement is personal. You spend your life serving others out of necessity, whether it's to raise children, make money to feed a family, or in the worst scenarios, because you are forced to work due to your circumstances. But when you get to retirement, and you have prepared for it, it's your turn to choose how you want to spend your time. Some people keep working because they enjoy that, some travel, some take up hobbies. I'd like to hear Evan's thinking behind his choice."

Here we go. I feel defeat coming.

"Lonnie, keeping Eva these last two weeks . . ."

"Four days, Dad."

". . . these four days made me feel alive. Sheryl's right. I spent my life raising you, supporting you, doing everything in my power to make sure you were successful. And having the opportunity to help you make that happen for my granddaughter is a breath of fresh air. For me, retirement was like a death sentence. What am I supposed to do all day? Sit on the couch and watch TV while I eat poorly and end up with bad health and die? I want my family to be my retirement. I want to enjoy the people I've worked so hard to support and care for all these years."

"Dad, what happens when the fuzzy feelings from a newborn wear off and you're ready to go off and spend your time doing something else?"

"Then if you want to send her to daycare, send her. But right now, I *want* to keep her for you."

"Mom, Dad, what are your thoughts?" David asked.

"Let the man do what he wants to do," said Jerry. "Caring for babies was never my cup of tea. But I haven't walked in Evan's shoes. I was blessed with three healthy children and a healthy wife. I'll never know the weight of only having one shot at parenting. Evan had one shot with you, Lonnie, and he made it count. If he feels this is an opportunity he wants to take advantage of, let him."

"If I were a woman, you'd gladly accept my offer," Dad said. Everyone around the table nodded in agreement except me.

"What about the daycare provider that's been set up?"

"Call them and tell them you've made other arrangements," said Sheryl.

"And will Grandpa and Nanna be on call when my dad cannot watch Eva, and we need help with childcare?"

"Gladly. This is our granddaughter too," said Sheryl.

"All in favor of Evan keeping Eva, say 'aye.'" And, unanimously, they all agreed that Dad should keep Eva. Now for the hard part. Do I completely reject all of them and send Eva to daycare, or do I listen and drop my case? Our parents are people of their word, and I honor them, but I was not pleased that they were forcing me into this decision.

"Lonnie, let's give it a chance. If we need to change up the plan, we'll change it, but let's give it a try," Dad pleaded.

"I seem to be outnumbered. I'll call the daycare tomorrow," I said as I headed to the kitchen.

"Lonnie, what's wrong?"

Dad had followed me to the kitchen. "Dad, you're supposed to be done working."

"Watching Eva is not work. She sleeps most of the day anyway."

"She does now, but that won't last long. Dad, I don't want you locked into another job."

"This isn't a job, Lonnie, it's my granddaughter. I want to be able to enjoy my grandkids, and having the opportunity to watch one of them grow before my eyes is an opportunity I don't want to pass up."

"Promise one thing, Dad."

"What's that?"

"The day you come over and you feel like you are obligated to come, tell me, and we'll enroll her in daycare."

With hesitation, he agreed. I gave him a hug as a sign of truce.

"Is it okay to come in?" Sheryl asked. I nodded yes. "Evan, Jerry and I would love to take Eva on Mondays. Neither of us have anything scheduled on those days, and we want a piece of the action too."

"Well, I guess it's settled," I said.

"We'll renegotiate the terms when she turns one," Sheryl taunted.

That brought chuckles from all of us. I really didn't understand why everyone was okay with this. Why was I *not* okay with it?

The evening ended cheerfully, but I continued to ponder the decision while I busied myself with preparations for Monday. Once everyone went to bed and Eva finished her late feeding, I headed to the office to get in a diary entry.

> **I'm starting to wonder if there is something wrong with me. How is it that everyone feels good about Dad taking care of Eva but me? I don't want Dad to give up his time to babysit. . . . I don't want to give up my opportunity at work. The pregnancy was a glitch in my plans. I love my daughter. I wouldn't trade her for . . . a promotion.**

I stopped recording, because the truth was, I preferred the promotion. I wanted to have both, but there would be days when one would overpower the other, and on those days, which would I prefer? My daughter or my job? I had a twinge of remorse for being so self-absorbed, but I also felt defensive at the notion of having to sacrifice my career for my child. I spent the first half of the weekend building a case for sending the child to daycare, and now I was defending my need to have a career. Right or wrong, I was done thinking. I was going to bed, so I could be ready for tomorrow.

Return of the Mack

My first task of the day was to call the daycare. What excuse would I use? My dad is having a retired-life crisis and wants to be the nanny for my eight-week old? Honestly, I didn't owe them an explanation, but I was still trying to give myself one that made sense. The call went smoothly as apparently this happened frequently. I did lose my non-refundable deposit. I wish I had thought of that when I was pleading my case. Still would've lost.

The morning routine went without a hitch. Dad was taking this first Monday to give Sheryl and Jerry time to get their future Monday schedules planned. He arrived a few minutes early, which was helpful. Johnny had an assignment he hadn't finished over the weekend, and Dad helped him with that while I finished getting dressed. The commute was light for a Monday morning. When I got to the office, I was feeling productive, on time, and ready for my first meeting. I was dominating my day. And then I got my calendar reminder for my pump time and . . . I had forgotten to bring the pump.

I immediately went into panic mode. I couldn't get off schedule. It would affect my milk production. I couldn't walk around all day with leaky breasts. Not only would I end up in an involuntary wet t-shirt contest, but I'd be in miserable pain. My phone dinged. Dad sent me a picture of Eva taking a nap. A lightbulb went off. Dad could bring me the pump!

"Hey, Dad, how are things going? I saw the pic. She's so cute when she sleeps."

"I figured that would brighten your morning."

"I actually need a huge favor. I left my breast pump at home, and I really need it. Do you think you can bring it to my office?"

"Sure can. When do you need it?"

"I kinda need it as soon as possible. It's in my office on the floor."

"Okay, I'm walking back that way now. I want to make sure I get the right thing." I could hear him fumbling around. "Is it this black bag with the tubes hanging out of it?"

"That's it. Just stuff the tubes in the bag and call me when you're on your way. Dad, do you remember how we practiced securing the car seat without the base?"

"I got it, Lonnie. I'll call when I'm on my way."

"Thanks, Dad, you're a lifesaver."

"I know. Aren't you glad I was here with Eva and not lounging in my recliner watching time fly. You would have had to leave work and come all the way home."

Touché.

All the anxiety triggered a letdown, and I dug in my purse to find an extra set of nursing pads. I came up empty. I couldn't take this emotional roller coaster ride. I was trying to work! I headed off to another meeting, my mind completely preoccupied with my breasts. I muscled my way through the meeting and when I stepped out of the conference room, I heard a commotion at the front desk. I headed down the hall to check out what was going on.

"Lonnie, she's beautiful!" said one of our graphic designers. I saw Dad and headed over to him while everyone oohed and ahhed over Eva.

"I've got your *bag*, and I bought you a little something special," he said as he handed me a very familiar bag that held something he knew I loved. The aroma from the bag cut through my anxieties. I gave him a big hug.

"Lonnie, is this your dad?"

"This is my dad, Evan Lee."

"Any connection between their names, Eva and Evan?" someone asked.

"Yes, she is named in honor of her papa." I glanced over at him, and he had the proudest look any man could ever display. In that moment, I gave up my argument for daycare. Who cares? If he's happy, that's all I want.

"Okay, everyone, Evan needs to get back to his papa duties with Eva." There was all kinds of "cute baby" chatter going on as the crowd dispersed. I saw Dad and Eva to the door and quickly headed to the pumping room with my laptop. The day was saved.

I got home a little late. David had already started dinner, and the boys were playing with Eva on the floor in the living room. I sat on the couch to watch them.

"Babe, wake up," David said, as he gently rubbed my leg.

"Was I asleep?"

"Out like a light, Mom," DJ chimed in.

"Sorry, guys."

"Mom, you're a busy lady. It's okay to take a nap," Johnny said.

"Thanks. You all are the best." I pulled myself off the couch and headed to the table for dinner. David had already fed Eva. That meant I'd be pumping after dinner. We ate, I pumped, we prepped for tomorrow, I headed to bed. David came in and jumped in bed next to me.

"What's up?"

"I got the job."

I sat up to embrace him. "I'm so happy for you. When do you assume the position?"

"The question is when can *you* assume the position? Don't you go back to the doctor this week?"

I gave him a playful push. "Seriously, when do you start in your new role? We need to make sure we're prepared. Are your hours going to change?"

"Hours will be the same. Travel is the part we'll have to stay on top of."

"Anything coming up in the next month?"

"I haven't asked, but I'll do it in the morning. How are you doing?" He wrapped his arms around me.

"My emotions are always up and down. It's all these hormones. I don't know if I can do this for a year."

"Let's not think that far in advance. That's going to overwhelm you. Let's just talk about this week. Give me a rundown of what you have on your plate."

"This week is actually light. I have my appointment on Thursday, but I can't think of anything else I have scheduled."

"Do you need to take a night off and go out with a friend?"

"I don't know, maybe."

"Let me know if that turns into a yes. Any day but Thursday when you already have a date with me."

With that he hopped out of bed and went to his closet to finish preparing for tomorrow. I surrendered to a few hours of sleep.

When Thursday rolled around, once again I barely made it in time for my OB/GYN appointment. The morning had been filled with meetings and reports due. Will had been easing me back into work, so he was completing some things for me, but each week he had added more onto my plate. His expectation was that I'd be at full capacity sometime in the next month.

I ran into the OB/GYN's office and got signed in. When they called me back, I ended up waiting for twenty minutes before the doc came in. Because the appointment was scheduled two weeks ago at my last visit, there were no convenient appointment times. This was right in the middle of my scheduled pump time. I had put my pump in the car just in case I didn't make it back to the office in time.

When I finally got an audience with the doc, the pelvic

exam was first, followed by our Q&A. The pelvic exam checked out okay. I could resume sexual activity.

"This pregnancy was a surprise for you, Lonnie. Are you wanting to have more children or should we discuss some more permanent forms of birth control?" Dr. Branch asked.

"I'm going to need something permanent."

"Do I need to prescribe an immediate temporary form of birth control while you are awaiting the permanent option?"

"There seem to be too many side effects with those drugs."

"There are side effects to most birth control medications, but you need to weigh the options, mommy of four or mommy of three."

"Well, since you put it that way, I may consider it. Will the birth control help my emotions? I've been all over the place since I've gone back to work. Will it affect my milk supply?"

"Those are excellent questions. The chances of getting pregnant before Eva is six months are lower because you are breastfeeding. So there's your first line of defense. Pills, patches, injections, implantable devices, and vaginal rings all have side effects not limited to . . ." She listed every unwanted side effect known to man—well, womankind.

"You sound just like the commercials on TV." We both laughed. "With all that I have going on with work and a new baby, I don't want to manage side effects too. Until I'm ready for the permanent fix, we'll stick to condoms."

"Okay. As far as the emotions go, if you don't want to take any medications, you can try meditation, exercise, some dietary things, delegating tasks, the list goes on."

"Well, doc, I think I'll try exercise first. I love to do that, but I haven't gotten around to reintroducing it to my schedule."

"All right, I think we've got a game plan. If anything changes, you can follow up with me or with your primary care physician if it's simply a medication thing. When you're ready for the permanent fix, come see me."

I checked the time after I got back to the car. There was

no way I was going to get in my pump session once I got back to work. I looked at my pump in the seat beside me. If I pumped now, I'd be late for my meeting. The thought of pumping elicited that tingling in my breast. I quit thinking about it and got myself set up and began pumping.

After watching the clock a few minutes, I came up with a grand idea. Drive to the office *while* I'm pumping since my hands are free! Brilliant idea. I fastened my seatbelt—safety first—and headed back to work. I unhooked from everything, straightened myself up, and ran into the building, feeling mighty accomplished. And only a couple minutes late for my meeting. I have no idea if it's legal to drive while pumping milk, but it worked great, and I'll be innocent until proven guilty.

When I got home, the house was unusually quiet. I looked around for the kids, but I didn't see anyone. David called for me from upstairs. I headed up. He was in the bathroom, dressed in a robe, holding a red rose. Old school R&B music was playing in the background. The tub was filled with bubbles, and a glass of sparkling cider was sitting next to some lubricant. The dude has covered all bases. I suspected we had grandparent babysitters to thank for the quiet.

"Welcome home. May I help you relax after a long day at work?"

"Why, yes, I think I'll accept your assistance." The rest of the evening has been censored due to its mature nature.

Over the weekend, David and I made time to discuss our schedules for the coming week since he would begin traveling. It looked like that would be happening at least every other week with his new position. We also took time to discuss our finances. We decided that we'd put the money we were going to spend on daycare into our savings. If we needed it later for daycare, we'd have some money already accounted for. And if we didn't use it, it would go right into the college fund. New week, here we come.

One of my first meetings on Monday was to discuss customer appreciation week. We take this very seriously at our company. Simply dropping off cookies and business cards isn't enough. We take a deep statistical look at what we have been providing the client and if their needs have changed. We try to customize our gift to them through the product we provide. This day was filled with meetings with each department to analyze their accounts and see where we could step up our game.

A few teams had clients who triggered some red flags, meaning the clients were potentially dissatisfied or were entertaining going with a different service provider. The long-time client who had been considering leaving prior to my maternity leave was still on the red flag list. We had come up with an initial strategy to address this, but the numbers and feedback weren't changing as much as they needed to. I decided to take the client file home for an indepth review. There was no balance between work and life today. The scale tipped toward work. The more I pondered how I could balance the two, the more frustrated I became. Balance didn't seem possible. I decided not to chase my thoughts down an emotional rabbit hole and just accept that my life would be imbalanced. For now.

Fenugreek Tea with Breastfriends

Wednesday marked the first evening breastfeeding support group. I had been looking forward to it. Everyone had agreed to come to tonight. No designated drivers this time. It would be a kid friendly evening with the ladies. Dad brought Eva to meet me in the parking lot at my office after work.

Entering the door marked "Breastfeeding in Progress" felt so good. I thought back to the day when I was sentenced to breastfeeding support group and how I hated the thought of entering this room. But I will always treasure what transpired between then and now.

"There's Eva," said Mary. "It's been a few weeks. Let's see how she is measuring up."

I set the car seat down, Mary unbuckled Eva's straps and pulled her up into her arms like a seasoned pediatric nurse, not too much affection but plenty of care. She walked Eva over to the changing table, and I took a seat along the wall. The only other mom in the room was quietly nursing her baby. I give a courteous wave and then dug in my diaper bag for a nursing cover. I had skipped my afternoon pump session, and my breasts were at the point of leakage.

"Hey, Lonnie!" Sasha exclaimed as she walked in, hurrying over to give me a hug. She looked glamorous as always. I peeked into the car seat to see Scarlett wearing her signature oversized bow. Rachel followed Sasha in. I hugged her and asked how her return to work was going.

"It's been okay," Rachel said. "I'm having to supplement with formula. It's too hard to get a break to pump. I'm okay with that as long as she's getting the nutrition she needs. Sasha has been feeding Scarlett meat and potatoes. Look at that girl! She's huge."

We looked at Sasha as she pulled her chunky infant from the seat, rolls at every joint.

"Is she accusing me of feeding my baby table food again? I've got good milk." She held Scarlett so they were cheek to cheek and then kissed her neck rolls. "Where's Queen NIP?"

That would have been a perfect moment for LeeAnn to walk in, but instead, in came Tish. Much to our surprise, her son Micah came toddling in behind her. She had no reason to be at this night group for moms who couldn't make it to the day groups. She gave me a cold "Hello" as she made her way to the other side of the room. She greeted the other moms in the room a little more warmly than she did me.

"Queen NIP!" Sasha exclaimed. LeeAnn smiled and playfully blew off Sasha's remark. She headed to me and gave a hug. "So, are we going out after this?" We all laughed.

"There are no designated drivers tonight," said Rachel.

"Welcome, ladies," said Mary, "to the first Breastfeeding Support Group, Evening Edition. I think everyone in the room has attended one of the weekly sessions, but in case this is your first time, the evening sessions are held once a month for our working moms. How many of the moms present are back to work?"

Rachel and I raised our hands along with the mom who arrived before I did.

"So, the rest are you must be here because you can't get enough of the weekly sessions. I'm flattered. Go ahead and bring the babies over one at a time, so we can see how they're progressing. Once I've seen everyone, we'll chat a little bit and then go home. While at the changing table, be thinking about questions you have."

I got Eva latched on and my whole body gave

a sigh of relief as she worked on emptying the first boob. I looked over at LeeAnn. She had a troubled look on her face. "What's wrong?"

"Is that child walking?" LeeAnn asked indignantly.

"He is. Some walk earlier than others."

"I'll share my thoughts during our after party. I'm going to get my baby weighed." She took another glance at Micah stumbling around the room and shook her head.

Rachel made her way back from the changing table a little bummed. "Emma hasn't gained much from the last visit. Mary thinks it's just Emma getting used to drinking the formula. She won't drink enough of it. I wish I could make her more of my milk, but it's tough."

"You're doing good, don't get discouraged. As long as she's eating and growing and pooping and peeing, it's good. Not all babies are hams like sweet Scarlett."

"Where's Grace? She said she would be here tonight."

"I'm not sure. I'll text her. If she doesn't answer, I'll check in with her tomorrow when I get to work."

Mary got our attention and said, "Okay, ladies, let's start our discussion. I want to hear how the transition back to work has been for our working moms."

Rachel shared her struggles with getting in pump times and having to supplement with formula. Mary educated us on the benefits of formula and how it's not mother's milk, but it's a good alternative if milk production is down. Then everyone looked at me. I guess I should talk now.

"It's been different. I'm pumping just enough to keep out of my frozen milk supply. Nothing much more to report."

"You're a pro, Lonnie, making it look easy. I want to talk tonight about the emotional roller coaster breastfeeding can have on a working mom." Mary went into a pretty intense lecture on the baby blues. The mom that arrived before me had tears rolling down her face as Mary talked about the symptoms of postpartum depression. When Mary acknowledged her outward show of emotion, the mom completely broke down, sobbing with a precious baby boy in her arms. To my surprise, LeeAnn was the first to walk over and console her. What came next is probably no surprise. A group of seven women huddled around a fellow mom exchanging tears, tissue, and encouragement.

When the snot cleared, Mary dismissed the majority of us so she could spend some time with our comrade who'd fallen to the baby blues. The ladies and I agreed we'd go grab a quick bite to eat. On the way out, Tish stopped to speak to Sasha.

"Will you be at the weekly group next week?"

"I will," Sasha happily replied.

"So what brought you out tonight, Tish?" LeeAnn interjected.

"I couldn't miss the inaugural session of the evening group," Tish replied without turning to acknowledge LeeAnn.

"I see your little one is walking. How old is he now?" LeeAnn asked.

Once again without turning to acknowledge LeeAnn, she replied, "Ten months. Sasha, I'll see you next week." Without acknowledging anyone else, Tish left the room.

"You see how I tried to be cordial," LeeAnn said defensively.

"Save it for the recap," said Rachel as she held the door for the rest of us.

"Thank you, Mary," LeeAnn called out as we were leaving. I waved to Mary and followed the crew down the hall.

Our city frequently has new little shops opening. It's one of the things I love about living here. It's always fresh. We all drove separately to an area of the city that was being revitalized with lots of boutique shops and restaurants that appeal to those with a sophisticated palate. I questioned why we were going to this area at this time of night with infants. The last time we let Sasha pick the venue, I drove home with four buzzed friends.

I parked in an open spot a few shops down from the cafe. Tonight's location specialized in herbal delicacies. Of course, this place was no secret to LeeAnn. Every product, from the teas to the cookies to the soups, had some kind of beneficial herb.

"Hi," LeeAnn said to the girl at the register, "we'd like everything you have with fenugreek in it."

"Well, we have a tea and some cookies with fenugreek," the young lady behind the counter answered.

"I'd like to have 4 of each." LeeAnn signaled for us to sit in a corner booth near a large bay window. We headed over to the booth and got the infant-bearing car seats situated.

"What made you choose this spot?" Rachel asked Sasha.

"LeeAnn and I came here last week, and I fell in love with this place. The food is good, and good for you, and I love the view."

She was right. The bay window opened up to a view of the night sky and the mountains in the distance.

"All right, ladies, tonight, instead of alcohol, we'll sip on this fenugreek tea. If we're going to drink, let's boost our supplies while we're at it," said LeeAnn.

The young lady behind the counter brought over a plate of cookies and four cups of tea. LeeAnn lifted her cup into the air and said, "To breastfriends."

"To breastfriends," the rest of us said as we raised our tea cups.

We caught up on what had been going on with each other, the babies, work, life in general, and of course our favorite pastime, discussing why Tish had had perfect attendance at the support group since her first child was born. When the plate and our cups were empty, we adjourned until next month.

After getting Eva's car seat locked into the base, I closed her door and looked at that beautiful nighttime sky. I would never have experienced this quirky little shop in this picturesque part of town if I hadn't crossed the threshold of that room in the pediatrician's office. I never would have met these amazing ladies who have made this change in my life manageable. My long-time friends and family couldn't empathize with me on this new season. But these ladies had the struggles and stresses that I did. And the diversity in age and life experience added an irresistible flavor to the group.

I chose to do a voice recording of my diary entry of today while I was driving home. The boys were still up when I got in. David had fallen asleep in the living room. I got everyone upstairs and into bed. Tonight was David's night to tend to Eva, so I didn't feel any pressure to go to sleep as soon as I hit the pillow. I didn't know what was in those cookies and the tea beside fenugreek, but my sex drive was boosted along with the milk supply. I woke David to take advantage of that perk.

"Tell me more about what's going on," Will said, opening our meeting to discuss our account that was in jeopardy.

Each of us poured over the packet sitting in front of us. Besides Will and me, Travis, the director of Media Planning and Buying, Leonard, and a few specialists working directly on the project were there. We looked at what we were providing and what we were billing and compared that data to what was offered by of some of our competitors. The problem was clear. The price of supplies needed for this client had gone up, and we were still passing the costs onto the customer.

"If costs for the supplies increased, why didn't we find another supplier so this client wouldn't be charged more?" Will asked.

"We have a contractual agreement with that supplier. We were able to adjust the prices according to our initial strategy, but the renegotiated price is above what the competition is offering," Travis reported.

"There's always a way to adjust the price. Did we discuss the price increase with the client prior to sending out these invoices?"

While Leonard spouted off excuses, I felt yesterday's fenugreek kicking in. I started leaking. I was not confident in my breast pads' ability to hold back this leak.

"Can we take an early lunch? I want us to have some fuel before we start making a plan for how to attack this issue," I suggested.

"That works for me. Twenty minutes and then we'll come back," Will said.

I beelined for my office to get my pumping supplies and headed to the pumping room. It was such a relief when the pump began to extract the milk. I closed my eyes and listened to the rhythmic hum of the breast pump. That led to a little siesta, and I woke to milk spilling onto my lap. The bottles were overflowing with milk! I'll need to lay off the fenugreek. I looked at the clock in the room. I only had two minutes left for my lunch break. I scurried to cap the bottles and clean myself up, stashed the milk in the fridge, and ran back to the meeting room.

As I gathered my thoughts at the table, I looked down at the papers scattered in front of me and saw a wet blotch on my shirt. At this point, I had no way to hide it. I also have no desire to be part of this meeting. But I overrode those concerns and forced myself to engage. The meeting revealed the flaws that had taken months to build up, resulting in an unhappy client. We came up with a good plan to turn this around. The meeting adjourned only for a post meeting to commence with Will and Travis.

Will said, "This account has been active for many years, and we've never had any issues with meeting their needs. I know the supplier personally, and if there has been a rise in material costs, we should have been able to negotiate a better price and then figure out a way to minimize the impact on the client.

"Lonnie, this is a prime example of the importance of thoroughly reviewing the reports submitted monthly from each department head. You're looking for trends. And we all should have kept a close eye on this account. I'm confident that we've got a strategy to turn this around before it leads to anything further. Travis, thank you."

Will dismissed Travis and said, "Lonnie, I'm not coming down on you. This is a good learning experience. I just wish it wasn't such an important account. Are you feeling comfortable with the position, and do you feel you have enough support to be successful?"

"I'd be lying if I said I felt comfortable all the time. Discomfort just shows I have something to learn, and I'm not afraid to learn from a situation."

"Okay, I just want to ensure that you've got this." He gave me this look as if he was expecting me to reassure him. So, I obliged.

"Yes, I can and will handle the situation. I still expect your assistance. This is the first time I'll be walking through this type of situation in this role."

"You know you have my support. How's the family?" he asked, grabbing a bottle of water from a basket on the counter in the conference room.

"Everyone is good. My dad is helping out by keeping Eva while we're at work. How is your family?"

"They're adjusting to the demands this position places on me. Speaking of demands, I'm supposed to be taking my wife out tonight, so I'm going to head out. We have a conference call in the morning. We'll talk some more then. Have a good night."

"Thanks, you too, Will."

He hurried out of the conference room. I let him get a head start, and then I left for the day as well. I'd missed lunch, I was due to pump or feed, I had a headache from this situation, and all I wanted to do was go home and sleep. I called my dad and asked him to hold off giving Eva another bottle. I also asked him to order a pizza, because I was not cooking.

When I got home, Dad and the boys were laboring over some math homework. The bewildered look they gave me signaled they needed help.

"Dad, thank you. You can go. I'll finish up with Johnny after I feed Eva. DJ, answer the door when the pizza comes. I'll be in Eva's room."

Eva was just rousing from a nap. I got us comfortable in the rocking chair, and she latched on eagerly. Rocking back and forth in the chair I could hear Dad tell the boys goodbye. A few minutes later the doorbell rang and the smell of bread, cheese, and mega meat reached the room. Once Eva's mealtime wrapped up I fully intended to induce a food coma from this pizza. My day was stressful. Several slices of pizza should ease my troubled mind.

TLC – Tender Love and Castor Oil

Well, the sleep coma was cut short by Eva's overnight feeding appointment. And although the sleep was good, the resulting heartburn was a price I wished I didn't have to pay. Today would be day two of David being out of town. I was already thinking I was gonna need a little something to take the edge off and the day had barely started.

Eva was a little fussy this morning, but there was no fever or sign of anything wrong. I just held her and did the best I could to groom and dress myself with one hand. When I finally made it downstairs, I was surprised to see breakfast on the table and a cup of orange juice at my place. DJ had already left for the bus stop.

"Did you make this breakfast, Johnny?"

"I made your orange juice. DJ made the rest."

"You did a fantastic job." I gave him a high-five. "Can you take your sister and see if you can make her happy?" He took the squirmy infant and headed to the living room.

Dad made his entrance at the perfect time to sit with me for a few minutes.

"How you holding up with David being gone?"

"If I didn't have you all, I'd be up a creek, in a psych ward, somewhere other than here."

"You're doing great, honey. When is he coming back?"

"He'll be back late tonight," I said with toast in my mouth.

"Anything this weekend?"

"Honestly, I don't know. My brain has been consumed with making sure I get everyone where they need to be without looking like a zombie. What are you doing this weekend?"

"Do you remember Mr. Arlington that used to live down the street from us?" Bracing myself for him to say he was going to this man's funeral, I nodded my head. "He's retiring and his wife is throwing him a party, so I'm going to that tomorrow night."

"That sounds fun, Dad. How are he and his wife doing?"

"They're doing well. They bought a property somewhere south a few years ago. They go there a few weeks out of the year and rent it out the rest of the year."

"Awesome. Have you thought about doing anything like that?"

"Haven't thought about it," he replied nonchalantly.

"Dad, Eva has been a little fussy this morning. She doesn't have a fever or anything outwardly wrong, but please keep an eye on her."

"Will do. I'll give her some castor oil."

"Dad, you wouldn't!" He laughed and headed to the living room where Johnny and Eva were.

"You go on to work. I'll get Johnny to the bus stop."

"For real, Dad, don't give that baby anything but milk and TLC."

"Tender love and castor oil?" I gave him a death stare as I grabbed my things and hurried to the car.

Of course, traffic would be horrible today. Whatever minutes I had gained by leaving the house a little early were lost. I took a minute to calm myself before entering the building to shake off my white knuckles from the crazy commute. I knew the first agenda item for the day was executing the strategy we had come up with yesterday for our unhappy client. This required every department head. My meeting prep was interrupted by a knock on my door. It was Julia.

"Good morning. I wanted to pop in before the meeting to share a few things about this account. I would like to pitch this idea to the group, but I wanted to get your buy-in first. Losing this account would be bad news for all of us."

I listened to Julia's ideas and the research she'd done on the client. Her information and ideas were well thought out. I invited her to share her strategy in the upcoming meeting. I could tell she felt empowered. That gave me joy. I felt my blood pressure return to normal. I quickly pulled my notes together and sent them to Danielle to print out for the meeting.

I arrived in the conference room first, followed by Julia. The others trickled in. I recapped the initiative to control and correct the damage with this particular client and described each director's role, tasking them to make this initiative their top priority, then signaled for Julia to take the lead.

Her input sparked positive discussion and led to everyone at the table rallying behind this initiative. I honestly don't think I could have elicited that response today, so I was glad she had come by this morning. As we broke from our meeting, I stopped Julia and thanked her for her input before returning to my office to get my pumping supplies.

As I sat in the room with my pump humming its mesmerizing tune, I reached for my phone to call Dad only to realize I left it in my office. I didn't even bring my laptop in today. I needed a break from that screen anyway. I closed my eyes and let the pump's hum soothe my frazzled nerves. That moment of relaxation made me think I should take this time every day to unwind instead of rushing in, doing work, and then rushing back out into the world.

I really wasn't much good the remainder of the day. I was tired. I felt like maintaining homeostasis was all my brain was capable of right then. I think I drove home on autopilot. When I walked in the house, I was greeted by the sound of Eva crying. I realized I hadn't called to check on her. I hurried over to pick her up and then headed to the kitchen for today's report from Dad.

"How did she do, Dad? I forgot to call and see if she was still fussy."

"She was a little fussy off and on. I gave her belly rubs."

"Thanks, Dad. I see you made dinner."

"One of your childhood favorites. What time did you say David was getting in?"

"His flight gets in around eleven thirty. We'll all be asleep by the time he gets home."

Fast forward to eleven thirty and guess who's awake? Starts with an "E." Yep, fussy Eva. I breastfed her, changed her, rubbed her belly, walked with her, rocked her. At midnight David walked into the bedroom, and I rolled over and signaled for him not to make any noise. Eva had just fallen asleep in the bed with me. Babies don't get to sleep in my bed. Never have, and I didn't plan on changing that policy. He tiptoed to our bathroom and closed the door. Now I had to try to move this baby back to her room, because I knew David was going to want to talk. I prayed that was all he'd want to do, because everything else *would* be rejected.

I very carefully wrapped Eva's blanket around her and carefully scooped her into my arms. I made my way across the hall to her room and gently laid her down. SUCCESS! We'd see how long it lasted. If she woke up within the next three hours, I'd be in selective hearing mode.

I informed David that he was up next for Eva duty. I laid my head on my pillow and closed my eyes. I gave David appropriate nods and "uh huhs" until he gave me my kiss on the forehead, indicating we were done for the night. I was already done. He had just caught up.

Much to my surprise, it was eight a.m. when I opened my eyes. The house was quiet. I went to Eva's room to see if she was ready for her morning feeding, but she wasn't there. I headed downstairs and DJ was playing video games while Eva was sleeping in her bouncy seat.

"Good morning. Was she crying? How long have you been up?"

"I heard Dad up with her late last night, so when I heard her going for a while this morning, I decided to get her. I gave her a bottle that was in the fridge and she went back to sleep."

"Thank you for taking care of your sister."

I got myself a cup of green tea and headed to the home office. It'd been a few days since I'd done a video. I needed to pump before the baby woke up, so I quickly recapped the highlights of the week. As I pressed the red button to stop the recording, I heard Eva. I slumped down in the chair and let my head drop onto my chest. I pulled myself together and headed into the living room to get her. I took her to her room and went straight for the changing table. Her brother had fed her but not changed her diaper, which at this point was leaking. I put her in a clean diaper and got us situated in the rocking chair.

I stroked her fuzzy patch of hair as she sucked away. I started envisioning us doing girl stuff and teaching her about her body and how to be a lady. I found myself beginning to verbalize everything I wanted to say to her. I told her no one is to touch her body and no one should speak to her in a degrading way. I told her that she was beautiful and that no one but her defined her beauty. While I was giving these life lessons to an infant who only had the capability of crying when she had a basic need, I saw David watching us from the doorway.

"You forgot to tell her that she'll have a curfew and that she won't have a boyfriend until she's thirty."

"She'll have a boyfriend before then. There will be so many milestones in her life. I don't want to miss any of them."

"You won't miss a moment," David said.

My phone rang. It was my dad. I motioned for David to put him on speaker since I was still feeding Eva.

"Good morning, family. Did I leave my glasses over there?"

"We can check in a few minutes, Dad."

"If they are there, I'll stop by and get them on my way to this party."

"Wait, what kind of party is this, Dad?" David asked.

"A retirement party."

"What's your curfew, young man?" David asked jokingly.

"I won't be in before curfew tonight," Dad said with a chuckle. "What are you all doing today?"

"Not much. DJ is going to hang out with some friends."

"Well, tell DJ to have fun and be safe. And if you find my glasses, call me and I'll come get them. Talk to you all later."

"Bye, Dad," David and I said in unison.

"One thing I'd like to do today, Lonnie, is plan out next week. I'll be out of town again."

I'm quite sure I scared him the way my head turned on my neck as I glared at him. "How often are you going to be out of town? I wasn't aware that this would be a weekly thing."

"I don't think it was clear at the time the position was presented to me. But after this first trip, it's becoming apparent that I'll be traveling more than we initially thought."

I dropped my head into the one hand I had free. "I'm going to be honest. I don't know how this is going to work. New baby, managing this branch, and you out of town."

"I get it, Lonnie. That's a lot for all of us."

"Correction. It's a lot for me."

"*Okay.* Let's talk about how we can decrease that feeling."

"Correction. It's not a feeling, it's a reality. How are we going to decrease my actual responsibilities while you're out of town? What happened to, 'Whatever is necessary to share the responsibility'? What happened to making me shine?"

"Well, your dad is here during the day. We can get some meals prepared over the weekends so your dad can heat them up and dinner will be ready when you get home. The boys can help out with some of the household stuff."

I had no response at the moment. Those sounded like viable ideas, but anything that fell through would be back on my plate. I was not pleased. But if I kept talking, I was going to say something that would hurt his ego. So, I pulled back my emotional reins. "Can you get all those things in order and let me know what days you'll be out of town?" I laid Eva over my lap to burp her.

"I can do that. Do you think those ideas will work?"

After a moment of irritated silence, I replied, "We can give them a try."

"Good, we'll give it a try. This week I'll be out of town only on Tuesday. But the following week, I'll be gone for about three days. I can see if my mom is available to help those days." He kneeled next to the rocking chair. "I know it's stressful with all these changes coming at once, but we're strong enough to make the adjustments. I need you to be okay, and whatever you need to be okay, I want to make sure you have it."

I didn't make eye contact with him. His words sounded nice, and he's a man of integrity, but I knew how exhausted I was the two days he was gone this week. Dealing with that every week would not be okay. I really just wanted to sulk in my negative thoughts and bad attitude, but this man was not going to leave me alone. I stood from the rocking chair and handed him Eva. "Can you get her washed up and dressed for the day?"

"Sure," he said.

I still gave him no eye contact. I got dressed and headed downstairs to look for Dad's glasses. I found them after about fifteen minutes and texted Dad that I would bring them to him. I needed some fresh air. As I walked out the door, I hollered out to everyone that I was dropping off Papa's glasses. I mounted my phone and recorded a diary entry while I was driving. I needed to get this off my chest. Seeing Dad would help too. I pulled up to his house and made my way to the door and knocked. I have a key, but I only use it if he's not there.

"Hey there, Lonnie," Dad said as he opened the door. "Thanks for bringing those over."

"You're welcome, Dad. You have a minute? I wanna talk."

"I always have time for you. You want something to eat?"

I made my way to the kitchen and he followed.

"So, what's on your mind?"

"David's job is requiring him to travel more often than we thought. I was exhausted with him being gone two days. I'm glad he got the promotion, but the travel part makes me nervous. We've had so many changes. I need him at home. But if I make this all about me and what I need, his ego will be damaged." Dad laughed. "Go on, give me your man's point of view."

"David takes great pride in providing for you and the kids. I'm sure this promotion brings in more money. But most of all, he loves what he does and wants to be respected for his work."

"I respect him for what he does, but this puts me at a disadvantage."

"How did he respond when you told him that he's putting you at a disadvantage?"

"He suggested we prepare meals over the weekend and have you heat them up so I won't have to cook. And the boys are going to do more of the household chores. He will also ask his mom to help when he's out of town."

"What's the problem then?"

"Dad, I'll be up with Eva at night, working fifty hours a week, and doing all the other duties I normally do. When he's there, I can just call on him to help. You and his mom won't be with us twenty-four seven. There will be times when I'll have to fend for myself," I said to justify my point of view while I ate a bagel with cream cheese.

"Lonnie, you're being anxious about a situation that is controllable. Take his suggestions, and if they don't work the way you need them to, tweak them, and move on. The last thing you need is resentment about his job."

"I know you're right, Dad, but I still feel overwhelmed and upset that I have to do this by myself a few days every week."

"You're not by yourself. David suggested three sources of help. Me, Sheryl, and the boys. I know your cousins would be willing to help. You just need to ask."

Once again, I had nothing to say. He was right. I had help.

"It takes work to organize all those people."

"If he's offering you help, let him organize the help," Dad said flippantly as he fixed himself a bagel and poured a cup of coffee. "You're still breastfeeding, so you can't have coffee."

"I can have decaf, but what's the point of drinking it without caffeine? You both are right. I'm just fighting to be mad. I need a minute to adjust my thoughts."

"Take your time. Have another bagel. I'm going to get my clothes ready for tonight."

I took him up on the offer for the second bagel. I plopped down on the couch. My eyes closed without my permission. When I opened them, I saw the table we gave Dad for his retirement. "And the story continues," I whispered. Everyone's story always continues. It's up to us to determine how it continues. I let that sink in. The more I thought about how I wanted my story to continue, the more my anger melted away. The alternative story was sad and depressing, so I let the anger go. I got up and put away everything from my bagel snack.

"Dad, I'm better now. Thank you for the bagels and the talk," I yelled up the stairs.

"Okay, honey. I'll talk to you later. Thanks for bringing my glasses."

"No problem. Anything for you. Have fun tonight."

"I will. Make sure you lock the door on the way out."

"Will do."

I locked the door and headed to my car. I called David to ask if I needed to pick up anything while I was out.

"Yes, I want you to pick up something that you can enjoy. I know you love those chocolate raspberry scones. Please stop and get one for yourself."

"Thanks, David. That's a great idea."

"Will you be home soon? I want us to get our chores done so we can watch a movie tonight and spend some time together."

"What movie will we watch?"

"We haven't been to the movies much this year. We should be able to find a good one to stream."

"Sounds like a good idea. I'll see you soon."

I ended our call and drove to the bakery near our home. I began to think of everyone who could help me. There were so many people. When I got to the bakery, I texted David all the people he could contact and how they could help us while I was waiting to pick up my scone. When I got home, my mother-in-law was in my kitchen.

"Hi there, Lonnie. I'm getting some meals started for you."

"Thank you, Sheryl. It smells amazing in here."

"I've got two dishes for the days David will be gone. David said he's ordering pizza for dinner tonight, and you all are having dinner with us tomorrow. We've got you set for most of the week, girlfriend."

It was a good day with everyone pitching in to help. Eva cooperated too. We were all ready for pizza and a movie when evening rolled around. The day ended well, much better than it had started.

The Apprentice

Monday rolled around and I was tired. Last night Eva had put in the most hours she'd ever slept, but I was still dragging. The thought of having to deal with the failing account at work was stressing me before I even got to the office. I tried to shake the heaviness before leaving the house. I didn't have the capacity for any more stress. I took a cleansing breath and focused on the things that I could do today.

Sheryl showed up early and managed Eva while I got ready. Traffic was favorable to me, and when I got in the office, I only had a few emails that needed my immediate attention. My individual meetings with my department heads went well and then it was time for pumping.

It was a smart decision to make pump time a meditation and quiet moment in the day. I'm not consistently quiet, but today was one of those days that I could be. I pushed worries aside and focused on good things. I'm doing a good job at work, we have a healthy baby, and I'm fortunate to be pumping milk from these ancient breasts.

I regretted this quiet time was only about twenty minutes of my day. Every woman needs more than twenty minutes of awake time to herself. Shame on me. But it was hard to see where another twenty would come from.

I had to strategize for the meeting regarding our unhappy client. I had a call with Will right after that meeting to give him the status on our progress. I had a Hail Mary plan in my back pocket if the team doesn't come through.

When I entered the conference room, the team had already begun discussing their tactics and how effective or ineffective they had been.

"Travis, what can you tell me about the expensive supplier? Were we able to get them to budge on the supplies for our client?"

"They aren't giving us enough of a cut to please the client. I've spoken to our rep, the manager, and the VP. They said they can't go any lower because of supply chain issues."

"Have you looked for a new supplier? We may have to deal with the contractual issue, but I'd rather go through that than to lose this client."

"I do have some other contacts I can reach out to."

"I need that done today, Travis, and I'd like to know what they are quoting for the supplies we need. Leonard, is there anything in their account history that looks amiss?"

"All of the account information is straightforward. There weren't any billing errors. We do offer some of our broadcast clients certain discounts based upon the level of services they buy. I can find a way to offer that and backdate it a few months."

"I like where you're going with that, Leonard. Run the numbers and let me know how much that costs."

After the meeting, I made three calls. One to the supplier, one to the client, and then one to Will.

"All right, Lonnie, what's the status?"

"The team has been working diligently with the client. We're exploring the cost of giving this client a discount and backdating it. I'll have the numbers this afternoon. I have a meeting tomorrow with the VP at the supply company. I wasn't able to get a meeting with the account manager for the client until next Tuesday as he's on vacation."

"Sounds like a solid plan. Do you want me to go with you to the meeting next week?"

I had to think hard and fast about this. If he goes,

I'll look like an apprentice. "No, I think I can handle it. I'll have Julia go with me. She's got a good handle on how we are addressing this."

"Good. Let me know those numbers when you get a chance. I've got another call I need to get on. Keep up the good work."

"Thanks, Will." When I hung up, I realized that my hands were sweaty and my neck was hot. I decided to take my extra twenty minutes right now. I lay my head down on my desk and closed my eyes as if I were in kindergarten. The only bad thing about being a kindergartner for twenty minutes is that I was much older and more fatigued, which meant that twenty minutes ended up being forty minutes of sleep time. I opened my eyes at the sound of someone knocking on my door.

"Come on in."

"I've got those discounted numbers for you, Lonnie. They get us close to what the customer is asking for."

Leonard slid the sheet across the desk. I studied the numbers.

"You doing good, Lonnie? I know it's got to be hectic carrying the load you're carrying."

"Thanks, Leonard. I have a great team here at work and very supportive family at home. With everyone's help, I get life done. These numbers give us what we need. I'll get them to Will."

"I'm glad to be a part of the team, Lonnie, and happy you've got good help at home. Have a good night."

"Thanks, Leonard." I quickly forwarded the numbers to Will. They were a little steep, and I wasn't sure we'd be able to sign off on this. If I could get the supplier to help us out when I met with him, we might not have to put out this much.

Will replied quickly.

> Thanks for getting those numbers to me. I want to see how these meetings go before we just hand our customer money. I think it would be in our best interest for me to

go with you to this meeting next week. This client has been with us for a long time, and I want to make sure you are successful. If any negotiations go on, I want us to be prepared, so instead of Julia, bring Leonard. Follow up with me tomorrow after you meet with the supplier.

Thanks
Will Cleveland
Senior Vice President
Mendallmen Inc.
111-222-3333

Well, it was official. I was an apprentice. Trumped by my boss. Well, if he wanted to negotiate this, I was done stressing about it. He could have it. I'd do what he asked and see how this all played out. I decided to go home. I needed to get a jump on tomorrow since David would leave town tonight. I gathered all my things, leaving the building and all the worries of the job at the threshold. Both would be waiting for me tomorrow.

I got home to the smell of Sheryl's Mostaccioli that Dad heated up. She knows how much I love that dish. I could hear David upstairs zipping his suitcase. Eva was cooing at Johnny. DJ was at the table doing homework. It was a beautiful sight. I headed to the office to shoot a video. There were so many feelings today that I needed to get off my chest. David came in as I was finishing and jumped in front of the camera.

"Anything she says about me has not been verified."

I pushed him out of the camera shot and ended the video.

"I wanted to kiss my bride before I head out of town." He gave me a big smooch.

"Let me know when you get there."

"Will do. Hopefully, Eva will put in another night of good sleep."

"I hope so. I've got a meeting tomorrow that will require some hardball negotiations."

"Since when have you been playing hardball?"

"Since this account has gone south."

He embraced me from behind the office chair I was sitting in. "Get it, Mom. I'll text you when I get in."

We walked downstairs together. I watched him kiss all the kids on his way out.

"I don't get a kiss?" asked Dad.

"You know I love you, Mr. Lee," David said, giving him a bear hug. "Bye, family!"

We said bye in unison and off he went. I sat down for dinner and released Dad to go home. The night and next morning went smoothly, and I headed to work in good spirits.

Travis got me all the details regarding the supplier I was meeting with that day. I read over the contract and reviewed the invoices. Travis even went as far as to contact the supplier's manufacturer to verify that there were actual supply chain issues. Everything checked out. After my briefing, I headed across town to meet with this supplier. Much to my surprise it was less formal than I expected. The offices were above their warehouse and turned out to be quite trendy despite the grungy work going on below.

In anticipation of my request to lower the price, the VP showed me documents authenticating the shortage of certain materials that are used in the supplies we provide our client. I inquired if there were other supplies that met the same goal made of different materials. We spent a considerable amount of time exploring those options only to come up empty. So, hardball it was.

It was a sloppy game of hardball, but I got them down to a reasonable price for our supplies. With this win, we should be able to appease the customer. I thanked him for his help and headed back to my office feeling good about the situation.

An impromptu meeting with Travis and Leonard let us start putting together a deal for my meeting with our client next week. The day's recap with Will via email had good information to report. I was drained and in pain since I hadn't pumped. I decided to go home and relax in my victories.

I hooked myself up to the breast pump before pulling out of my parking spot. Sweet relief. It was so sweet, I didn't realize I was going over the speed limit until I saw the lights flashing in my rear view. I quickly snatched the bottles from the horns, pulled over, and unhooked the pump from the car's charging port. I made sure the breastfeeding cover was on straight, but the horns of the breast pump were still secured inside the hands-free pumping bra, and I didn't have time to remove them. I looked like I had on a bullet bra from the 1950s.

I put down the window and did my best to conceal the horns with my arms.

"License and registration please."

I fumbled around in the glove compartment and came up with the registration. I handed it to the officer and looked at him with pitiful eyes.

"I also need your license, ma'am."

I was so preoccupied with hiding my breasts that I forgot to get the license. And wouldn't you know, my purse was in the back seat. I informed the officer that I was going to get my purse from the back of the car. There's no hiding the bullet bra now. I quickly reached around to grab my purse and resumed my guarded position as I rummaged through my wallet to find the license. As soon as I saw him heading back to his motorcycle in my side mirror, I quickly freed myself from the hands-free bra and pulled the horns of the breast pump away from my body. I tossed everything into the pump bag. By the time the officer walked back to my vehicle, I looked somewhat normal. I was now wearing the nursing cover as a scarf.

"Ma'am, were you aware that you were driving ten miles over the speed limit?"

"No, sir, my mind was preoccupied. Is it possible to have a warning? I have a very good driving record, and I'm typically very mindful of how fast I am driving."

"You do have a clean record. This time I will allow a warning. Make sure you watch your speed."

And with that, he handed me my license and registration and headed back to his motorcycle. I sat there for a moment with my eyes closed. I took a cleansing breath and opened my eyes. I put the car in drive and drove home, completely focused on my speed. I had a few irritated drivers speed past me with glares. I ignored them. I just needed to get home.

I dragged into the house. Dad had dinner ready, the boys were arguing about who was going to drink the last of the juice, and the baby was crying. I picked up Eva and went right to the rocking chair. She latched on and started sucking. I closed my eyes. Tears begin to leak between my clenched eyelids. All I wanted was to get in my bed and sleep. I heard a soft knock at my door.

"I'm heading out, Lonnie."

"Thank you, Dad. See you tomorrow."

"Love you."

"Love you too."

I heard him go down the stairs, and I resumed my silent tears. When Eva was finished, I burped her and attempted to reel in my emotions. As she burped, I heard activity happening on the opposite end of her digestive system, followed by the all too familiar smell of poop.

There was another knock on the door. "Mom, we're done cleaning up the kitchen," said DJ.

"Are your clothes out for tomorrow?"

"Mine are. I don't know about Johnny."

"Make sure Johnny has his clothes out. I'm going to lie down in my room. If I fall asleep, make sure you and Johnny are in bed before nine."

"Are you going to eat dinner?"

"Not tonight, honey. I'm very tired. Make sure all the food is put away."

"Okay, Mom."

I got Eva cleaned up and then took her to my room.

I put her in a bouncy chair next to the bed and lay down with my eyes closed. I heard Johnny running up the stairs and into his room. Less than a minute later I heard him running back down. My guess is that he pulled out some random combination of clothes and then ran back downstairs to resume some activity he shouldn't be engaged in during the school week, like playing video games. Prior to my life changing OB visit, I would have enforced the rules. But I was tired and overwhelmed. So I kept my eyes closed and dozed off.

Around midnight I heard David coming in from his trip. I looked over and saw Eva next to me. My breast was hanging out of my shirt. I was completely disoriented and had no recollection of getting out of the bed to pick her up or of nursing her. It actually scared me. What if I wasn't fully awake, and I dropped the baby. I tried to shake my panic, but my adrenaline was rushing at the thought that I wasn't fully awake while caring for my infant. I scooped up Eva and took her to her room. She would be safer there. I went back to my bed and waited for David to come up.

"You awake?" he asked.

"Just enough to tell you hello and welcome home."

He whispered, "Hello to you too." He kissed my forehead and stepped away. I seized the opportunity to go back to sleep.

Overwhelmed

I wasn't necessarily refreshed in the morning, but I was functional. David's travel has exacerbated my already high stress levels. I didn't have much space left for emotions. I was feeling kinda blah. Ever since David started traveling, I hadn't felt as affectionate. I wouldn't consider this baby blues, but I was no clinician.

I shrugged off my thoughts and dragged myself into Eva's room for a morning feed. She was sound asleep. I assumed she needed a few more minutes, so I headed to my bathroom to shower. As the warm water ran over my body, I couldn't help but notice my fleshy abdomen. It reminded me that I planned to begin working out after I had Eva. It sounded good, but I struggled seeing where I could fit that into my schedule even though it would help both my emotional state and my abdominal situation. I stood under the warm water longer than I should have, trying to wash away my cares.

"You okay in there?"

"Yes."

"I fed Eva about three hours ago, so she may sleep a little longer."

"Thanks, D."

"No problem. You need me to get anything for you?"

"Make sure the boys are getting ready."

"Done," he left the bathroom, and I finally started washing

my body. When I got out and stood in front of the mirror, I was a little concerned about how tired and aged my face looked. Now, I'm no spring chicken, but I looked better than this earlier this year. I tried to erase the stress and sleep deprivation that has crept across my face using makeup. I pulled out a pick-me-up outfit and spent a little extra time on my hair. I looked at my face once more in the mirror and gave myself a nod of approval. I looked ten times better than I did a half hour ago.

Eva finally began to stir. I said good morning to her, and she smiled at me. "Mommy looks like a real person this morning, doesn't she?"

Her grin got bigger and her eyes were wide open. I got her latched on, and she put her little fisted hands around my breast as if she was holding it. She held her gaze on my face, and I couldn't help but stare at hers. I was amazed at how often her features changed. She had always resembled Johnny when he was a baby, but she was beginning to show her unique features. We switched breasts and after she was full and drowsy, I got her changed and ready for Papa.

I heard Dad downstairs talking to the boys, so I took Eva down to him.

"Good morning, Dad."

"Good morning," he replied in a super chipper tone.

"You sound exceptionally joyful this morning. What's up?"

"Nothing, just glad to be here."

"Eva has a well-baby visit scheduled today. Do you feel comfortable taking her? It's at ten forty-five."

"No problem. Is the office still over there by the high school?"

"Yes. Thank you, Dad. Ten forty-five. See you this afternoon."

I hopped in the car and pulled up my favorite podcast. I thought about my current state in life and decided to find a podcast relevant for new moms instead. I found one and played it during the commute. I felt a little more empowered when I pull into my parking spot.

The morning started with a voicemail from Will, so I quickly give him a call back.

"Nice work getting them to come down. That'll make the meeting next week a bit easier."

"Thanks. I must admit it wasn't pretty, but I got the job done."

"That's all that matters. Let's meet with Leonard on Monday at two to prep for the client meeting."

"Okay, I'll send an invite to you both."

"Sounds good. Have a good day, Lonnie."

"I will. You do the same."

I hung up and thought about how I could have better handled this mess so Will didn't think he needed to step in. I decided not to mess up my good vibes by being critical of my leadership skills. I looked over some more emails and saw one from Grace. I had forgotten I reached out to her.

> Hi Lonnie. Sorry I'm just getting back to you. I've had to take a few days off to stay home with Jackson. He's had a cold. I'm not supposed to take any days off during my probation period, but they've been very understanding. How've you been?
>
> Grace Williams
> Secretary
> Mendallmen Inc.
> 111-222-1234

I picked up the phone and called her.

"Thank you for calling Mendallman, this is Grace."

"Hi, Grace, this is Lonnie."

"Hey, Lonnie. Did you get my email?"

"I did. I'm sorry to hear Jackson has had a cold. We're heading into that cold and flu season. It's so hard when they're this little."

"I had to stay home with him a few days because Mom had it too. Technically, I was caring for both of them."

"Did you get sick?"

"I didn't, but I was super tired after waiting on them hand and foot and passing out meds. I felt like a nurse."

"I'm glad everyone is better."

"Me too. So what's new? Have you seen any of our BSG friends?"

"We all went to the evening support group a few weeks ago. We missed you."

"I totally forgot about that. I had to get a new phone and lost all my numbers. Did you all go do something fun afterwards?"

"You know we did. LeeAnn had us at this shop that had all these herbal teas and desserts. We had fenugreek tea and cookies. Fenugreek is supposed to increase your milk supply. Eva was very fussy after drinking my fenugreek infused milk." We both laughed.

"Well, when's the next one? I'll go just to hang out. I stopped breastfeeding earlier this month. I wasn't able to pump as often as I should have while at work, which meant I had to start supplementing and now we're fully on formula."

"Formula is available for just that reason. The next group is in two weeks on Wednesday. I'll send you a reminder. What's your new number? Send it to me, and I'll share everyone's contact info with you."

"Thanks, Lonnie. I gotta go. I'll talk to you soon."

"Okay, bye."

I left work a little early. David was home early today too, and Dad had already left by time I got in.

"Did Dad say how Eva's appointment went?"

"He said it went well. Her progress sheet is on the table."

I sat at the table and read over her progress.

"David, when are you traveling again?"

"I will have to travel for two days next week."

"Can you ask your mom to help out with meals?"

"Yes. I went ahead and got dinner going."

"Thanks, babe. I'll go work on laundry."

I headed upstairs to my room and was greeted by Mount Clothesmore on my king size bed. If I didn't fold these clothes, I'd be sleeping on the couch. I sat and began folding, and the more I folded, the angrier I got. I didn't have time for this! Then I began thinking about Sasha. She had someone who helped her. How could I get that deal? I grabbed my phone and called her.

"Lonnie, how are you?"

"I'm actually a little overwhelmed. I was calling to ask you about your housekeeper. Where can I get one?"

"Are you looking for someone all the time, weekly, or once or twice a month?"

"Maybe I can start with once or twice a month."

"Are you wanting someone who cooks and cleans or a little more than that?"

"Mostly cleaning, maybe cooking."

"I have a few recommendations, and I have a few friends who have help a few times a month. I can ask them about their housekeepers."

"Thanks, Sasha. Can you text me their contact info when you get it?"

"I sure can. Other than being overwhelmed by housework, what else is new with you? How's Eva doing?"

"Eva actually had a well visit today, and she's growing fine. Much improved from how we started off."

"Scarlett is off the charts as usual. I was concerned she was getting too big too fast, but the doc said once she starts moving she'll thin out. I guess my milk is premium stuff." We both laughed. I really needed that. "So when's the next time we can all get together?"

"You're great at organizing those things, Sasha. I'll wait to hear from you."

"We've got evening support group in two weeks. Maybe we can do something afterward like we did last time. Let me think of some baby friendly places."

"I talked to Grace. She's not breastfeeding anymore, but she said she'll come to hang out at the next group."

"Oh, that's a bummer that she's not breastfeeding anymore. I know her situation is tough."

"Yeah, Jackson and her mom were sick with something respiratory."

"Oh no, not the baby! Are they better?"

"They are better." I heard David downstairs calling everyone to the table for dinner. "The dinner bell is ringing, so I've got to go. Thank you in advance for the recommendations."

"You're welcome. I'll send out a text with our next rendezvous spot."

"I'm looking forward to it. Talk to you later."

My family assembled at the table. We did our usual run down of everyone's day and then I popped the question.

"What do you all think about getting a housekeeper?"

"Why do we need a housekeeper, Mom?" asked DJ with a straight face.

"I agree. We have help with childcare and food. Why *do* we need a housekeeper?" David asked.

"Well, it would be nice to have someone help with the laundry and cleaning up around the house, especially now that Dad is traveling. I have a very busy schedule at work, and I don't get much sleep at night with your sister, so I need some help around the house."

"Let me get this straight," Johnny said excitedly. "This person would do all of our chores?"

"No, not all of your chores. This person would come a few times a month and help with the cleaning I'm not able to do and the laundry that piles up. It will make life easier for me. I know I've been able to handle it all in the past, but things are different. I'd like to try this out to see if it helps us."

DJ and Johnny were definitely open to someone doing their chores for them. Little did they know that their chores would still be there for them. For the moment, I had them on my side, so I omitted that detail. David was still processing the idea.

"Let's talk some more about it later, Lonnie. Is that okay?"

"Sure," I said, adding a smile. But I'm not taking no for an answer.

After dinner, David had the boys clean up the kitchen, and he headed upstairs to work on the laundry. I took Eva to her room for our evening routine of feeding, changing, rocking, and then bedtime. This had become my unwind time. I knew it wouldn't last long. She'd get more mobile and would want to get down and move.

I checked on the boys. They were preparing for tomorrow and getting ready for bed. I was so grateful for their independence. Especially with having a baby in the house. I went to help David fold the laundry. He had brought the mountain of clothes down to a plateau. I sat on my side of the bed and started folding.

"I think you should go ahead and get the housekeeper. I just needed a minute to process the idea. The workload doesn't get any lighter when I'm gone, and I'd feel more comfortable knowing you have the support you need. So go ahead and find someone."

"I've got a few recommendations. I'll start calling them and have them come by for an interview so we can get someone we are all comfortable with."

"That works for me." He walked around the bed and wrapped his arms around me. "I think I should take you out for dinner tomorrow. I'll get a sitter lined up."

"I like that idea." We folded clothes and chatted for another hour. I didn't tell him about getting pulled over. That would be my secret. With all the laundry folded and put away, we got ourselves ready for tomorrow. All that chatter led to a more pleasurable end to our evening. We'd sleep good tonight.

I was so excited to be going on a date with my husband. It'd been a while since we'd gone out, just the two of us. He sent me text messages throughout the day with details about our evening. I ran through my closet in my mind, trying to decide what to wear. When five o'clock came around, I shut everything down and headed home. Dad was just starting to change Eva when I arrived. Apparently, she had a blowout. As soon as I walked into the room he said, "Perfect timing! Mommy will take over from here, precious." He gave me a hug and left the room.

"I thought you loved me, Dad," I shouted.

I got Eva all cleaned up. The doorbell rang, and I heard Johnny answer the door. I stepped out of Eva's room to see who was at the door. It was the sitter. I signaled for her to come up so I could give her the run down on Eva's schedule. Tonight was her first time with Eva. She was very familiar with the boys, but they weren't the ones she was getting paid for tonight.

After I got her oriented, I got myself ready. I wasn't happy with my outfit choices, but postpartum mommies can't be choosy. I abandoned the search for something sexy and went with what I could fit into. I tried to doll up my hair and face to make up for the slowly receding maternity weight. I could hear David downstairs giving last instructions to the sitter and the boys. I gave myself one more glance in the mirror and went down to meet David. He greeted me with flowers and escorted me to the car.

"You look lovely, my dear."

"Thank you, kind sir. I can't wait to see the dinner menu," said the breastfeeding mom who couldn't fit in her clothes.

David chose the restaurant where I had had my interviews. We pulled up and he chose to valet the car. He held my hand as we walked in. There wasn't a bad table in this place. Whoever designed it made sure every detail spoke to the senses. The host pulled out my chair, and David took my jacket.

"Do you know why I chose this restaurant?" David asked as he settled in his chair.

"No. I assumed you liked the menu."

"It's a good menu, yes, but I chose this restaurant because this was the place where you had a major victory. The labor and delivery room was technically the place of your most recent victory, but I'm sure you don't want to go back there." We both laughed at the thought of that.

"Wow. You put a lot of thought into this."

"I know this year has easily been the most challenging you've had in a long, long time. I wanted to remind you that you are winning." He took my hand. I started to tear up. I grabbed my napkin from my lap and dried my eyes. I spent a lot of time on my makeup. I couldn't ruin it thirty minutes into this date.

"Thank you, David. I feel like all I've done this year is stumble forward. To others it looks like expertise, but to me, it feels like chaos."

The tears really started flowing. The waiter came to get our drink orders. David ordered for me, never letting go of my hand.

"We've been through all sorts of things together, and we always come out on top. This season of our life will be no different."

All I could do was nod my head. The waiter brought our drinks and, seeing my emotional state. offered to give us more time to look over the menu.

"Order whatever you like, babe. Tonight, we're celebrating your victories."

We talked about old times and new times and laughed a lot. It was great to really talk to each other, this time at an elegant restaurant table instead of at the foot of Mount Clothesmore. On the way home, David took the scenic route. I've said before how beautiful our city is at night, and tonight was no different. We stopped at this park that is at a higher elevation than the city, and you can see a portion of the skyline, all lit up and beautiful, the sky without clouds, the stars putting on a most brilliant show. We got out and sat on a nearby bench.

I pulled out my phone to record a video.

I've been doing these videos along this journey so one day I can look back at how I maneuvered this season of my life. David did something very special tonight, so I'm including him in this video. I want to be able to look back and encourage myself with what he's said.

I signaled to David to share what he shared at the restaurant.

Well, tonight, we had dinner at one of the last places where Lonnie had a major victory this year. It was the restaurant where she had her final interview for the position she now holds at her job. I wanted this night to be a reminder of all her victories during this challenging season of being a new mom again, breastfeeding, running a branch of her company, and being my wife. You truly are a strong lady. I'm glad you're mine.

My victories may look impressive to others but feel chaotic to me. That's it for tonight.

I stopped the recording and kissed my husband.

We didn't stay out there much longer because the night air was becoming chilly. We were welcomed to a quiet home, all children sleeping. We paid the sitter and rewarded ourselves a second night in a row. That doesn't happen much at this stage in our marriage, but no one's complaining tonight.

The Pump Up Mix

David left next morning for work travel. Will was at our branch today to meet with Leonard and me. We also had an all-hands meeting. The first topic was finalizing our customer appreciation week plans. We followed up customer appreciation week with an employee appreciation event. That was always tons of fun. I'd been hands off with the planning of that event, but someone would expound on it today.

I was on a call when Will came. I motioned for him to have a seat while I finished the call. We had about fifteen minutes before our meeting with Leonard.

"We've got our all-hands meeting today. The department heads will share their plans for the customers, and the team planning the employee appreciation event will present today as well," Will said.

"Awesome. I was able to catch up with an old contact from the client we're meeting with tomorrow. She shared that they've gone through some organizational restructuring and a lot of the people we're used to working with have moved to different areas or are no longer with the company. She also said that they conducted an audit of all their expenditures earlier this year, and that's where all this is dissatisfaction with our pricing is stemming from. They were able to get lower quotes from some other guys around town, hence the pressure on us to match or beat our competitors."

"So, we're going into this meeting without any solid rapport."

I wished I had known this earlier. "Do you think the numbers we put together are going to be good enough? If not, our only advantage is our quality and the longevity of the partnership"

"I agree with you, but if we're dealing with someone who's only concerned about the numbers, the quality argument doesn't stand a chance."

"Since this has been a long-time customer, are we willing to take a loss by matching the prices?"

Will shook his head in uncertainty. "This is a big account. If we can't match and we lose the account altogether, we'll have a hard road ahead of us landing an account of that size. And we may run into the same pricing issue."

"So, either way we're going to take a hit, Will. I don't want any of our employees to be affected. It'd be better to take a loss in revenue by matching than to risk the cost of losing them altogether and trying to find an account to replace them."

"I agree, but I don't want to just give in."

I did! I didn't want this added stress. At this point in the conversation, Leonard came in. We went over our proposal that would bring us close to matching the main competior's pricing. We decided to start negotiations with our original proposal, and then we'd move to our second line of defense, which was to actually match what they were asking. We discussed who would speak on what topic in the meeting. I wasn't feeling so insecure about having Will come along. I needed his expertise. But I still needed to take a strong stance. Ultimately, any follow up will be my responsibility.

After lunch I switched gears to prepare for the all-hands meeting. I got all my things together for the meeting with five minutes to spare before start time. Then I realized I had forgotten to pump. I don't know how I could have forgotten. My breasts were ready to overflow. I got the meeting started and, of course, my breasts started leaking. I made it through intros and the agenda before handing the meeting over to Will. I instructed the department heads to follow Will with their reports.

I cut out at the back of the room and rushed to my office, closed the door, and grabbed fresh nursing pads stashed in my desk. I quickly switched out the wet ones with the dry ones. A quick trip to the bathroom made sure I was put together before I went back into the meeting.

Will happened to be standing in the back of the room when I slipped back in.

"Hey," he whispered, "I'm going to head out. I'll come by here in the morning, and we can all ride together to the meeting."

"That works. See you in the a.m."

He slipped out the back, and I moved back to the front of the room in between department head presentations. Once everyone had spoken, I closed out the meeting and made my way back to my desk to finish up the day. It took me an hour with interruptions, but I finally escaped the office. I put in a call to Dad to let him know not to feed Eva even if she got a little fussy.

After Eva and I exchanged services, the boys and I had dinner. I was in this mood where I didn't want to think about anything, so what better thing to do than watch TV. I put on some mindless show that I could watch with the boys and we laughed our way through two hours of TV. On a school night! Once I saw the clock, I jumped up and scurried the boys off to bed. I put Eva in her crib and went to my bed. I decided to record this moment of complete exhaustion while the bedside lamp was still on.

> **It's 10:30 on a Monday night, and I wasted two hours of my life watching TV with my kids to avoid thinking about work and the fact that I have to do this alone. If I were in my right mind, which I am not today, that would have never happened. I'm trying to maintain the strength of a leader at work and be all things to this family when I get home. But I guess I should be grateful I only have to do this alone one or two days a week. I think about Grace who has to do it on her own twenty-four seven. I'll survive.**

I stopped recording, put my phone on the bedside table, and closed my eyes. The next time I opened them, I saw a sight that shook me out of my sleep. Eva was next to me, nipple halfway in her mouth. I probably fell asleep feeding her. She was fine, but not having any recollection of doing this for the second time alarmed me. I looked at the clock. It was a little after three a.m. I got up and took Eva to her crib and came back to bed. It took a while to get back to sleep, but I finally did around five, only to be rudely awakened by the alarm clock forty-five minutes later. I hit the snooze button. The next sounds I heard were my second alarm and my dad's voice downstairs. I sat up and looked at the clock. I nearly fell on my face trying to get to the bathroom. I'd overslept!

Thirty minutes later, I ran down the steps and waved goodbye to everyone. Of course the traffic was horrible this morning, causing me to pull into my parking spot close to nine-thirty. Leonard and Will were sitting in my office.

"Good morning, gentlemen," I said between huffing breaths.

"Good morning," they said in unison.

"Do we have everything we need for the meeting?"

Leonard confirmed he had all the documents we needed.

"Awesome, who wants to drive?"

"Well, you look like you could use a minute to catch your breath, so maybe I should drive," said Will.

I tried to remain cool on the outside, but inside I was mortified by my tardiness. My confidence began to dwindle and my breasts began to tingle, signifying they were about to start leaking.

"I'm going to run to the restroom and then we can head out. Back in five."

I briskly walked to the bathroom. As soon as the door closed, I started to cry. Okay I'll rephrase that. I started to ugly cry, snot and all. I got that out of my system, fixed my face, checked my nursing pads, ready to face the world. Leonard and Will were putting on their jackets. I grabbed my purse, and we headed off to the meeting.

I opted to sit in the backseat of the car, hoping they'd talk to each other and I'd only have minimal input to whatever conversation they had. I closed my eyes and tried to pull myself out of this ditch of misfortune and emotional collapse. The timing could not have been worse.

"You asleep back there, Lonnie?" asked Will.

"No. I'm going over the numbers and what I'll say." My eyes were still closed. Dig deep, Lonnie, and pull yourself up.

"Whenever I go into an important meeting like this one, I play my motivational mix. Are you okay if I play that?" Will asked, looking in the rear view mirror.

"Sure, I'm open for motivation."

What happened next was unsettling. When I heard the music, I opened one eye to see Will dancing in his seat like he was in a boy band. The electronic tunes and foreign accents were not what I expected to hear.

"Is this K-pop?" Leonard asked, slightly shouting. "My daughter loves this stuff."

"I don't know why, but it gets my head in the game," Will said as he fist pumped with one hand and steered the car with the other. "You like K-pop, Lonnie?"

"It's new to me." I had to project my voice to be heard over this noise. I hated it.

Leonard and Will bobbed their heads and completely immersed themselves in this music. It made me feel nauseous. This was totally having the opposite effect on me. The longer the music blared, the angrier I got. Luckily for me, the client's building was not far from our office. I was the first one out of the car.

The meeting began with introductions and the flowery we-love-having-you-as-a-client jabber. This was my major role. Leonard jumped in with the numbers, and Will tagged in with the hardball. This new team had no rapport with our company, but once we delivered our plan and stated the value we brought to the table, we were able to negotiate a price that was comparable to some other bids they had received without completely breaking the bank for us.

As soon as we got in the car, Will celebrated the win with an exuberant "Yes!" Leonard gave him a high five, and then they both turned to give me a high five. I indulged them, but I was completely drained from the whole ordeal.

"Let's go have lunch. Great job, team!"

"Let's try that sushi bar south of downtown," Leonard suggested.

"Yes! I know which one you're talking about! Lonnie, does that sound good for you?"

"Not my favorite, but I'm sure they'll have something else on the menu," I said with little enthusiasm.

"Are you sure? We can pick something else," Leonard said.

"Yeah, let's do something else. How about a deli?"

"I know a great one not far from here," Will said.

When we sat down with our food, it dawned on me that I hadn't eaten breakfast. That explained some of my anger earlier. As I got the food in my system, I was able to switch over to being genuinely excited for this win as opposed to smiling hard enough to mask my physical and emotional fatigue. We recapped the meeting and talked through how to compensate for this deal we just made. After much discussion, we ended up back at that supplier. We'd have to explore the cost of breaking our contract with that company to find a lower cost supplier.

On the way back to the office, Will decided to play his "equilibrium" mix. Before I could object, in fear that I would once again be exposed to K-pop, the operatic sounds of a tenor flowed through the car.

"This helps me to re-center myself after a tense meeting," Will said.

I'd learned more about Will through his music than I think I wanted to know. We'd worked together for many years, but today was TMI. When we got back to the office, Leonard went on his way, and Will followed me into my office.

"Are you okay? This was a big win for us. Granted it's a partial win because there's still work to do, but you seem disengaged."

"Dealing with this issue has been exhausting. I'm just trying to 're-center.' It will take a little more than a tenor to get my equilibrium back. I'm okay."

"All right. If you need something, let me know. I'm going back to my office."

"Thanks, Will."

"Lonnie, you're doing a great job."

I sat at my desk, numb. Mentally done for the day. The tingle in my breasts reminded me of my obligation to pump milk for my infant. Which reminded me that I ran out of the house without the pump. Oh well. I read emails and returned phone calls until it was time to go home.

I dragged myself to the car and put in a call to Dad to hold off on feeding Eva. I had to hold the seatbelt away from my chest the whole ride home, because the pressure was causing further discomfort to my engorged breasts. As soon as I walked in the house, I grabbed Eva and went to our rocking chair. She relieved my pain. I relieved her hunger. Win win.

Dad stayed to eat dinner with me and the kids. I unloaded all my emotions from the day, and he, being the loving parent that he is, listened without judging me. After we got the kitchen cleaned up, Dad went home, and I sent the boys to bed and put Eva in her crib. Once my head hit my pillow, I didn't blink twice before I fell fast asleep.

I was on time this morning. I was relieved and actually excited to focus on something other than that troubled client account. Customer appreciation is coming, employee appreciation is coming, and I can't believe Thanksgiving is around the corner. Because I had time, I took the opportunity to pump today. The pump hummed, and I tuned into the rhythmic sound and closed my eyes and cleared my thoughts. After about fifteen minutes, I looked down and found my bottles weren't full. I adjusted the horns on my breasts and turned the suction up a little higher and sat for another five minutes. I didn't get much more. I sat there for a moment trying to process why there wasn't more milk.

When I got back to my desk, I did a search for "where's my breastmilk?" What I read made me sad. I did this to myself. I hadn't kept up with my pumping while at work, and the added stress had likely cut down my milk supply. The thought of not being able to give Eva breastmilk because I wasn't diligent with pumping came across as selfish, and I felt regret. And then a little anger. How was I supposed to be successful at work and a successful breast feeder at the same time? I wanted to cry. So I did. I shifted from crying over the problem to fixing the problem. I looked up all the things I could do to boost my milk supply and strategized how I could incorporate them.

On the way home, I got a call from David asking me to pick up a few things from the store, so I made the shopping detour.

I walked in the house and was greeted by dimmed lights and music playing.

"David?"

"I'm in the kitchen." There was a candlelit dinner ready for us. "The kids are with Lizzie. He pulled out my chair and motioned for me to sit. I let him serve me. "So, how was your day? Your dad told me you've had a rough few days. What else can I do?"

Although he was sincere, I struggled giving him an answer. "We already have help with childcare and meals. We've discussed having someone come in to clean. I can't think of any other bases that we can cover."

He looked discouraged. "Lonnie, I don't want to see you overwhelmed."

"And I don't *want* to be overwhelmed. But to get through this stage in life, I don't see me avoiding that." I hated that this wasn't going the way he may have imagined, but the truth was the truth.

"Maybe taking the promotion at work wasn't the right decision for me so soon after your promotion and all that we have going on."

I wasn't in the mood for any melodramatic male self-pity. "David, if we don't take advantage of opportunities when they come, who's to say they will come again? We take them when they come. No regrets." I took my plate to the sink and rinsed it off. "Let's go pick up the kids and get ready for tomorrow."

He brought his plate over to the sink and gave my shoulders a quick massage. He grabbed his coat and went out to start the car. I put our dishes in the dishwasher and joined him. Not much was said on the way to Lizzie's. We are usually able to squash any disagreement we may have, but I was not willing to initiate the truce tonight. David took a turn off the highway before we got to Lizzie's exit and pulled into a Guppies Frozen Yogurt. He went through the drive through and ordered our favorites.

We ate our frozen yogurt in more silence. I was not trying to be mad. I truly didn't have anything to say. We picked up the kids and got everyone home and in the bed. Before I went to sleep, I asked David about his travel for next week.

"I'll only be gone Tuesday next week. We travel in the morning, and then we'll be back that night. I'll call my mom and see if she can come over Sunday and cook for us." He scooted closer to me and laid his arm over my side. "I love you," he whispered.

"Love you too."

David's request for his mom to cook on Sunday evolved into us hosting Sunday dinner. Somehow the whole Peterson clan was invited. And unfortunately, they *all* accepted.

Much to my surprise, dinner went without a hitch. I hope Thanksgiving goes this smoothly. Aunt Madeline is hosting this year. The mention of Thanksgiving prompted me to think about Friendsgiving. I usually organize and host this with Jackie and Lisa. I hadn't even thought about it this year. I was surprised they hadn't reached out. While I was thinking about it, I sent them a text letting them know I couldn't host this year. They popped back quick responses saying they would plan our Friendsgiving for the Sunday after Thanksgiving.

David was already snoozing when I got in the bed. I got comfortable and closed my eyes to sleep. If Eva woke up overnight, he'd be on duty since he went to sleep first.

Security

Customer appreciation week finally arrived, and the office was filled with excitement. The act of giving always brings out the best in people, and customer appreciation week brought great vibes and creative ideas to put a smile on our customers' faces. There were singing telegrams, billboards with thank you messages, candy and food galore all over the city expressing Mendallmen's gratitude to its customers.

But the highlight of this week was the monthly evening breastfeeding support group. I made sure Grace was included in the messages regarding the after-group festivities. Eva and I arrived early to the session so I could catch Mary before group to talk about my milk supply.

Mary wasn't there yet, but Tish was. I said hello and set Eva's car seat on the opposite side of the room. Not a fan of awkward silences, I started a conversation.

"So, are you still going to the daytime group every week?"

"I am."

"What brings you to the evening sessions?"

"I don't want to miss out on any new information."

She doesn't want us unsupervised in *her* breastfeeding support group.

"I'd think you'd know all there is to know by now."

"I'd think the same about you given your *seniority*."

"I was a little rusty. I've certainly benefited from the group.

How about you? What benefit do you get from weekly attendance for all these years?"

"I enjoy sharing my experience with new moms. It's the highlight of my week."

"Do you work or volunteer somewhere during the week, outside of this group?"

"I'm a stay-at-home mom. That's full-time work."

"True." I said with a slight chuckle.

"What's funny?" I heard the offense in her voice though I wasn't trying to argue with this woman.

"I agree with you. Stay-at-home moms are on duty around the clock. I take my hat off to you."

"You're patronizing me. Ever since you started coming to this group you've come off as if you know everything. You suggested having this evening group because you were intimidated by me and hoped I wouldn't be involved. But I take this group seriously and, regardless of who comes, I'm all in. You can't push me out."

Now I was laughing. "This evening group was proposed so that *working* moms like me and others in the group could continue to benefit from *Mary's* knowledge. I don't see this as a place to spout off my knowledge about anything. I do that at my *job*. I come here to learn and gain support from other moms."

"I see your little *clique* here. They come just to see you. You all use this as a social club. I attend to make sure that this group is not being abused."

"The whole point of us *being* here is for us to socialize with other mothers who are experiencing the same things. That is not abuse of the group. The only thing out of order is your sense of ownership of this group. Mary doesn't need a watchdog. She's quite capable of moderating the group. The only person who feels intimidated is you, as evidenced by this conversation."

As I was speaking "my clique" came in, and they stood there in silence with their mouths hanging open, watching this heated dialogue.

"Whoa, what's happening here," LeeAnn jumped in.

"Speaking of watchdogs, here's yours," Tish spouted off.

"Tish, I hope you enjoy the group tonight. That's what *I'm* here to do. This conversation is over."

Luckily, Mary came bustling into the room, effectively putting an end to the dispute.

"Well, hello, ladies and babies," Mary said, oblivious to the tension in the room. "I heard from two more moms who are on their way, so we'll give them a few minutes to arrive. Who's first to the table?"

I headed to the table first and discussed the milk supply issue with Mary. She coached me on a few things as she weighed Eva.

"I don't suggest you run out and start her on formula. Give yourself a week to get your supply back up. If it doesn't improve, you'll need to come see me and we can determine a strategy for supplementing."

"I really don't want to do that, but I'm having a hard time keeping up with work and pumping. I feel horrible that this is even an area of conflict for me."

"Don't beat yourself up, Lonnie. Breastfeeding is important for the first year of her life. You working will benefit her well into her college years. Supplementing is not a sign of failure. It's just that, a supplement. We're going to talk a little about this as a group." She dismissed me from the table, and Eva and I went to sit down.

"So, what was all that about?" LeeAnn asked. Rachel and Sasha were leaning in to get the scoop as well.

"We'll talk later." I fumbled around in my diaper bag, hoping she'd leave it alone.

"Okay. Let me know if you need backup."

"LeeAnn, we're too old for that."

"Maybe you are." I glared at her. "I'm just saying."

Mary's advice for the evening was about keeping stress levels low and finding peace throughout our day to maintain a healthy milk supply. The past week, and even this evening, my stress levels had been through the roof. I usually handle stress well, but I'm no fool. I know stress works on you even though you think you have it under control. We finished the night with a deep breathing exercise. I needed that.

Tish hung around to speak with Mary after the group. I knew she would voice a complaint, but I decided to put my energy toward hanging out with my friends. Tish could have her false sense of leadership. We regrouped in the parking lot to make sure everyone knew where we were going. I let them know that Grace would meet us there. LeeAnn tried to talk to me as I was getting Eva's car seat snapped in, but I said we'd chat at the cafe. She seemed a little put off, but so was I. I needed a moment.

Tonight's cafe was a kid friendly coffee house. It was very vibrant and there was music appropriate for little ones. A play area was set up in the front of the cafe and the tables were positioned so that you could see the play area from anywhere in the cafe. Grace had arrived before we did and reserved a large booth that accommodated us all.

"Did I miss something? You all look like somebody committed a crime and you're all trying to hide it."

Everyone looked at me.

"There was a heated conversation in support group. It's not worth revisiting. We want to hear about you and Jackson," I said cheerfully.

The other ladies turned their attention to Grace and the direction of the conversation changed for the better. We chatted for an hour over nonalcoholic beverages and baked goods. Sasha proposed the idea of a Friendsgiving brunch the Saturday after Thanksgiving. Everyone agreed it was a great idea. I was beginning to feel overwhelmed with my Thanksgiving schedule, but I agreed to it as well.

As we all gathered our things and babies to go home, LeeAnn pulled me to the side.

"Are you okay?"

"I'm fine, LeeAnn. I can handle myself. Tish said what she needed to say, and I gave my response. It's all good."

"Lonnie, don't go home and internalize that woman's foolishness. She's not worth your time."

"Thank you for the advice. I'd appreciate it if we just let it go and not talk about it anymore."

"Sure," she said, throwing her hands in the air.

"I'll see you all the Saturday after Thanksgiving at my house," Sasha said as she got in her car. We waved goodbye to one another and went our separate ways. I can't lie, the adrenaline from that spat was still lingering in my veins, but I did my best to focus my thoughts elsewhere. When I got home, David attempted to pull me into a romantic moment. My mind was far from romance, but I gave him what he was after. At three a.m. I found myself in our home office starting an entry to my diary to get some of these negative emotions off my chest so I could get some sleep. I felt much better afterward and was able to get a few hours of sleep.

By the weekend I had successfully moved on from the incident at BSG. LeeAnn had texted every day since Wednesday to check on me. She always shared something funny or a photo of a piece of furniture she was working on. I was grateful for her friendship. The employee appreciation event this week was another pick me up. But on the flip side, I was not looking forward to David's upcoming travel. Next week was going to be busy with Thanksgiving, brunch with Dad, and two Friendsgivings.

The boys were getting excited for Thanksgiving break. Talks of Christmas were starting to pop up.

"Mom, are we going to put up the Christmas tree the day after Thanksgiving?" Johnny asked.

"Yeah, Papa can help when he comes over," DJ said.

"Maybe we could go help Papa put up *his* Christmas tree the day after Thanksgiving. What do you guys think about that?"

"I like it," DJ said.

"I'll call him and see if that's okay. Or I can ask him when he comes over to watch Eva."

"We should buy him a special ornament for his tree," Johnny suggested.

"That's a great idea. We'll shop for one this week. Boys, I need for you to get your things ready for the week. Dad will be out of town the end of the week, so we need to be prepared."

"Mom, why does Dad go out of town all the time?" Johnny asked.

"He goes for work. He's a regional manager now so he has to make sure people are doing what they're supposed to in other cities," DJ explained.

"Is he going to do that forever?" Johnny asked.

"I'm not sure, honey," I replied.

The boys and I started prepping for the week. David had gone to the store to pick up diapers. He came home with diapers and dessert for the two of us. After the kids went to bed, we watched a movie and ate double chocolate cake.

"We haven't had time to talk about how things have been for you the last few days. How are you doing?" David asked.

"I'm doing fine. The week of Thanksgiving is going to be very busy for me. I'm trying not to let it stress me out."

"How are things at work?"

"Much better now that our unhappy account is back on track. This week is employee appreciation week. There's a fun day planned for everyone on Wednesday."

"What day do the boys get out of school the week of Thanksgiving?"

"They have a half day Tuesday and they are out Wednesday through the rest of the week. What days are you out of town?"

"I'm in the field Thursday and Friday this week and again on Monday."

I kept looking straight ahead so my facial expressions wouldn't reveal the hateful thoughts that were going on in my mind. This traveling was getting old real quick. I knew we both worked and we both were in managerial positions, but I was getting the short end of the stick. I felt bad when I started thinking like this because I did have a lot of support, but I still felt the pressure of David's absence when he was out of town. He didn't have that pressure. I shifted my thoughts to keep from turning this semi-date night into fight night.

"Are you excited about Thanksgiving dinner at Aunt Madeline's house?" I said with a hint of sarcasm. He looked at me sideways with a smirk.

"The only thing exciting about that Thanksgiving dinner will be the food and the game. Mom Mabel ain't getting my money this year."

I laughed at that. "You say that every year. I thought you were letting her win on purpose."

"I *wish* I was just being benevolent. I don't know how she does it."

"That's what you get for gambling. You shouldn't be doing that in front of the boys anyway."

"We're pretty discreet about it."

"And kids are much more aware than you realize."

"True."

We sat for a few minutes, just quietly enjoying each other's presence. Then Eva started crying.

"It's your turn," we said simultaneously.

"No, babe, you stay here. I'll get her," David said.

"How about you go get her and bring her to me. That way we don't have to pull any milk from the freezer." I got situated on the couch and he laid her in my arms. I raised my shirt to get her latched on and looked up to see David curiously watching this mommy-baby feeding moment.

"What?"

"I'm just trying to wrap my head around how breasts that haven't produced milk in, like, 10 years are flowing again. No milk comes out when I latch on. And I latch on pretty regularly."

I rolled my eyes. "Different set of hormones, babe." He cuddled next to me while I fed our baby nature's perfect food for an infant, not for a grown, sexually aroused man. But this whole scene aroused him for sure and now he wanted to engage in the act that brought us to this point.

"You can't get pregnant while you're breastfeeding, right?" He said kissing me on my neck.

"How old are you? How old are we? We can't afford to play those games! Look at where it got us!"

He laughed. "I'll put Eva down, you go wait for me upstairs."

There's no need to elaborate on what happened next. Just know security was in place, so no intruders were allowed in. Good night.

Heads and Ankles Will Roll

Employee Appreciation Day had arrived. The company had rented luxury busses to pick up everyone from both branches and take them to a restaurant on the other side of town. The bus was charged with good vibes and interesting conversation as I walked the aisle greeting everyone on our bus. The restaurant was one of those places where you eat and play. Each person signed up to compete in their choice of pool, bocce, shuffleboard, or a board game. Co-workers from Main Branch and South Branch would be partnered for the competitions. I decided to be adventurous and signed up for shuffleboard. I'd never played, but from what I'd seen, it didn't look too hard or strenuous.

Both buses arrived at our destination at about the same time. I had to admit it was nice to relax and just enjoy the event, leaving the responsibilities to someone else.

"Everyone, welcome to Board. We are so happy to have Mendallmen here with us today. I'm Stephen, your Game Master for the day. We'll get you all prepared for competition. After competition, you will be served a meal. Are you ready for some good competitive fun?" He rolled his arm in the direction he wanted us to go, and everyone moved that way.

We received our game assignments and teamed up with our assigned partners from the other branch. The room got lively quickly as the natural competitor in each of us came out. I was teamed up with our CEO John Bianco's secretary, Marianne. Turned out she knew how to play shuffleboard. She's a frequent cruiser. Our opponents were Julia and another director from Main Branch.

After a dominant win over Julia and her partner, we moved on to compete against one of my designers on the creative team and an account services team member from Main Branch.

"Lonnie, let's put a hurtin' on these folks," Marianne said as I stepped up to take my turn.

Feeling pretty confident coming off the first win, I positioned my cue in front of the disc, leaned back to get momentum and lunged forward, propelling the disc down the court. But as I lunged, my ankle rolled and down went Frazier! The handful of people who were nearby came rushing over to see if I was hurt. I refused to take their assistance getting up off the ground. I knew my ankle was injured, but I couldn't let my pride be injured too.

I got up on my own and insisted we continue playing. The final play was up to me for the win. I switched up my stance so my weight was on my uninjured ankle and in true KarateKid style, I pulled out the win on a bum leg. I hopped to the area where we were going to eat and had one of the staff members bring me some ice.

"What happened?" Grace asked as she sat down next to me.

"Oh, I was trying to be the hero playing shuffleboard. It's fine, probably just a sprain."

"Really? Shuffleboard? Old people play that without breaking a sweat and you break your ankle," Grace said jokingly.

"Well, what sport did *you* play? I took a chance on trying something new and I won!"

"Since you asked . . ." Grace said with a playfully arrogant tone, "I competed in bocce. I have never played the sport before but dominated my competition."

"Congrats to you, Grace! Who were you paired with?"

"This guy named Rob. He said he was new to the company. I carried our team. He was out there throwing the ball like a shot putter. I think he actually broke one of the balls."

"Are you coming to Friendsgiving next week?"

"I'm planning on it. I've never been to a Friendsgiving, so I'm interested to see what it's like."

"Just food and fun among a small group of friends. Just another reason to get out of the house." I squirmed in my chair. The pain from my ankle was starting to set in. "Do you have any ibuprofen?"

"I don't, but there's a lady in the office who's a walking pharmacy. I'll ask her." Grace rushed off and Will came up.

"What happened here?"

"I was winning and someone from your branch pulled a Tonya Harding on me. I'm kidding. I rolled my ankle during a shuffleboard game. Nothing serious." Those words were coming out of my mouth, but the pain was saying otherwise. "What did you play?"

"I was in the chess competition. It's been a while since I played and it showed. My partner and I lost. But it was fun to sit and play again. This was a great idea. We should give the committee some bonus time off or something."

Grace came back and handed me two unwrapped pills. "Are you sure these are ibuprofen?"

"That's what she said."

"Grace, you've met Will, I'm sure."

"Yes, informally."

He shook her hand while I took the ibuprofen.

"How do you know each other?"

"Our babies go to the same pediatrician," she replied before I could.

"Small world! Well, Grace, it's great to get to know you a little better." Will meandered to another table, making his rounds.

By this time most people had finished their competitions

and our meal was ready. The committee announced the game winners. I had Marianne go up and receive our award. It dawned on me that I was going to have to drive home and this bum ankle was either going to tolerate the pain or I would be driving with my non-dominant foot.

The food and conversation were awesome. I saw a side of some of my colleagues I probably wouldn't have seen if we had done some type of formal sit-down event. The time ended sooner than we all liked. By three we were loading onto the busses to return to the offices.

My ankle had swollen, and the pain killer was barely taking the edge off. I propped up my leg on the ride back to the office and headed straight to my car when we got there. I thought about calling Dad to come get me, but I decided to try to get home. I put in a call to David to pick up the strongest pain killer he could get over the counter that wouldn't hurt Eva.

"So, you did this playing shuffleboard?" David asked sarcastically.

"Yes," I said, rolling my eyes, "We won. That's all that matters."

"Well, get home safely so I can take care of you."

"For like two hours. You're out of town early tomorrow."

"You've got all of my attention up until that time and as soon as I come home. I'll pick up some meals your Dad can start and DJ can finish."

"Thanks. I'm going to start driving. If it takes me more than thirty minutes, come find me."

"Okay, babe. Drive carefully."

I decide to drive with my non-dominant foot, one of the scariest things I've done to date. Needless to say I drove in the slow lane all the way home, with my blinkers on. When I reached the house, DJ was waiting at the door for me.

"Can I help you, Mom?"

"Yes, I'll need some help, honey." I got both feet out of the car and put my arm over his shoulders. He helped me onto my good foot, and I hopped into the house straight to the couch.

"Shuffleboard?" asked Dad.

"Yes," I said, annoyed.

"I thought that was a low impact sport that older people can play. I won't try that sport."

"But I won. How 'bout we talk about that."

"Did you win on the play you injured your ankle?"

"No, even better. I won on the next turn *with* an injured ankle," I said proudly. "Enough about me. How was Eva's day?"

"She had a great day. We got out and had some fresh air. She's really getting to be animated. I'm seeing less milk in the freezer. Are you bringing any home?"

"I haven't been bringing home as much. I feel awful. At this rate, we're not going to make it to a year with the breastmilk."

"Don't feel bad. She's had it up to this point, and she'll have a little more. You can only do what you can do."

"I could have done better, Dad." I started to cry. It didn't really take much because the pain I was in had me at the threshold of tears anyway.

"Lonnie, let's not focus on shoulda, coulda, woulda. Focus on where you are now and how you want to move forward." He squeezed my shoulder.

"Has she eaten recently? I can nurse her now."

"She's probably ready for dinner."

Dad got Eva from the swing and set her in my lap. He was right, she was becoming more animated. David came in with the pain meds and a glass of water. He made sure my ankle was propped and put some ice on it.

"Thanks, Dad, I'll take over from here," David said.

"I'll come over a little early tomorrow so you can stay off that ankle. Are you going to stay home tomorrow?"

"I hadn't planned on it. I'm hoping I can just prop it up and ice it for the night and be functional in the morning."

"I don't know, Lonnie, it's pretty swollen. You may need to have it looked at," David said.

"I'll check it out in the morning. As of right now, I'm planning to work tomorrow."

They both backed off, and Dad gave me a hug before he left. David brought a plate of food and put it on the table beside me. Eva sucked away and got a little fussy when one breast tapped out. I switched her to the other side, and she emptied that one in record time. I was not seeing how I'm going to be able to keep up with her. I handed her over to David so I could eat. I really just wanted to go to bed, but I was nervous about getting upstairs and not being able to get back down in the morning.

"Babe, I'm going to sleep down here so I don't have to manage the steps. Can you pull my navy slacks and the orange top from the closet and grab my toiletries and some underclothes?"

"Sure, honey."

I could feel the medication starting to kick in. I stretched out on the couch and David propped up my ankle and refreshed the ice. He covered me with a blanket, and I drifted off to sleep. I woke around two to the sound of Eva crying. I could hear David coming down to get milk. My ankle was throbbing.

"David, I'll feed her, just bring her here. Can you also bring me some pain killers?"

"Lonnie, are you sure? Shouldn't you be resting?"

"Yes. I need to do a better job of feeding and pumping. My milk supply is dropping."

He retrieved Eva and helped me sit up to feed her. When Eva finished, David helped me lie down. He sat on the far end of the couch and burped Eva.

"Just put her in the swing with a blanket so I can get to her."

He laid her in the swing, covered her, and came back to the couch. He grabbed the sofa throw, found a comfortable enough position, and fell asleep. I did too.

When my alarm went off, I woke to a throbbing ankle. The swelling didn't look any better. But being the strong woman that I am, I tried to get up. As soon as my foot touched the floor, I knew this wasn't going to work. I began sending emails letting those who needed to know that I wouldn't be in the office today, but that I would take all my meetings via phone or video at their regularly scheduled time. I looked at my calendar for the day and found an open window that would allow me to go to the urgent care.

David left. He wouldn't be back until late tomorrow night. Dad and I laid out the plan for the day. After two meetings via phone, Dad, Eva, and I headed to the urgent care.

"Mrs. Peterson, the good news is the X-ray doesn't show that you've broken anything. The bad news is you've got a significant sprain. I'm recommending a boot for you to wear, and you'll want to stay off your foot for a few days. Also, I'm writing a prescription for some physical therapy and stronger, longer lasting pain medication—yes, I know you're breastfeeding. This won't impact the baby. The nurse will bring you the boot and some crutches. If that ankle is not a lot better in a week, come back in." He handed me the scripts and left to help his next patient.

This was going to slow me down. I was in pain and irritated. I'd never used crutches before and frankly, I didn't want to learn. I called the office and asked Danielle to reschedule my meetings for the rest of the day due to my ankle and told her that I'd be available by email tomorrow. The nurse came in with my boot and crutches and gave me a crash course on how to don the boot and how not to fall using the crutches. I headed to the waiting area with a boot on my right foot and crutches under each arm.

"Dad, after we get these scripts filled can we stop by the bakery? I think I need one of those chocolate raspberry scones."

"Anything for you, Lonnie." He helped me hobble to the car while lugging Eva in her carrier.

When we got home, Dad helped me get situated on the couch with my leg propped and iced, and my scone, meds, and water handy on the side table. He sat on the couch next to me, holding the baby.

"You want to talk?"

"I really just want to cry. I want to be great at work, I want to be a good mom to these kids, I want to be a good wife, but I don't feel like I'm good at any of those things right now. And I can't walk," I broke into full ugly cry. Dad put Eva down and sat next to me.

"You are being unrealistic, Lonnie. You're doing fantastic in all those areas. Everything won't be perfect, but you're giving it your best."

"I don't feel that way, Dad."

"Feelings change. Don't base your position in life on feelings. You're performing well at work, this baby is healthy and growing, and your family is running well. Are you stretched? Yes. But the times in life when we are stretched are the times when we grow."

He looked at me to gauge if I caught what he was laying down. I nodded.

"I'm going to call Jackie and see if she can come over tonight. If not, I'll stay with you. I figure you may need a friend instead of Dad."

"Dad, I'll always need you. I couldn't have made it this far without you, that's for certain."

Eva was getting fussy so I motioned for him to hand her to me and I nursed her. There is something so calming about breastfeeding. It did more for me than the pain meds. When the feeding was complete, I handed her back to Dad to be changed, and I curled up and went to sleep.

I woke up to happy chatter. Once I was able to shake off that fog between sleep and awake, I realized Dad and Jackie were in the kitchen having a discussion with the boys about school. Jackie must have heard me stirring because she came around the corner.

"Well hello. I was wondering if you were still alive in here."

"Thanks for coming, Jackie."

"Of course. I'm going to stay tonight, and your dad will be back in the morning. He'll stay until David gets home. Do you need anything right now?"

"I gotta pee."

She helped me up to my feet and followed me to the bathroom, guarding me as I walked with the crutches.

"Thanks, I can take it from here, Nurse Jackie."

"Oh don't worry. I have no intention of wiping your bottom."

I closed the door and just sat in there for a few minutes. I'd spent so long on the couch, it felt good to sit up. I headed back to the couch to find the boys watching TV. Jackie had my dinner on a TV tray table. Dad said his goodbyes and left us in Jackie's hands.

Dad was right, I needed a friend here with me. She cared for Eva, made sure the boys had their things ready for tomorrow, and walked me to the bathroom. When all the kids were down, we watched a movie together and talked for a few hours before we called it a night.

"I'm so glad you were able to come over. I needed some girl time."

"I'm happy to share some time with you. You're not just a friend, you're family, like my sister."

"Thank you, Jackie." I felt myself give in to the medicated urge to sleep.

I woke to the smell of breakfast and the need to get this milk out of my chest. I sat up and looked around to see which adult was here with me. Jackie was still here.

"Jackie, did Eva eat over night?" I was trying to figure out exactly what time it was.

"She ate about two hours ago. I put some pain meds and water on your tray table. Do you want pancakes and sausage?"

"Sure. Did the boys eat?"

"They ate and they're getting themselves ready for school."

"I need you to move in."

"I don't think my crew could survive without me. They're grown but you wouldn't know it the way they act sometimes. And the little one, I don't have the words. He's lucky I love him."

"Good morning, ladies," Dad said as he walked in for his shift. "How'd everyone do overnight?"

"Everyone did great," said Jackie.

"Thanks again, Jackie, for coming on short notice."

"No problem, Uncle E. The boys have eaten, and Lonnie will be ready to feed Eva soon. She has meds on her tray table." She gave Dad a hug. "Lonnie, I'll talk to you later. Get well!"

"Thanks for your help, Jackie."

"Are you feeling better today? Do I need to bring you a bedside commode?"

"Not funny, Dad. Especially for you, because you'd have to empty it."

"You're right, I didn't think about that. You ready to eat?"

"Yes, it'll be good to have something on my stomach when I take this medicine. Dad, will you bring me that prescription for physical therapy? I need to get that scheduled. If they can help me get back on both feet, I want to start today."

He grabbed the paper and handed it to me. "The doc said you need to rest for a few days. Then you can go to physical therapy," he said in a parental tone.

I took a video of myself laid up on the couch, recounting my triumphant victory in shuffleboard, and the pain that victory rewarded me. I gave special thanks to Dad and Jackie.

At lunch Dad brought the plate he prepared for me and sat on the opposite end of the couch. He seemed a little nervous.

"Lonnie, we'll be having a guest with us the day after Thanksgiving."

"Who's coming?" I said with pasta in my mouth, totally expecting him to say one of his cousins or bowling buddies.

"I met a lady a few months ago."

I sort of froze, then lowered my fork. "A lady? Wow, Dad. You've never talked about anyone other than Mom."

"I know. This took me by surprise as well."

"I have so many questions."

"Shoot."

"How long have you been seeing this lady?"

"About two months."

"What's her name?"

"Linda."

"Is she employed or was she employed long enough to have her own retirement savings?"

"Yes."

My interrogation went on for about thirty minutes.

"Do you think you'll marry her?"

"That's a heavy question, Lonnie. I don't have an answer just yet. I wouldn't make that decision until you have had a chance to get to know her. I think you will like her a lot."

"Dad, I'm happy for you, but this is a lot to process."

"I know. Trust me. I've been processing it the last two months, asking if it is real. It's been so long since I've felt this way about a woman."

"Why didn't you say anything about her sooner?"

"I wanted to make sure she was a good person that I felt comfortable bringing around my family. I would never expose my grandkids to just anyone."

"Well, I'm ready to meet her."

"I'm ready for her to meet you all."

I shook my head and smiled. "Dad, you've been out of the game so long, how were you able to get back in it?"

"I've been asking myself the same question. I just keep showing up on dates and talking to her the best I know how. I guess I'm just being myself. Which is comforting because I won't have to keep up any pretense."

"You're right about that. Good work, Dad."

"Will you tell David and the boys before you all come over on Friday?"

"I'd prefer you tell them sometime this week, so you can answer any questions they may have."

"That's fair."

My couch bumming lasted the whole weekend. I decided to get up more often on Sunday to get used to being on the crutches. I was keeping my pain under control which helped me tolerate the extra activity. Dad said he would drive me to work Monday and Tuesday and David would drive me on Friday. I was able to make my way upstairs, slowly. It was good to sleep in my bed.

Monday and Tuesday were fairly quiet in the office. Many people took the whole week off for the holiday. I was glad about that, less walking I had to do. I actually took my pump times each day. On Wednesday I had my first physical therapy session. I have no words to describe the pain. Those folks have no qualms about hurting people. I wasn't looking forward to my second appointment on Friday. No pain, no gain I guess.

Confessions

Minus Eva and me, everyone in my house slept in on Thanksgiving morning. When I opened my eyes, the reality of having Thanksgiving at Aunt Madeline's house hit me. The one saving grace about Thanksgiving is the presence of other family, assuming they show up. Aunt Madeline has two sons and is divorced. One of her sons, Andrew, still lives with her. The other, Matt, no one has heard from in ten years. Aunt Teresa had two daughters. Sadly, one died some years ago. Her other daughter, Sherrie, lives somewhere overseas, so we haven't seen her in years either.

"Will any of your cousins be there?" I asked David over breakfast.

"Andrew will be there of course and rumor has it Sherrie is in the States. Not sure she'll be at dinner though."

"That'd be interesting. I wonder how Aunt Teresa would react to that. There is no common ground between that mother and daughter."

"To say the least."

"Are we supposed to be bringing anything?"

"Mom has us covered."

"I love your mom, babe."

While other women were likely four hours into an eight-hour kitchen shift on Thanksgiving, I was hopping around in my pajamas on crutches trying to decide what my daughter and I would wear to dinner. I gotta admit, I liked this. If David's family wasn't so hard core about Thanksgiving, I'd take my family out to eat instead of cooking.

We got dressed and headed over to Aunt Madeline's. I called my dad while we were in the car. He's always been so understanding about Thanksgiving. We often will have brunch the day after Thanksgiving or we may go out and see a movie. This day after Thanksgiving would be one for the books with his new *lady*.

"Happy Thanksgiving, Dad!"

"Why thank you. You heading over to Sheryl's?"

"Thanksgiving is at David's aunt's house this year."

"Well, enjoy."

"I'm going in to work tomorrow for a few hours, then we should be at your house about three. Where are you spending Thanksgiving?"

"I'm meeting Linda's family today."

"Dad, how serious is this? If you all are meeting each other's families, you must intend to make this long term."

"We're going to feel out each other's families before we talk about long term. It's safer that way."

"I'm eager to meet her. Represent us well, Dad. We won't be able to talk about how crazy her family is tomorrow since she'll be there."

He laughed. "I will represent us well."

"Love you, Dad. Enjoy dinner with Linda and her family."

"I love all of you. Tell David's family I said Happy Thanksgiving."

We pulled into Aunt Madeline's driveway. We all piled out and headed to the front door. I took a cleansing breath and rang the doorbell. A tall slim lady with a very pregnant belly answered the door.

"Lonnie," she exclaimed and pulled me in for a hug, "It's been forever since I've seen you!"

"It's good to see you!" I had no idea who she was.

"D! How are you?"

"Sherrie!" David exclaimed as he embraced her. "What is that attached to your stomach?"

"It's a baby bump. You should be familiar with this look. You getting a touch of dementia as you age?"

"Ha. Is there a man that comes with this bump? Where is he? We must approve all eligible bachelors before this occurs."

"No bachelor. Just me and the bump. Where's your princess? I have to see her."

David was carrying Eva in the car seat. He pulled her blanket back to reveal the XX version of our offspring.

"David, she's gorgeous." Sherrie stared at her in awe. "You guys come on in. Once you get settled, I have to hold this baby doll. Lonnie, why are you using crutches?"

"Shuffleboard injury."

The boys headed straight for the basement. All the men gathered there to watch football and do whatever it is men do on Thanksgiving when they aren't eating. We went to the living room to greet everyone. Aunt Teresa wasn't there yet. She was picking up Mom Mabel.

"Where's my princess?" Sheryl asked as she dried her hands on a kitchen towel. David pulled Eva out of the car seat. "Oh my goodness, look at that outfit! Lonnie, she's a doll." Sheryl hugged Eva and sat at the dining room table holding her.

"I've got her next," Sherrie said.

"Sherrie, when are you due?"

"I've got another two months, Aunt Sheryl. Feels like forever."

"Are you going to find out what you're having?"

"I don't think so. I want to be surprised."

"Keep the surprises coming, honey," Aunt Madeline said with a little cynicism.

"It's my first, so I want to fully embrace this experience. Lonnie, could you tell the difference between your pregnancies with the boys and Eva?"

"Uh, I don't recall. This last pregnancy was overshadowed by a lot going on at work and me being in total shock."

"But to have a girl after the boys, that must be a great feeling."

"You may want to ask me that a year or two from now."

"Are the boys just loving her to pieces?"

"They are. She lets out one little whimper and they come running."

"That is so sweet. I don't think this little person will have any siblings." She rubs her belly. "Good thing we have you all. Eva will be around the same age."

"Do you plan on staying in the States?"

"Yes, I will be staying in the States. I've had fabulous experiences traveling and living overseas, but it's time for me to settle down and live a real life. I don't want to raise this baby away from family, so I packed up my stuff and moved back."

This story lacked depth. It would make for a pretty entertaining evening as people inadvertently started spilling beans. I slipped away from the food preparation area to find Joanna and Lizzie. I leaned over to Joanna, "So what's the scoop on Sherrie."

"I don't know all the details. She just showed up pregnant last month. Mom has tried getting details from Aunt Teresa, but she's gotten nowhere. What did you do to your leg?"

"Shuffleboard injury."

Sherrie came into the room and sat in a chair near Joanna and me.

"Sherrie, where are you staying?" Lizzie asked.

"Right now I'm staying with a cousin on my dad's side of the family until I find a place. I've got some money saved up, so I should be able stay home with the baby for about a year before I need to go back to work."

"Must be nice. Are your parents excited to have you back and to have a grandbaby on the way?"

"They are excited for me to be home, but they are struggling with me being pregnant and no man in the picture. I know it's not what they envisioned for me, but I'm an adult."

"Well, take my advice," Lizzie said. "You will need

as much support as you can get being a single parent."

The doorbell rang. David looked out the window and announced Mom Mabel, Aunt Teresa, and Uncle Larry had arrived. Sherrie stood up with a nervous look on her face. David opened the door and greeted them. He took Mom Mabel's jacket and the dish that she brought. We all trooped into the foyer to greet them. Sherrie hung back to be the last to greet them.

"Mom Mabel!" Sherrie said with forced excitement as she hugged her grandmother.

"Well, look who decided to join us. And you didn't come alone," Mom Mabel said as she eyeballed Sherrie's baby bump. "Did you run off and get married while in Europe?"

"No, ma'am," she said bashfully.

"Is the baby's father in Europe?" Everyone looked to Sherrie, then to Aunt Teresa and Uncle Larry. Mom Mabel waited for an answer.

"David, can you bring that dish into the kitchen? Teresa, I need your help in here. You're late," Aunt Madeline called from the kitchen. David and Aunt Teresa quickly exited the awkward moment in the foyer, but Mom Mabel showed no sign of moving until she got an answer.

"Mother, come sit here in the living room," Uncle Larry said.

"Did you flee the country? Why is everyone looking around like there's something going on?" Mom Mabel inquired as Uncle Larry escorted her to a chair in the living room.

Sherrie took a deep breath and followed her father. She sat on the couch close to Mom Mabel's chair. Joanna, Lizzie, and I sat in the dining room with our ears and eyes glued on this interaction.

"There was a guy, for a long time, but we broke up. After that I didn't want another relationship, but I did want a child, so I opted for AI," Sherrie explained.

"What's AI, honey?" Mom Mabel asked, irritated. Joanna

was sitting on the edge of her seat, and Lizzie dropped her head in anticipation of what was coming next.

"Artificial insemination." Sherrie said with some hesitation. Mom Mabel just stared at her for a moment. Uncle Larry looked away out of the window.

"Well, were you able to buy the best sperm on the market, honey?"

Sherrie relaxed a little and chuckled. "As a matter a fact, I was."

"I hate that your baby will never know who its father is or who its people are, but if that's what you want, I hope it works out the way you planned. Lonnie, where's that baby of yours?" she said, turning her attention toward me. "And what happened to your leg?"

"Shuffleboard injury."

Lizzie retrieved Eva from Sheryl and handed her off to Mom Mabel. This Thanksgiving dinner was shaping up to be a memorable one right out of the gate! I headed into the kitchen to help. Lizzie followed suit.

"Aunt Madeline, is there anything I can do?"

"Yes, set the table and put the breadbasket in the center. Are you even able to do anything on those crutches? What did you do to yourself anyway? Make sure you wash your hands."

I looked over to Lizzie and quietly mocked Aunt Madeline as if I were a ten-year-old. Family gatherings have a way of pulling the worst out of you. After washing my hands, I took the tableware and breadbasket to the table and arranged them as best I could.

"Lonnie," said Mom Mabel, "are you still breastfeeding this baby?"

"Yes, ma'am."

"She's looking for a meal, and I don't even know how she located that territory on my body. It's long gone." Mom Mabel laughed.

Lizzie retrieved the little one from the old one and escorted me down the hall to the guest bedroom. I got Eva situated, latched on, and covered, and then there was a knock on the door.

"Come in."

"Is it alright if I hang out in here? I need to learn how to do this."

"Sure, Sherrie. Please close the door." I was a little reluctant about this.

"The pressure out there is a bit much," she said, taking a chair in the corner of the room.

"I'm going to go out on a limb and say there's a little more behind your story than just artificial insemination." I can't believe I just said that. I'm in no way an intrusive person, but the suspense was too much.

"I'll tell you because it'll come out sooner or later anyway. My parents know, which is why they are a little standoffish." She took a deep breath. "When I initially went to Europe, it was simply to travel for a season and then come back home. But while I was there, I ran short on cash and needed money. So, I became a surrogate mother."

I know my mouth had to be hanging wide open.

"This is my fourth pregnancy. I had two children for one couple in Russia. The third pregnancy was for a couple who didn't live in a country where surrogacy is legal. I took the chance and went through with it. We proceeded with the adoption after the child was born, and there were no problems. This last time I took the risk again with a different couple. About three months ago the couple decided they didn't want the baby because the ultrasounds were concerning for some type of birth defect, so they wanted me to abort the pregnancy. I refused, they nullified our agreement, and so here I am."

Tears began to roll down her face.

"I never breastfed any of those children." She paused to regain her composure. "I want to breastfeed this one," she said touching her belly. "It'll be my own this time."

The tears were rolling hard and nonstop as she tried to keep from sobbing. "I've cried an ocean of tears, and

I'm ready to face the fact that this baby will be my new life."

I was rather stunned and at a loss for words. I had a child attached to my breast, so I couldn't go over and give Sherrie a hug. I felt bad that after all she'd been through, her parents were acting strange. This woman and her baby deserved love and support.

"I breastfed the boys without a hitch. But when this little lady came along, we had trouble. The hospital nursing staff coached me the first three days, and then I went to a breastfeeding support group at my pediatrician's office. It helped with the technical and emotional deficits I was having with breastfeeding and being a new mom again. I'd start there and don't quit."

"When it's my turn, will you help me?"

"I most definitely will." I switched Eva to the other side.

"Does it hurt?" She was now leaning forward in her chair, wiping the tears from her cheeks.

"I'd be lying if I said it didn't. It does in the beginning because your breasts aren't used to that kind of force, but once the nipples have toughened up, you're good to go. Keep them moisturized and protected and you shouldn't have a lot of pain."

"Wow. Make sure I get your number before we leave."

Aunt Madeline called everyone to the table.

"Well, time for the main event," she said. She walked to the door, then turned back. "Thanks, Lonnie. I didn't mean to do all that emotional vomiting, but I think it will help me get through this evening."

I'm always amazed at the perspective and influence I now have because of this unexpected event in my own life. I caressed Eva's hair, and she turned her gaze to me as she finished up. I laid her across my lap and patted her back until she burped. Johnny came running up to the door.

"Mom, we're all at the table." He carried Eva down the hall. I followed. Everyone was seated around the table. I sat next to David, and he rubbed my shoulder.

"Andrew, you're the man of the house. Bless the food," directed Aunt Madeline.

Now before we go any further, let me paint a picture of Andrew: under-employed Mama's Boy. Let's proceed.

Andrew stood from his seat at the head of the table. "Everyone, bow your head. I'm going to start with a scripture and then bless our food. 'The Lord is my Shepard I shall not want.' God, we are grateful for everyone here today. We are grateful for the food. Amen."

"Amen," we all said in unison to this completely anticlimactic prayer. It was so poorly done, Mom Mabel, with her head still bowed, picked up where he left off.

"God, you deserve more than that." She glanced over at Andrew and bowed her head again. "For the stars in the sky, the breath in our bodies, young and old, we thank you. For roofs over our heads and being here together, we thank you. For the new lives here and those yet to come, we thank you. For every fulfilled prayer and the strength to keep going, we thank you. For every promise in your Book and this special family, we indeed thank you. For letting these old bones see another Thanksgiving with my offspring, I thank you. And finally, I thank you for the ones who have gone before us and those who are not here. Thank you for their impact in our lives and for bringing those who are lost home. And, God," she said with authority, "bless this food we eat, bless the hands that prepared it, bless the bodies that eat it, and I pray David's football team gets *whooped* today, so I can have some spending money for the week. Amen."

"Amen," we all say once again.

"I don't know if I'm totally in agreement with that prayer," said David.

"Larry, will you cut the turkey please," Aunt Madeline said, handing him the carving knife. "While he's doing that, we'll go around the table and each one can say one thing you're grateful for." Her voice was decidedly unenthusiastic. "Boys, go ahead and start."

"Video games," shouted Johnny.
"My mom," said Jordan. We all cooed over his response.
"My whole family," said DJ.
"My health," said Mom Mabel.
"My job," said Andrew.
"My wife," said David.
"Peace of mind," I said.
"Being gainfully employed," said Lizzie.
"For the future," said Joanna.
"For my family," said Jerry.
"For my grandbabies," said Sheryl.
"I'm thankful that a new year is coming and that this one is going," said Aunt Madeline.
"I'm thankful for my parents," Sherrie said intently.
"I'm thankful for my daughter," said Uncle Larry.
"I, too, am grateful for my grandbaby," said Aunt Teresa.

Sherrie came around the table and embraced her parents. There was silence as everyone joined in on the emotion happening on the other side of the table.

"Can you pass the sweet potatoes please," Johnny piped in, totally ruining the moment. We began passing food around, and the chatter rose around the table.

"So, Lonnie," Andrew said, "what's with the crutches?"

"Shuffleboard injury," every adult at the table said simultaneously.

The remainder of the meal was uneventful. When Mom Mabel had filled her gut, she had DJ help her to the basement so she could watch the football game. Everyone else finished up, and the men all made their way to the basement behind Mom Mabel. The ladies cleared the table and spent the next half hour chatting, putting away food, and washing dishes.

Aunt Madeline went to the foyer to grab her ringing phone. Everyone rushed to her when we heard the phone crash to floor. Sheryl got there first and found Aunt Madeline trying to pick up the phone off the floor.

"Hello," Aunt Madeline said. Sheryl stood close by, seeing

the concern on her sister's face. As she listened to the voice on the other end, Aunt Madeline began to do something I didn't know she was capable of. She began crying. And then, yet another shocker!

"I'm sorry. I'm so, so sorry. Can you forgive me?" Aunt Madeline pleaded though her tears. Sheryl was alarmed now and snatched the phone from her sister.

"Who is this?" she demanded. When the voice on the other end began to speak, Sheryl grabbed her bosom and handed the phone back to Aunt Madeline. Now everyone was alarmed. Joanna ran to the basement to get Andrew. Aunt Madeline took the phone down the hall and closed the door behind her.

"What's wrong," Andrew asked frantically.

"Your brother is on the phone," said Sheryl through her tears.

Andrew ran down the hall and burst into the room. By this time everyone had come up from the basement. Mom Mabel went to the room where Aunt Madeline and Andrew were. We all waited patiently in the living room, no one saying a word. David sent the boys back to the basement.

A few minutes later Mom Mabel came down the hall. "Everyone's all right. Matt is all right." She began to cry. Uncle Larry helped her sit down, and Joanna brought Mom Mabel a box of tissues. Andrew helped Aunt Madeline back to the living room. Everyone was looking at them, trying to understand what was going on.

"That was Matt. He was calling to wish us Happy Thanksgiving. He'll be home for Christmas," Andrew said as he wiped away the tears rolling down his face. David put his arm around Andrew's shoulder.

"I never shared this with any of you," Aunt Madeline said, "Matt has been in prison. When he went to jail, I was so angry and ashamed that I told him never to call again. I never said where he was because I was embarrassed. But I was so wrong." She broke down into sobbing.

My family gets animated when we get together, but I had never experienced anything like this with David's family. Mom Mabel, Sheryl, Aunt Madeline, and Aunt Teresa all embraced. Sheryl, in my opinion, is the only normal one in the bunch. After today's events, I saw why. Her sisters had been holding so much pain in their hearts concerning their children that they were hateful to others and maybe even jealous of Sheryl because her kids turned out so well. What a day.

"Anyone want pumpkin pie?" asked Uncle Larry, trying to lighten the mood.

"No. Get the sweet potato pie that I brought," Mom Mabel said. She rose from the huddle and moved to her seat at the dining room table. Uncle Larry cut a piece of sweet potato pie for her and let everyone else help themselves to dessert. After her last bite of pie, Mom Mabel beelined to the basement to watch the rest of the football game. The men were right behind her.

The kitchen chatter started back up again. Aunt Madeline was in the room with us, but she was quiet. When it was time to go home, Sheryl and Aunt Teresa opted to stay behind with Aunt Madeline who looked as if she needed the support of her sisters. So we ended up taking Uncle Larry home. Somehow, we also ended up with Jordan. Lizzie said she'd come to get him tomorrow.

All that excitement made me forget that I was supposed to go to work tomorrow. I laid out my clothes, nothing fancy. I'd likely be the only one in the office. After Eva's last feeding, we told the boys they could stay up for two hours, then had to go right to bed. David and I went to our bedroom.

"That was an interesting evening," I said.

"I can't believe they never told us Matt was in jail. He probably thought we all abandoned him."

"Sherrie told me her story."

"There was more to it?"

"Of course there was more. There was too much emotion

between them for her story not to have more depth." When I recapped her story, he was floored.

"What's with all these secrets in my family? This is information overload. I don't know what to do next."

"Well, Matt will be home for Christmas, and we'll be having another baby shower soon."

"That's one way to look at it." David climbed in bed next to me. "Do you *have* to go to work tomorrow?" He laid his head on my chest.

"I said I would, so I should. I won't stay the whole day. I want to be prepared for my meetings next week, and I want to spend the weekend just relaxing and not thinking about work. I'd rather have the technical pieces worked out tomorrow, so I'm not brooding over it next week when I'm flying solo."

"Got it."

We lay there in the bed in each other's embrace. He fell asleep before long. Food coma. I got up and went to the office to record a video diary entry. I didn't go into details about the events of the day, but I reflected on my thoughts earlier about having a different perspective and level of influence after being pregnant and having Eva. After making my entry, I headed to bed myself.

Emotional Attachments

I won't lie, I was a bit anxious and slightly terrified for the events today. First, I would go to physical therapy, so I was anticipating pain. Then I would meet my dad's *lady*. Who does that at his age? I really was happy for him, but I didn't know this woman! I didn't need anyone taking advantage of my father.

My PT session was truly pain and torture. This better get me out of this boot or I may file a complaint for cruel and unnecessary treatment. My office was deserted, a perfect environment for productivity. David and the kids came to get me around two thirty, and we headed straight for Dad's house. When we arrived, there was a late model Mercedes in the driveway. Already, I was forming a picture of this woman. She's a big spender with deep pockets or a big spender who wants everyone to think she has deep pockets.

"Boys, do you have the ornament for Papa's tree?"

"Yes, I have it right here," Johnny said proudly.

Eva was crying. I didn't think David fed her before he left the house, so my initial plan of interrogating Linda right out of the gate would have to take a back seat to this screaming infant.

"Are you good?" David leaned over and whispered.

"Yes. Why do ask?"

"You seem a little tense."

I brushed off his comment and got out of the car. David got Eva and her bag. Dad was waiting at the door for us.

"Here are my girls. Whoa, who forgot to feed the princess? That's her 'feed me or I'll scream' cry."

"Hi, Dad. I'm going right upstairs to feed her." I headed straight upstairs, no stopping to meet the *lady*.

I sat on the bed in my old room and got the screaming little person out of her carrier. She was stretching and not letting me get her calmed down, which was new for her. Finally, she came to herself enough to see that there was a breast being presented to her, and she greedily started chugging.

It had been a while since I had been up to my room. There were still some items from my childhood in view. I closed my eyes and tried to relax. David was right. I was tense. There was a screaming kid, a bum ankle, and a new woman in Dad's life.

There was a gentle knock on the door. I opened one eye and said to come in.

"You okay up here?" David asked as he sat next to me on the bed.

"Yes. Did I fall asleep?"

"You've been up here about thirty minutes. I was wondering if you were going to hide up here the whole time."

"When have I ever hidden from anything? I just fell asleep. Looks like Eva did too."

"Everyone is ready for you to come down. Do you need a few more minutes?"

"Yes."

He leaned in closer and started to massage my shoulders.

"Linda is a nice lady. She works as a financial planner. She's had an impressive career. I've never seen your dad in Mack mode. He really likes this lady." I just nodded. "You are not okay, Lonnie." He repositioned himself to look me in the face. "I'm going to have your dad come up here."

"No! I don't want him to be upset."

"Then tell me what's going on with you."

"This is a lot to take in, David. My life right now is a lot to take in. Look at me, an almost old lady breastfeeding a baby, a father in Mack mode, and floundering in a management role I've spent years positioning myself for."

"Wait a minute. Let me put your life into perspective for you. You are a woman in the prime of your life who is healthy enough to breastfeed a flourishing, growing baby. Your father has found someone who fills a need that none of us can fill for him. And the last time I checked, your branch was still a thriving business.

"Lonnie, I know this year has been different for you, for all of us, but everything that has come to us this year has been a blessing. Granted, these blessings require a greater level of responsibility, but they have added positive things to your life."

I couldn't argue with him. He was one hundred percent right. I hadn't been dealt any bad hands. I'd just had trouble managing all the great things that had been handed to me. "Thank you for that perspective, oh wise one."

"Now will you come down and enjoy all your blessings?" He held out his hand and helped me up with Eva.

Everyone was fumbling putting the artificial tree together.

"I always get a real one because I figured it would be hard to put an artificial tree together by myself," Linda said just as Eva and I made our presence known. She untangled herself from a pile of lights.

"Lonnie. Hi, I'm Linda." She walked over and grabbed my free hand with both of hers. She was a very well put together lady. No elastic pants for her, and her hair was trendy. Dad did good, based upon the cover.

"I'm glad to finally meet you. Is this little lady happy now? I don't think I've ever heard her scream like that," Linda said as she stroked her finger along Eva's cheek.

"You've met Eva before?"

"Yes, I have. She is the reason your dad and I met."

"Really," I said with one eyebrow raised.

"May I tell her how we met, Evan?"

"Go right ahead. Let's all sit down for this. Putting together a Christmas tree is a chore."

Once everyone got settled, Linda described how she encountered Dad and Eva in the grocery store. "I'm so glad I met Eva because she introduced me to Evan," Linda said as she looked at Dad. "May I hold her?"

"Sure. So I hear you're a financial advisor?"

"Yes, I am. I have been for several years after many successful years in syndication."

"You'll have to explain what that entails. But there are so many other questions I have. Can we come back to that?"

"Of course, I'm an open book."

Linda and I sat on the couch and watched the guys as they went back to assembling the tree while I ask fifty questions.

Question #2: Do you have any children?

"Unfortunately, I don't. I was married but it ended before we had children. Probably was for the best."

Question #23: Where do you live? (I really wanted to make sure she owned her own place and wasn't trying to move in.)

"I own a condo north of downtown."

"May I interrupt, ladies?" David asked. "We are ready to put ornaments on the tree, and the boys have a special ornament they'd like to share with Papa.

Johnny pulled the ornament from the box.

"Papa, we chose this ornament because it shows a grandpa holding a baby girl, just like you with Eva," DJ explained.

Dad admired the ornament and, with a tear in his eye, he placed the first ornament on the tree. "You all are always finding special ways to celebrate me. Thank you." He hugged the boys.

Linda and I took a break from the interrogation and joined in decorating the tree. David put on the radio station that was playing Christmas music all day. It was fun. Dad ordered pizza for dinner. Linda and I resumed the interrogation over dinner.

Question #47: What attracted you to my dad other than the cutie pie in diapers?

"He was genuine. He has always treated me like a lady. But his dedication to your family in caring for Eva is a trait you don't see in all men. He loves you all deeply. If I could win even a portion of that type of affection, I'd be full for the rest of my life." She reached over and held Dad's hand. They stared at each other as if David and I weren't in the room.

Question #62: (Yes, I'd asked that many questions.) Do you have any medical conditions that Dad should be aware of?

"I take my health very seriously. I'm active, exercising a few times a week. I used to be an avid runner. I take a few vitamins and have the body of someone 20 years younger per my PCP."

"Well, I'm really impressed, Linda. You seem like a candidate someone put together on a dating website. Do you have any questions for us?"

"I really don't have any. I just hope you all give me a chance to get closer to this fine man. It's evident that his life has been engulfed with raising a successful woman and devoting all his affection to this family."

"You've got my vote," said David. Everyone looked at me.

"He's a special man, Linda, and he deserves this type of relationship in his life. I'm all for it." Dad reached across the table and gave my hand a squeeze.

"Thank you, Lonnie."

"On second thought, I do have a question," said Linda. "How exactly did this shuffleboard injury happen? I've played shuffleboard many times without injury. This has got to be a great story."

Over cookies and ice cream I gave the hero's version of my epic shuffleboard match.

"I do have one more question," I said. "I know Dad spent Thanksgiving with your family. How did that go? Did they give the green light on this relationship?"

Dad and Linda looked at each other and began to laugh.

"Long story short, they tried to marry us last night," Dad

said. "Her cousin is an ordained minister, and he literally offered to marry us last night." They laughed.

"I don't know if you would've had a daughter if you had gone off and got married without telling me," I said.

"You know I'd never do that."

We packed up our family and loaded ourselves in the car. Dad and Linda waved at us from the front door as we pulled off. The thought of that being a permanent picture in my life was starting to settle in. I wiped a tear from my eye. David put his hand on my leg and gave me a look of reassurance. I put my hand on his, and we rode in silence.

On the way I got a text from Sasha outlining the events for tomorrow's Friendsgiving. I was supposed to bring a side dish. I asked David to swing by the store to pick up something for me to take.

The guys piled out of the car at the market, and I stayed with Eva, who was sleeping. I took the moment to add a video to the ongoing chronicles of my life. I spoke about my conversation with David and tried to expound on why I felt the way I did. All I needed was a couch and a licensed professional to complete that moment. I wrapped up the self-led therapy session when I saw David and the boys on their way back to the car. Fifty percent of the items purchased were unnecessary.

Once the kids were off to bed, David and I snuggled in bed and talked.

"I know today was tough, but I'm proud of you." He held my hand.

"He's my dad. The closest person to me besides you. I don't want him hurt or abused. He's protected me my whole life and has done everything in his power to make my life full. I feel the responsibility to return that to him during this stage in his life. I can see Dad really cares for Linda, and she seems to care for him. She'll make his life full and, to a certain degree, protect him. They'll take care of each other."

"Healthy relationships prolong your life, so this will increase his longevity."

"You're a well of wisdom today, Mr. Peterson."

"I always have been," he said in a pompous tone.

We capped our night off the way lovers do and then got in some much-needed sleep.

When I arrived at Sasha's house, Maria answered the door. With a quick look at my crutches, she hurried to the car to get my contribution to the Friendsgiving feast while I hobbled to the bench by the door to remove my shoes. Maria walked me to the room where everyone was gathered.

"Lonnie! Lonnie? What's with the crutches?" LeeAnn exclaimed.

"Oh my goodness!" Sasha chimed in.

"She came about that injury in the most valiant way," said Grace.

"Let's hear it," everyone said.

I targeted a chaise in the corner of the room and plopped down, letting the crutches fall beside me. Sasha brought a pillow for me to prop up my leg.

"Here's the short story. I brought home the shuffleboard victory for my team at Employee Appreciation Day at work. With one good leg," I said proudly.

"No short versions! This is Friendsgiving. We want the full monty, baby!" None other than LeeAnn.

"Has she had drinks already?" I asked the room. Everyone burst into laughter.

"I have yet to sip on anything except this refreshing sparkling water our good friend Sasha has provided for us."

I fully disclosed how the ankle injury came about and the physical therapy that had followed. I wasn't alone with such a tale. Rachel had broken a wrist playing badminton a few years ago.

I hauled myself off the chaise with a little help, and we moved to the kitchen to eat our shared bounty.

"Sasha, is this turkey left over from your dinner yesterday?" LeeAnn asked.

"You know it. Enjoy."

"We'll be eating turkey for days at our house," Rachel said.

"We ate at my in-laws, so no turkey leftovers at my house," I said.

"Oh, Lonnie, I forgot to tell you that I met your Dad the other day. He was at the entrepreneur fair with Eva and some lady," said LeeAnn.

"Linda."

"You never told me your dad was in a relationship."

"I just found out."

"What?! Was he keeping it a secret?" Rachel asked.

"No, he just wanted to make sure she was worthy of meeting the family."

"So what do you think of her. I don't know anything about your dad. I'm assuming he's widowed," said Sasha.

I told them all about Linda and that she had my approval.

"That's good. We don't need Pops hooking up with a schemer," said Grace.

"Trust me, I grilled her yesterday. She's not your typical *mature* woman. She's still working and has made a good life for herself. She's in shape and still works out. My dad is going to have to keep up with *her*."

"Does anyone have any exciting news or something fun on the horizon?" LeeAnn asked, shifting the conversation.

"I might be moving," Grace said. "I've been saving my money for a down payment on a house. My mom covers most of our necessities with her disability check, so I've been able to save most of my checks."

"Grace, that's awesome," I said.

"I'll be finishing my bachelors in the spring," Rachel reported.

"Oh my gosh, friend! You didn't tell me!" Sasha squealed.

"They were able to fast track me and use some of my experience toward my degree. I'm so happy. This will really put our family in a good place," Rachel said.

"I'm proud of you, Rachel," I said.

"I landed a contract with the city to design some pieces for city hall. They are going through a redesign," LeeAnn proudly announced.

"Way to go, girl," said Sasha. "Get that exposure."

"I'm excited. This will be one of my biggest projects."

"What about you, Sash, what's new?" LeeAnn asked.

"Well, I was hoping to share this a little later, but Scarlett is going to be a big sister," Sasha said sheepishly.

Everyone was exuberant over this news, talking at once in our excitement.

"You didn't try to use breastfeeding as your only contraception, did you?" Rachel asked.

"We weren't trying, and, yes, I thought you couldn't get pregnant when you're breastfeeding," Sasha admitted.

"Thank you for disproving that theory. I will make sure my meat is packaged before it comes into the store," Rachel said.

"That makes me anxious just thinking about it. One baby barely able to walk and the other one hanging on your breast. Grateful for my little ones, but I'm done," LeeAnn said.

"I was done and look what happened to me," I said. Everyone laughed.

"Abraham and Sarah over there adding to the bloodline," LeeAnn sniped.

"You do not have any room to talk, LeeAnn. You're my age." I shot back.

"I'm in your age *bracket*," she said with air quotes.

"Whatever. I've got an interesting conversation starter. Would you ever consider being a surrogate mother?"

"Do I get to have sex with the father?" LeeAnn wanted to know.

"LeeAnn!" Sasha exclaimed.

"I'm just asking."

"I don't think that's how those arrangements go," Rachel said.

"I would if the money was right," said Grace.

"I don't know if I could carry a baby for nine months and not get attached. Or to have another woman rub my belly when what's inside is hers," I said.

"I'm with Grace, if the money was right, and if I wasn't married, I'd take that job," LeeAnn said.

"I wouldn't be able to do that. I'd be too attached," Sasha said.

"Being pregnant is such an intimate process. Having two other people that you don't have a connection with be a part of that process would be awkward. I wouldn't do it," Rachel said.

"What made you ask that question, Lonnie?" Grace asked.

"There was some chatter about it at our Thanksgiving dinner."

"Man, the chatter at our dinner was out of control!" LeeAnn said.

"LeeAnn, if your family is anything like you, I would've loved to have been there. Pure entertainment," said Sasha.

"My mom and I went out to dinner. With her and Jackson not feeling well lately and me working, no one wanted to cook or be in the house," Grace said.

"Thanksgiving is a huge production for our family. There's every dish you could think of, the best china on the table, Santa comes and takes pictures with the kids. It's a big to-do," said Sasha.

"I would have never guessed," said LeeAnn sarcastically. Sasha walked over and gave her a little shoulder shove. "So how does that work with Santa showing up a month early?"

"Oh, we tell the kids Santa stops by Memaw's house on his dry run before Christmas, because she makes the best cookies in the world."

"Lying to the children," said Rachel. "I'm going to tell my kids the truth about Santa as soon as they start trying to make a list for him."

"Dream crusher! It's fun to believe," said Grace.

"I agree, believing in the *truth* is fun, believing a lie never ends well," Rachel said.

"Are you carrying childhood scars from when your parents told you Santa wasn't real?" LeeAnn joked.

"No, I just don't want a fictitious person taking credit for my show of love with my hard-earned money."

"You've got Santa trauma. We set out cookies and milk, the Elf on the Shelf moves every day, we leave a little soot in front of the fireplace, put out apples for the reindeer . . ." LeeAnn explained.

"That just proves my point. All that credit to Santa when you are the one creating that sense of joy for your kids."

"Being the creator of joy gives you joy as a parent. *That's* the credit that you as a parent get," I said.

"Lonnie, your kids are old enough not to believe in Santa. When did they stop believing?" asked Sasha.

"My older son found gifts in our closet when he was in the third grade. We told him we worked as contractors for Santa when he gets too busy to make sure all gifts get delivered on time. When he found most of the gifts, he concluded that Santa was too busy for him, so he stopped believing because he was offended at Santa." The room erupted with laughter with that story.

The evening went on with random, fun, at times serious conversations about everything under the sun. Sasha brought the get together to a close as she had another engagement that night. We ended our Friendsgiving with a toast to a great friendship forged by the milk from our breasts! (These were LeeAnn's words, of course). We said our goodbyes and planned to meet up again after the next evening BSG.

I was glad to have that outing with friends but was ready to get home and rest because I had another outing tomorrow. Conversation with Lisa and Jackie was so much easier because of our history. We'd eat, play a card or board game, and talk about everything. It'd be easy. With my BSG friends, our relationship was so new and the conversation range so wide, it took a lot more energy. I got home, and David was ready to cater to my needs. I breastfed Eva and then headed upstairs to get my leg propped up and iced.

The Beginning of the End

Monday started out busy after the holiday. On my way to my first meeting, Leonard tried to corner me to share something, but because he's random sometimes, I told him I really needed to get to this first meeting but we could talk after that meeting. The first meeting only took about 20 minutes. I hobbled back to my office and, of course, Leonard was waiting at the door.

"Come on in, Leonard."

"Have you checked your email this morning?"

"Not yet. I had to run straight to my first meeting. Why, what's going on?"

"ACM is ending their relationship with us and going with a cheaper provider."

"What?! We met their demands and brought the price down! Close the door, please." I quickly pull up the email from Gayle at ACM.

I sat back in my chair in total disbelief. I forwarded the email to Will. "Do we know why? Have you reached out to Gayle?"

"I did call her. She said the other company came in with better prices and at this time they want to pursue working with this other company. I asked her if we could meet again to come up with a number that worked better for them. She said not at this time. It's like they've already closed the door," Leonard said, defeated.

The Beginning of the End

"I'm going to call again." I dialed Gayle's number and put her on speaker. I got two rings, then an answer. I expressed to Gayle my disappointment that they still were not satisfied. She explained that managing costs was their top priority and our prices were higher than our competitors. I tried offering a steep discount, but she still didn't bite. I finished the call letting her know we would look forward to an opportunity to earn their business again and wished them future success.

I could feel tear-filled rage rising deep within. My phone rang. It was Will.

"This is Lonnie, you're on speaker with Leonard and me."

"Lonnie, are they serious?" Will asked. He was pissed.

"Yes. I just got off the phone with Gayle. I offered them a ten percent reduction in the price point we negotiated, and she said it didn't match what they've been offered."

"Leonard, did you run some numbers to see if we could get lower?"

"Good morning, Will. I spoke with Gayle before I met with Lonnie this morning, and I got the same responses. I did take a minute to calculate if we could accommodate their price point and unfortunately we would be paying them to be our customer, which in the long run would put us in the red. Not having that client will be inconvenient, but the potential of securing some new clients has a better chance of profitability than essentially paying a client over time."

You could hear Will cussing under his breath. "Lonnie, you need to call the CEO. Explain to him the importance of longevity and customer service with our company. Do you still have his card?"

"He's the next phone call after this one," I said.

"I can't believe this. Leonard, remind me what the numbers say about our revenue without ACM and how much new business we'll need to drum up to replace that client." Leonard starting rattling off numbers, and they didn't lie. We were going to take a hit from losing this client. We would need at least three smaller clients or another big one like ACM to break even.

"Lonnie, your team needs to hit the pavement and get some new clients in," Will said.

"I'll be meeting with those individuals shortly. Do you have any other advice?"

"Let me know how the CEO call goes, and we'll talk again right before lunch."

"That works. Talk to you later," I said.

"I'm going to get some numbers prepared, so we have a target for the type of clients we need to bring on to replace ACM," Leonard said as he was leaving my office.

"Thanks, Leonard. Will you close the door behind you please."

Once the door was closed, I dropped my head in my hands. All that work to come up empty. I wish I had some fight in me. I needed to find some. There must be some in there somewhere. But if I couldn't give this customer the price they were asking for, why bother? No. Your branch depends on this, your company depends on this. Act like your job depends on this! Because it just might.

I called Leonard. "Find out who their billboard provider is. I need to know who their equipment supplier is. I'm going to setup a meeting with ACM's CEO. Find out who is selling these supplies and at what price. We're not going down like this."

"What about the contract with our current supplier?"

"Screw it," and I hung up.

I pulled out the business cards given to me when Will, Leonard, and I visited ACM and dialed the number for the CEO, expecting to get a voicemail. And I did. I left a message explaining our oversight in the new price offering and that we'd like to schedule a meeting in two days to speak with them again. I hung up and asked Danielle to schedule a meeting with all the directors this afternoon. Even though our billboard services were only a portion of our offerings, we needed to get to the bottom of why we were being priced out.

I shot Will an email outlining my plan to meet again

The Beginning of the End

with ACM's CEO and that I was meeting with the directors this afternoon to find out how we were being priced out for the billboard services.

Before the day ended I got a return call from the CEO, Jim Nguyen, at ACM. He agreed to meet with me over lunch on Thursday. I'd put my team in a high-pressure situation, but I needed them to raise the bar. We'd been a staple in the marketing sphere for a while, but that wasn't going to keep us safe. We had to up our game to stay in it. Here we go. I found some fight.

I got home a little later than normal. I could smell dinner cooking. David was feeding Eva.

"Did she just start drinking that bottle?"

"Yes. You want to switch?"

"Yes. I didn't pump again today." David and I switched places, freeing him to finish dinner preparation. I got Eva latched and feeding. She seemed a little frustrated shortly into the feeding. I wondered if she's already emptied one side. I switched her to the other side. She quickly finished that side as well, but still seemed hungry. I called for David to bring me the bottle he started her on. She gulped down most of the bottle and finally seemed satisfied. I laid her across my lap and burped her. She was getting to the point where she could burp on her own, but I think we both enjoyed the routine.

On Tuesday the office was in a tizzy trying to uncover who these lower-priced billboard equipment suppliers were. They were calling contacts they had from previous projects, searching the internet and cold calling competitors to find these companies. Every team in the branch was working on preparing me for this meeting. The next two days were going to be long. All this for one customer. Well, I figured ACM would only be the first, then we'd receive other breakup emails. I'd rather stay ahead of the trend than go through this drama every time.

By Wednesday the team was able to start providing numbers and had narrowed down the search to three options that were considerably less expensive than our current supplier. By early afternoon the team had compiled a spreadsheet with pricing and services provided by each of the three companies. I sent the sheet to Will to get approval to break the contract with our current supplier.

"Lonnie, we're losing money staying with this supplier!"

"I know."

"I'll get our legal consultants on the phone to see how we can do this and how much it'll cost."

"I'm meeting with Jim Nguyen tomorrow. I want to be able to tell him that we can compete. I plan on speaking with someone from each of these suppliers before the day is out to get a ballpark figure that I'm assuming will be similar to prices our competitors for the ACM account have received."

"I like it, Lonnie. I'll get back with you with an opinion from our legal consultants."

I had made all my phone calls by the end of the day and the quotes I received were far less expensive than what we were currently paying. I knew ACM was monitoring their bottom line, so I was going to need the most attractive price. Although I hadn't made any agreements with an equipment supplier, I had the numbers I needed to pitch to Jim. This time, I was going in alone. I intended to come out victorious. None of that K-pop foolishness.

Thursday morning I fueled myself with coffee. I'd been avoiding it since I was breastfeeding, but my performance today took precedence. I pulled out the lowest pair of heels I owned to wear later and popped some pain medication to prepare for the inevitable ankle discomfort that would come from making a power play with my outfit. I pulled my hair back into a neat ponytail and went neutral with my makeup. David gave me a motivational speech before he left the house, and Dad gave his dependable affirmation. I flooded my mind with tips on negotiating from a podcast I frequented on the ride to work.

When I got in, the first few hours resembled a busy

newsroom with information floating between hands and multiple briefings. I gave Will the rundown of the position I would be negotiating from. I left an hour before my twelve-thirty lunch meeting, which was only thirty-five minutes away.

Once I arrived, I spent the first ten minutes meditating in the car. I took off my boot and flat shoe and slipped on those low heels. I went in the restaurant and found the perfect booth. I made a trip to the ladies room to make sure I looked the same way I did when I left the house this morning. I got back to my table and flipped through my documents once more to make sure I had the content in my head and the papers to show Jim as needed. I asked the waitress to bring water for Jim and me and instructed her to wait for my signal before coming to the table again.

Jim arrived promptly at twelve thirty. I stood and let him catch my eye. We greeted each other and shook hands before being seated. I could tell from his demeanor that he was simply here to hear me out and that he had no intention of making a deal. I switched my negotiating stance to a more direct approach.

I pulled out my documents and I ran down the numbers with him. I compared what we were charging, what competitors charge, and what we were now going to offer. The document also included numbers on the effectiveness of the advertising we have provided for ACM.

He leaned in and examined the numbers with me. He asked a few questions and then requested to take the documents I prepared to review them with his team. I gave him my card and reiterated that Mendallmen was interested in providing ACM services for any current work or new projects they had on the horizon.

I sat back down after sending Jim off with thanks for his time and motioned for the waitress to come over.

I was ready to open the gates to my stress-infused appetite with the most damaging item on the menu *and* a stop for frozen yogurt on my way home. I sat there for an hour eating my way back to a normal emotional state before returning to the office. I knew everyone was eager to hear the outcome of the meeting.

"Did they bite?" asked Travis.

"Did the numbers make sense?" asked Leonard.

"How are you feeling?" asked Julia. I was somewhat surprised that she asked that. She and I had come a long way.

"After a thousand plus calorie lunch, I feel good. At least for now," I said with a laugh. "As for ACM, we made a good case. Jim took our information back to review with his team. Now we wait."

Since I wasn't likely to be super productive the rest of the day, I took a pump break. It was nice to be back in that room, with nothing but the hum of the breast pump occupying the space with me. I closed my eyes and tried to relax every muscle in my body. When the milk quit dripping into the bottles, I turned the pump off and looked at the scant two ounces in each of the bottles. There is no way I can keep this up. And I think I'm okay with that. Sad, but okay.

Next up, I called Will.

"How'd it go?"

"I could tell he wasn't interested when he sat down. But once I pulled out those numbers, his interest was piqued. He asked a few questions and took the documents I prepared to review with his team. I'm going to send a thank you email before I leave today."

"All right. I hope we hear back soon."

"I feel confident this will turn in our favor."

"I trust you, Lonnie."

I spent another hour responding to emails and then I headed to Guppies for frozen yogurt. I thought back to the day I found out I was pregnant with Eva and how I cried all over this steering wheel. Here I was several months later, spilling frozen yogurt on the steering wheel, rewarding myself for a strong performance. No matter how it turned out, I performed well today. I'd performed well since that day I found out I was pregnant. Change is never easy but when you grab it by the horns and ride it out, it changes you into someone greater and stronger. I felt stronger today. I did a video describing my day and the thoughts and feelings that resulted to add to my growing documentary of this season in my life.

My phone dinged. It was a message from Grace to our BSG friend group text.

> Ughh, Jackson is sick again. Does anyone have any tips on removing snot from a baby's nose when he keeps fighting you? And they're making me use this nebulizer, and I can't keep it on his face!!

She ended it with several emojis expressing her disgust.

I put the phone down with the intention of responding later. I knew the others would respond immediately and before I could even finish the thought, my phone dinged. I turned the ringer off and returned to my empowering moment for just a few more minutes before heading home.

When I got in Dad was still there, so we chatted. I told him about my day, and he told me how enchanted he was with Linda. I remembered how, when David and I were dating, Dad would let me go on and on about how I felt about David, and now I felt as though I was in his shoes. I liked it. I was glad he had Linda. It gave our relationship a new angle.

The changing of the guard occurred, and I gave David the same run down of my empowering day.

"You want to go out for dinner to celebrate?" he asked.

"I'd rather wait until I hear back from ACM. Will you make hamburgers for dinner?" As if I needed another meal. My commitment to go to the gym after Eva was born came back to my remembrance. I guess my brain was signaling me that today's food consumption was warranting time at the gym.

Friday in the office was much quieter, but anticipation was in the air. Around two I received an email from Gayle at ACM reporting they were interested in retaining our service. She requested to move forward. I didn't know whether I should dance or cry. With a bum ankle, I did the latter. I grabbed some tissue from my desk and soaked it with tears and snot. Grabbed another tissue and repeated. After about three cycles, I fixed my face and called Leonard. I handed it over to him to communicate to the rest of the team.

Now the next hurdle was getting out of the old contract and into a new one with some other company. Luckily, I could be more hands off going forward. I relayed the good news to Will and entertained the occasional drop-ins from various people congratulating me on saving the account. It was saved, but in no way did I see it as something I had done on my own. I simply led my team to a victory. And to congratulate them for their hard work, I sent out an email that afternoon giving everyone the option to take a half day next Friday. I was winning on all fronts!

That night Dad and Linda joined us for dinner to celebrate this big win at work. Linda fit in well with our family. This will work.

Saturday morning my phone started dinging. I chose to transition in and out of sleep rather than responding to life. When I did look at my phone, I saw multiple messages from the BSG friends. Panic set in as I read the messages. I called Grace immediately, but my call went straight to voicemail. I tried LeeAnn next.

"Hey, what's going on with Jackson?"

"Grace had to take him to the ER early this morning because he wasn't breathing well. They ended up admitting him."

I could hear the emotion in her voice. She knew this situation all too well.

"Have you talked to her?"

"Yes. She's a mess, Lonnie. And her mom isn't well either."

"Can we go visit at the hospital? She shouldn't be alone."

"I asked her if we could come. She said they are still

figuring out everything, and she'd let us know when she learns more. I'm freaking out, Lonnie. This could go bad," LeeAnn said.

I'd never heard this in her voice. It was fear. I'd only known her a few months, but she had become an instant friend. I'd heard strength and power in her voice. Sometimes anger, often orneriness. But never fear. The fact that she was feeling this way made me scared.

"I'll call again and see if I can get through to her. Will you and Sasha work on getting some meals together for her and her mom? Rachel would be good at putting together a little bag for her with things to use at the hospital to make her more comfortable."

"Lonnie, you are a voice of reason. I'll do that. Please call me back as soon as you know something." You could hear the anxiety in her voice.

I called Grace again and on the fourth ring she answered.

"Hey, Lonnie."

"Hi, Grace. What's going on with Jackson?" I tried to use the calmest voice I could, even though LeeAnn's demeanor had gotten me a little nervous.

She started to cry. "He's having trouble breathing," she said between sobs. "It's RSV."

I had heard of RSV but not dealt with it personally. LeeAnn would be the best person to comfort Grace, but she was a basket case herself just hearing about Jackson's situation. "What are they doing for him now, Grace?"

"He's got machines and lines everywhere. He's on oxygen, and they are giving him fluids through his arm."

"Stay focused on Jackson getting better, Grace. I know you're scared, but you can't help him from a position of fear. Find your strength. Can we take turns to sit with you so you're not by yourself?"

"That would be good."

"Okay, I'm going to talk with the ladies. One of us will come by every day. Will you please give me an update on Jackson whenever they give you any new information? Call me if you just need a listening ear."

"I will, Lonnie. Thank you. Having supportive friends is so helpful."

"Sasha, LeeAnn, and Rachel are working on some meals for you and your mom. Let your mom know we're coming with food."

"Thank you, Lonnie. I will." She sounded completely emotionally distraught.

"One of us will be by starting today. Remember, stay strong for Jackson."

"I'll try, but it's so hard seeing him like this."

I reached back out to LeeAnn, Rachel, and Sasha. We coordinated days to sit with Grace at the hospital and take meals to her home. Sasha made meal recommendations, Rachel said she'd put together the care bag, and LeeAnn was first up on the visiting schedule. We planned the visit and meal assignments through the weekend. We'd regroup on Monday to plan going forward.

I couldn't focus on anything but Grace and little Jackson the rest of the day. I found myself checking my phone constantly, looking for an update. The first update came from LeeAnn after her visit.

"Lonnie, I had to leave the room to pull myself together. I didn't want her to know that I was freaking out, so I told her I needed to take a phone call. He's stable, but he's on oxygen and has lines all over the place like Grace told us."

"How is Grace?"

"Not good. She's worried about work, worried about her mom, and devastated that she couldn't prevent this with what she was doing at home with the breathing treatments and suction. Lonnie, I don't know what to say to her."

"It's okay, LeeAnn. We don't have to say anything. Just having someone there with her will help her."

"I know. I just feel helpless."

"I know what you mean. I do too. We just need to stay positive for Grace."

You Can't Control Everything

My sleep was terrible that night. David tried to sympathize with me, but it was unfruitful. I got up in the night to feed Eva. I usually walk back to bed with my eyes closed, and I'm asleep before my head hits the pillow. But tonight my eyes stayed open. My mind ran toward every negative thought. Every time I dozed off, my eyes popped open a few minutes later. Finally, I gave up on sleeping and focused on resting my body.

Eva and I were rocking in the chair when the sun came up. She had finished eating a while ago, but I couldn't bring myself to put her back in her crib. There are moms who don't get to hold their babies. I wanted to cherish the opportunity to hold mine.

That afternoon I picked up soup and a sandwich for Grace's mom and some pastries for dessert or breakfast. They lived in a small two-bedroom unit in a duplex. The steps up to the front door were in disrepair. I rang the doorbell and, after several moments, I heard movement behind the door and then locks turning.

A woman with a small frame and slouched posture opened the door. The heavy smell of cigarette smoke greeted me before she did.

"Are you Lonnie?"

"Yes, ma'am. I'm one of Grace's friends. I came by to bring you dinner."

"Come on in, honey." She stepped back for me to enter. It was extremely modest. I could see a bouncy seat next to the couch and a small TV on a sagging shelf. I followed her to the kitchen. She reached for the bags in my hand and was racked with a coughing spell. I put the bags on the counter.

"Thank you so much for helping us out," she said. She sounded short of breath.

"We want to help you and Grace while Jackson is recovering. Is there anything I can do for you while I'm here?"

She looked around. "I can't think of anything, honey," she said, coughing again.

"Are there any errands I can run for you?"

She looked through the bags I brought in. "No, it looks like you've got me set, thank you."

She began walking toward the door, so I followed her. I was becoming short of breath trying not to breathe in the nicotine-laden air. She opened the door and said thank you. I stepped outside and negotiated the decrepit steps. When I turned to wave goodbye, she had already closed the door.

I rode home with the windows down, uncomfortably cool from the winter air, trying to reduce the heavy stench of cigarette smoke. I went straight to the laundry room when I got home and threw the outfit I had on in the washing machine. I put on an old coat of David's hanging on a nearby hook and started the washer. I leaned my head against it, feeling completely overwhelmed for Grace. No wonder Jackson couldn't breathe. I struggled to breathe in that house.

"Is everything all right?" David asked. I guess I looked a little strange standing at the washer wearing an old coat.

"I don't know how that baby is going to stay out of the hospital living in that house. The air is thick with cigarette smoke. I could hardly breathe." Tears started running down my face. David pulled me in for a hug and held me.

"We can't change some things, babe," he whispered in my ear.

"I know, I know." I pulled away and wiped my eyes. "Everyone's shot in life is so different. Grace shared how she was saving up to put a down payment on a house for them. She's going to be out of work and that's going to affect her savings. If the stench in the air is any indication of how much her mom smokes, Jackson won't have a chance where they are now or in a new house. Grace seemed so happy with where she is in life and now this." I wiped a few stray tears from my eyes.

"It'll be okay, Lonnie."

"It's my turn to visit them at the hospital tomorrow. I hope he's getting better."

David massaged my shoulders. "It'll work out, Lonnie, don't worry."

I heard his words, but I couldn't internalize them. Later that evening we got an update from Rachel via text.

> Sorry I don't have better news. When I left they were preparing to take Jackson to the NICU because his breathing was worsening. Grace isn't holding up very well. I stayed long enough for her to calm down. The nursing staff is really good. Pray for her.

There were several messages back and forth. The thought of Jackson in NICU was so hard. I stayed up most of the night watching TV, trying to chase the negative thoughts from my mind. In the middle of the night Eva woke to eat and I sat with her in the rocking chair the remainder of the night, intermittently crying and holding her so tight that she roused from her sleep. I was living the good life with a healthy family. Grace had nothing but uphill battles to fight.

I thought about when my mom died. I remember the sadness I felt that I wouldn't see her again, but I remembered how everyone rallied around me and Dad. And how Dad did everything in his power to make me happy and remind me of the things we loved about Mom.

"She'd want us to remember her that way," he would say. And then he would talk about events that we shared together that were happy. I'd lay in bed at night and cry. He would hear me and come in and kneel next to my bed. He'd stay there and talk to me until I fell asleep again. I could only imagine the grief he felt dealing with my pain and his too. He probably left my room and cried on his own pillow. He never let me see his sadness. He was always encouraging me, showering me with love. He did it so well, David would always joke about having to change his last name to Lee because I wasn't going to leave my dad.

When Monday morning came, I texted Grace asking if I could call her. It was several hours before she responded. I was already at work.

"Hello?" The fatigue in her voice was clear.

"Grace, it's Lonnie. How is Jackson? Rachel told me he had to be moved to NICU."

"He's stable."

"I'm coming by after work. I called your manager and told her Jackson was hospitalized and that you would likely be out for a while."

"Thanks. I called too."

"Don't worry about work. When you're ready to come back, your job will be there, I'll see to that."

"Thank you, Lonnie."

"Is there anything I can bring you when I come this afternoon?"

"Some hope would be nice." My heart broke into ten thousand pieces.

"I'll bring as much as I can carry, Grace," I said, wiping tears from my eyes. "Is there anything specific you want to eat?"

"I haven't really been hungry. You can bring something, but I don't have a preference."

"I'll be there this afternoon, Grace. Please call me if you need me or think of anything you want me to bring."

"I will."

"Be strong for Jackson."

"It's hard, Lonnie. It's so hard." She began to cry.

"Grace, try to keep thinking about the best scenario."

"I'll try. I really will. I'll be glad when you get here." All ten thousand pieces of my broken heart were ripped in half.

"A few more hours and I'll be there, Grace."

I couldn't stop the tears from falling from my eyes. The tissues were in rotation for several minutes. I had a meeting in five minutes. I had no desire to participate. All I wanted to do was be with Grace and Jackson.

At four, after all the meetings for the day were done, I left work quickly before anything else came up. It had been a long time since I'd been to Children's Hospital. I'd never had to come for any of my own children, only to visit others. The brightly colored entrance was eerily welcoming. The lobby was vivid with playful hues and large, clever sculptures. I approached the information desk to check in and got directed to the yellow elevators with the giraffes painted on them.

I rode to the seventh floor and followed the arrows to the double doors that enclosed the NICU. I walked in, looked around to see where the room numbers started, and followed the path around the nurses' station in the middle of the unit to room 710. I knocked on the glass to announce myself. The curtain was drawn so I couldn't see into the room.

"Come on in, Lonnie," Grace said.

I pulled the curtain to the side and there was Jackson, in a hospital crib, oxygen mask on his face, IVs hooked to three bags of fluids hanging on a pole. He looked lifeless, although you could see his chest rising and falling. Grace was under a blanket in an oversized reclining chair in a corner of the room. She sat up when I came in. I dropped my things on a counter close to the door and quickly made my way to her. I hugged her and held her tight. She cried. I cried. We sat for a while, chatting about anything other than her current situation.

"What'd you bring to eat, Lonnie?"

"I'm kinda lazy, I bought the same thing I got your mom the other day, soup and a sandwich."

"You're not lazy. I think I'll have it." I took the food from the bags and checked my phone for messages while I was close to my purse. I set the phone down on the counter and carried the food to Grace. I pulled up a chair next to the recliner.

"I love tomato soup," she said after the first bite. "Mom used to make it quite a bit in the fall. She doesn't cook as much now. Thank you guys for taking food to her. She said Sasha brought a buffet." We laughed.

"Sasha is over the top," I said. We spent another hour together. She picked up Jackson and held him tenderly for a few minutes, then let me hold him. "He's going to pull through, Grace, I know it."

"I hope you're right, Lonnie."

"You asked me to bring some hope, there it is." We smiled at each other and there was a knock on the glass.

"Come in," Grace said.

The curtain pulled back and in walked Tish. I got up and placed Jackson in the crib, mindful to position him the same way he was when we picked him up.

"Hello, Grace. Mary and the rest of the breastfeeding support group wanted to show our support."

"Thank you. Come in."

"Grace, I'll see you another day this week. I'll let you two visit." This was not the place to have a run in with Tish.

"Okay. Thank you, Lonnie."

"Call or text if you need anything. We'll plan out who will take meals tonight, and we'll let you know who's coming which day."

I acknowledged Tish as I grabbed my purse, but she ignored me and walked toward Grace. Tish was the last person to send over to represent the breastfeeding support group. I wonder if Mary realized that.

When I got home, there was chaos going on. Eva was

screaming while Johnny was trying to console her, DJ was in the kitchen burning something, and David was upstairs packing for his trip. I went into Mommy mode. I grabbed Eva and started consoling her while instructing DJ on how to fix this dish he started without incinerating it. Once DJ was on a roll, I sat down to breastfeed Eva. She was getting more fussy lately because she wanted more than what was in my breast. I was having to use my stored breastmilk, which was depleting the supply Dad needed during the week. David finally came down and jumped in to help with dinner.

I set the table and soon we were all seated and eating. Eva was big enough to sit, reclined, in her highchair, so she was a part of meals now too. I was fully engaged in everyone's stories today. Internalizing and cherishing them all. After what I've been experiencing with Grace, I don't want to take anything for granted.

Once the kids were off to bed, I helped David finish packing, and we lay in bed for a while just embracing each other. He knew I was still shook up about Grace's situation, and he knew this was the best way to support me at that moment. I love that about him.

When I woke in the morning to Eva's cries, I looked over and David had already headed out of town. I could hear the boys downstairs, I looked at the clock and rolled out of bed. I hadn't intended to fall asleep when I did. I was supposed to get the schedule for food and visits together for Grace. It would have to wait. I was solo until tomorrow night. I headed to Eva's room and saw why she was upset. She's rolled up against the rail in the crib and couldn't figure out how to roll off the rails. I scooped her up and fed her what I had in my breasts. I guess it was enough because she didn't fuss. I took her down and put her in her highchair while I fixed myself something to eat. Dad arrived and I got ready for work. Another morning in the Peterson household.

Within thirty minutes, I was out the door. Midmorning I remembered I needed to have someone take dinner to Grace's mom. I looked for my phone to get the text messages rolling. When I dug through my purse, I didn't see it. I dumped everything onto my desk, and it wasn't there. I called home and had Dad tear the house up looking for it. He tried calling it and there was no answer. I had never activated the feature that locates your phone if you lose it. I was paranoid about a stalker being able to find me. I know it's silly, but now I was kicking myself because I needed to find my phone!

My desk phone rang.

"This is Lonnie."

"Hey, it's LeeAnn."

"Hey, what's going on. I just realized I don't have my phone."

"That's why I'm calling. Grace called me this morning and said you left it at the hospital. She gave it to Tish to give to Mary, so you should be able to pick it up at BSG."

"I need my phone before then. Ughh!"

"Well, I'd pick it up for you, but I don't know if she's dropping it off today or bringing it to the group."

"I'll figure it out. How is Grace this morning?"

"She sounded better. She said Jackson is using less oxygen today, moving around a little more."

"I'm so glad to hear that. So who's taking food and visiting today?"

"I'm taking food, Sasha is visiting. I thought maybe we could all go before BSG on Wednesday. Rachel can take food to Grace's mom that day."

"That's a great idea. I'll reach out to Mary about my phone."

"Cool. Well, I'll see you tomorrow. We'll meet at the hospital at four."

"Thanks, LeeAnn. See you tomorrow."

I called the pediatrician's office to speak to Mary, but of course she was off today! The remainder of the day was filled with meetings. Traffic was horrible on the way home.

Dad wasn't able to start dinner because there wasn't anything to cook. So I ended up getting the kids fast food. Once we were all fed and prepped for the morning, I wasted no time falling asleep. The days when I was solo completely exhausted me.

There was so much to look forward to on Wednesday. I'd get my phone, I'd get to see Grace, and David would come home! It was a new day and I was feeling optimistic. Eva was sprinkling in some full nights of sleep every now and then, and it was working in my favor today. Dad rolled in, I rolled out.

David called midday informing me he'd be home earlier than anticipated, which would work out great. He could bring Eva to the group for me. At three thirty I headed to Children's Hospital. The whole crew was there. Jackson had done well today, and he didn't require NICU status anymore. He would be changing rooms later that evening. Grace was in good spirits, which made it easier for us to joke and laugh like we usually did.

"Support group starts in about a half hour. We need to get ready to go," I said.

"Oh, I'm not going tonight, Lonnie," Sasha said, "I went yesterday during the day."

"I have class tonight, so I won't be there either," Rachel said.

I look to LeeAnn. She sheepishly looked down. "I didn't bring Wind, and I don't have time to go back and get him and make it to group tonight. Sorry."

"You and Tish will get to spend some quality time together," Grace said. Everyone else laughed.

"Ha ha. You all are going to leave me hanging? Okay. I'll remember that." I gathered my things and gave everyone hugs on the way out. David was waiting for me in the parking lot when I arrived at the pediatrician's office.

"Thank you for bringing her. How was the trip?"

"It went well. I've got the boys. I'm going

to take them to get something to eat. Your Dad said there wasn't anything to make for dinner. Do you want me to pick up anything for you?"

"I shouldn't be here too long. I'll grab something on the way home."

"See you at home then." He hopped back in his car, and I waved to the boys as they pulled off.

Mary was with a mom at the changing table when I got there. I walked over to Tish.

"Hi, Tish. Did you bring my phone?"

"It's over by Mary's table."

"Thank you." I glanced at Mary's table and sure enough my phone was there. I undressed Eva so I could get to the table next. As soon as that mom picked up her baby, I made a fast move to the table.

"Well, hello. Looks like you lost something."

"I left it at the hospital when I was visiting Jackson and Grace."

"I haven't heard the latest. How is Jackson?"

"He's better. He'll move out of the NICU later this evening."

"Oh, I'm so glad to hear that. What's new with this little lady?"

"She's eating more, but I'm producing less. She's rolling some."

"Let's talk about the producing less first. Are you planning on trying to boost your supply, or are you wanting to move on to formula?"

"I don't think I can increase pumping and feeding times, so I'll have to start her on formula. I'm not excited about that."

"No one ever is." She educated me on my formula options while she weighed Eva. "Make sure you transition her to the formula so you can see which one she'll take. We don't want a situation where she won't take any formula and her weight drops."

I took in all the advice and quickly dressed Eva. I grabbed

my things, making sure I had everything this time. A quick stop to pick up a salad for my dinner and I was on my way home.

I scrolled through my messages and emails while munching on my salad. Didn't miss too much. The boys and David came in around eight. He went straight to bed, worn out from traveling. I stayed up a little later with the boys. Before I went to sleep, I got a text from Grace that Jackson was moved to a regular room. Perfect way to end the day.

By Friday, Jackson was released to go home. Grace made the decision to put him in daycare since her mom wasn't consistently well enough to care for him. It was going to affect her savings for a house, but she'd rather her son be healthy. I was pleased with that decision because the more time he spent out of the house, the better for his lungs. The daycare provider happened to be a retired nurse, so Grace felt comfortable with Jackson in her care. All good news.

We spent the weekend in full Christmas mode. Shopping, putting presents under the tree, and getting the exterior of our home decorated. Well, we hired someone to do that last part. A week that started off with heavy emotions had a great ending.

All Good Things Must Come To an End. Or Do They?

Everyone was in the holiday spirit the week before Christmas. There was lots of cheer flowing through the office and plenty of food to be had. Productivity was a little lower due to this, so I had to be a bit of a Scrooge and remind people that we still had work that needed to be done.

I was at my desk when I got a call from Jackie.

"Hey, cousin, what's going on?"

"Lonnie, have you been keeping a video diary?"

"I have," I said suspiciously.

"It's on the internet, Lonnie."

"What! Wait, that's not even possible."

"Lonnie, have you shared that with anybody?" Her voice was urgent.

"No, I haven't shared it with anybody. I did lose my phone a week ago, but I had it back in like twenty-four hours."

"Lonnie, who had your phone?"

I stood up from my desk. "There's a chick in my breastfeeding support group who hates my guts, and she had my phone." I sank to my chair. "Where can I find the video online?"

I typed *ancient mom* in the search bar. Up popped a still shot of me and David in the ultrasound room. My heart sank with fear of what I'd see.

"The end of the video is where it gets bad. This has 500,000 views already and it was just posted over the weekend," Jackie said.

All Good Things Must Come To an End. Or Do They?

I pressed play. The video played our first ultrasound visit. Every minute of it, including cutting back to me sobbing on the table. At the end, a link appeared: "Click here for more Ancient Mom content." I clicked the link and there were several of my video diary entries. Not all but some were there, some that I did not want to be seen. Including the entry after our girls' night out at that club. There was even one detailing my feelings of being an apprentice at work. I didn't need to look at any more. I clicked the button to "Report."

"Jackie, I'll have to call you back." I hung up the phone.

I clicked the appropriate options and filled out the form allowing me to state my concerns about the video. But then there was nothing else I could do. I started sending emails to the video platform the video was on. I even tried calling. I called David and gave him the run down.

"I'm on it, Lonnie. I know some people who can help us with legal aspects. Don't say anything to anybody about this."

When I went back to the search page, there were already memes from the videos. This was horrible. I panicked. What if my friends saw this? What if my boss saw it! I called Danielle and told her I had an emergency and had to leave the office.

I gathered my things and hurried home. I had no idea what I would do when I got there, but I had to get home. When I got there, David was already home. He was in our bedroom on the phone with someone. He motioned for me to come over and put the call on speaker.

"Lonnie, this is Claude Cruise. He's the attorney who is going to help us. I've already reached out to the persona, Ancient Mom, that posted the videos, and Claude is going to need some information from you to verify your identity in order to have the video removed."

"I'll do some research on this username and see if I can track down the person who uploaded the video. Lonnie, do you have any idea who would've uploaded the videos?" the attorney asked.

"I cannot tell you who uploaded the video, I can only tell you who had access to my phone. There's a woman in my breastfeeding support group named Tish. She has been trying to discredit me within our group."

Claude asked questions about the group and the other people mentioned in the videos. I answered his questions. When the call was over, I just sobbed in David's arms. There were no words, no motivating speech, nothing that could console me. After I couldn't cry another tear, I curled up on the floor. For a while David quietly wrapped himself around me. Then he got up and went to get me a glass of water. He set it next to me and left me alone.

The evening went on, but I didn't move. David sent everyone to bed and came back to the room where I was still curled up on the floor.

"Lonnie, I've given you alone time to process all this, but now I need you to get it together. You haven't done anything wrong. You will have to defend yourself, but you will win. Everyone mentioned in those videos knows you, and they know your character. So I need you to get up and let's figure out how we will attack tomorrow."

I didn't move. I didn't want to. David got back on the floor with me and whispered in my ear.

"Just the other day you boasted about how powerful you felt. You still are powerful. Don't let this woman steal that from you. It's not hers to have. You will not hide from her. Or anyone for that matter."

"You're right, David."

"If I'm right, get up and be the powerful woman you are."

"I don't want a pep talk right now. I know what you're saying is right. I will get up. But let me do this on my own terms. Please give me some more time alone."

He left the room. I could tell he was getting upset. But I wouldn't be forced to do anything right now. I sat up and thought about how this could impact my relationships. It was already creating tension in my marriage. It could impact my friendships and my career. But I was not going to lie here and be a victim. I was not going to let Tish's hateful act take my life. I took a sip of my water and headed to the bathroom. I changed into my pjs and crawled into bed.

When morning came, I proceeded to lead my life as if yesterday's event hadn't occurred. David tried to talk to me about yesterday, but I refused. I told him I was moving on from yesterday and thanked him for checking on me.

I went to work as usual. I got a few looks, but no one mentioned the video. But that was short lived. Text messages started coming, and around lunch time I saw a call from Grace. I immediately answered it.

"Hi, Grace..." she cut me off.

"What's the deal with this video?"

"I think Ti...." She cut me off again.

"I don't appreciate the fact that you put my personal business in a video. I've been through too much to put up with this elementary school mess. Don't bother talking to me, and you better not mention me in another video." She hung up.

And so it began. Rachel and Sasha reached out before the day was over. They were understanding. They knew I didn't post the videos and didn't take offense at them. I was hoping to hear back from the lawyer or the video platform. The only communication received from the video platform was an email, but it said there was a complaint filed against *me*. I didn't understand how this was possible and there was no way to reply to the email. When I got home I showed it to David.

After reading it several times and referring back to the profile on the internet, he put two and two together.

"Lonnie, they used your email and name to make this account. This email is asking *you* to take the video down."

We scrambled to pull up the website and used the forgot-your-password function to try to gain access into the account. But we didn't know the answers to the security questions, so that didn't work.

"They're trying to make it look like I did it! This is identity theft!"

"Calm down, Lonnie. You're going to need to get a new email address and change the password on your phone and your email. If you used that password for any other app, you'll need to change it. Claude will help us sort through all this." David put in a call to Claude and filled him in.

On Friday I reached out to LeeAnn. I was hoping her response would be the same as Rachel and Sasha's. The call went to voicemail.

> *You've reached LeeAnn, please leave a message. If this is Lonnie, communications with you have been suspended until further notice.* Beep

I left her a voicemail apologizing for getting her involved in this. I told her I had nothing but love for her and that I hoped to speak with her soon.

I hung up with a heavy heart. It didn't matter if I defended myself, she was still hurt. A lot of people close to me would be. DJ even saw the video and was put in a situation where he had to defend our family. I can't believe how heartless Tish was to do this. She could have handled her beef with me within the support group, but she involved people that had no idea who either of us were. She involved the world.

On the way into work, Dad called.

"Morning, Dad."

"When life gives you lemons . . ." He paused for my response.

". . . make lemonade."

"That's right."

"Dad, there's no sugar that can make this a good pitcher of lemonade."

"There's always sugar, Lonnie. You may have to pull it from some unexpected places. You know I was reading the nutrition label on some fresh chicken, and it had two grams of sugar. Who knew? But there is a way to turn this in your favor."

"We have a lawyer working with us. He can turn this in our favor."

"That's all good. The lawyer is simply going to bring justice, but justice doesn't always bring peace. You didn't do anything wrong. You were simply sharing your perspective on your life and how each person interacted with you. You didn't discredit anyone."

"I did, Dad. I ranted about Tish in some of those videos."

"I didn't see anything like that."

"They weren't included in the videos online, but I'm sure she saw them."

"Well, when you talk to your lawyer, maybe you can share those videos to paint a picture for motive."

"That's a great idea, Dad."

"Keep an eye out for the sugar, honey. Love you. Try to have a good day."

"Thank you, Dad, I love you too."

When I got to the office, the word was out. Leonard was the first to corner me.

"Lonnie, did you know there is a video on the internet with you and your husband in it."

"I'm aware, Leonard." I think he was surprised that I knew. I kept walking toward my office. I opened my email only to find more "heads up" emails. I responded the same way to them all.

> I am aware of the videos, and actions are in motion to have them removed.

All my meetings today were awkward. I took my pump break just to remove myself from public access. The pump break yielded two ounces of milk. Just like everything else in my life right now, in a dwindling state. I plowed through the rest of the workday and headed home with relief that it was Friday. On the way home, I got a phone call from the video platform. I explained the situation, and they removed the videos and disabled the account. I inquired if there was more information they could provide as to who opened the account. The only thing they could see was that the account was opened on Sunday. All the other info was my own. Well, at least the videos were down.

I spent most of Saturday in the bed. I didn't take any phone calls, and I didn't check my email. David brought me breakfast in bed and brought Eva to me for snacks, since I wasn't really producing enough for a meal. Jackie and Lisa came by in the afternoon to sit with me and cheer me up. They went on and on about what criminal things they were going to inflict on Tish. We laughed a little, but I cried a lot.

"We love you, Lonnie. Forget all those other people," Jackie said.

"But what if I was talking about you guys in those videos?"

"We've been friends long enough that whatever you'd say would be true. I couldn't be mad about it," Lisa said.

"I'd be mad, but I wouldn't cut you off. My kids have done worse, and they live with me," Jackie said. "We brought you a little something."

Lisa handed me a bag and inside was a white box and a card. I opened the box and there was this little red microphone.

"Don't let that heifer shut you up," said Jackie.

"What she said," said Lisa.

"Thanks, guys." I hugged them both.

I went to bed early again, but I couldn't sleep. This time it was because the Italian dinner they brought me didn't agree with my stomach.

Sunday went pretty much the same, morning in bed, afternoon with family. This Sunday it was David's family. My stomach had recovered from yesterday's dinner, so I was ready to dig into whatever Sheryl was fixing. Joanna and Lizzie discussed the videos with David and me. The videos had elicited all kinds of emotions and opinions from family, friends, and even strangers. I took some time to go through my emails before bed and there were a few emails requesting an interview or to buy my video. The spam was already on the upswing.

With Christmas week in high gear, gifts were accumulating under the tree. At night our home looked like a little gingerbread house and Christmas music played all day. David had headed out of town early this morning. His last trip of the year. Christmas Eve was on a Thursday this year. I planned on being out of the office starting Wednesday and returning on Monday. I was ready for the break.

We started our morning routine as usual. Dad arrived and the boys and I left. Traffic was light this morning as some people started their holiday a little early. When I got to the office, I found a voicemail from Will asking for a return call. This did not bode well. I called.

"Will, it's Lonnie. Returning your call."

"Lonnie." He paused. "You're aware no doubt that there's a video on the internet with you in it."

"I am aware. The video was removed last week."

"I need to let you know that the legal team is in the process of determining if some of the content was damaging to the company."

"I didn't mention the name of our company in any of those videos, Will."

"I know, but if people are able to trace you back to our company and to our clients, that could pose a problem."

"Will, is there anyone I can talk to in legal? I don't see where the company would be at risk."

"If a senior member of our company makes it known that they are being treated like an apprentice, it could jeopardize our ability to hire top talent in the future."

I leaned back in my chair and let out a frustrated sigh. "So, what now?"

"They'll have an answer for me tomorrow. If you don't mind me asking, how'd the videos get out there?"

"Someone I've had run ins with had access to my phone and uploaded the videos using my personal information."

"Unlucky. Sorry to hear that. Do you have a lawyer?"

"We do."

"Well, I'll be in touch tomorrow. I hope this pans out well for you."

"Thanks, Will."

I could tell this was NOT going to pan out well for me. That lawyer better be able to build a strong case for me. If my job was impacted by this, it was on!

I couldn't concentrate the rest of the day. I even tried pumping to clear my mind. The results only made me more stressed. I did as much work as my troubled mind allowed. I wrapped up everything around three and went home.

Dad sat and chatted with me over a cup of coffee. He endured my crying over the possibility of disciplinary actions at work. He shifted my focus to the things that were good in my life.

I recalled the words I shared with Grace about not facing the situation from a position of fear but instead being strong, not focusing on the worst that could happen but concentrating on the best possible outcome.

Tuesday morning came. I arrived at the office a ball of nerves on the inside, a well-put-together corporate woman on the outside. I sweated so much during the morning hours that my deodorant was no longer providing any odor protection. It was 2:37 when Will's call came through.

"Lonnie Peterson."

"Lonnie, it's Will."

"So what's the verdict?"

"The legal team, John, and Brian have decided to ask you to take an extended paid holiday. We will meet with you on Monday January 4th to discuss how to proceed. The staff will only be notified that you will be out of the office until the New Year. No action is being taken right now outside of you taking an extended holiday."

"What are your thoughts on this?"

"I feel it's harsh, but I see their point of view. It also gives you time to sort this stuff out."

"Will, have a great holiday. I'll see you in the new year."

"Same to you, Lonnie."

I packed up my things for my extended holiday. David called to check on me. I replayed the conversation between Will and me.

"Are you serious, Lonnie? Claude has time to meet with us tomorrow, so we can talk through how to handle all of this. I can't believe Mendallmen is doing this."

"I need a break anyway. I'm not sweating it anymore. What's done is done. I'm ready to move forward. I've cried too many tears and lost too much sleep."

"What if you go into the meeting and they fire you?"

"Their loss," I say flippantly.

"Lonnie, what about us, our livelihood?"

"We can look at our finances and work something out." I could hear his frustration on the other end.

"We've got a lot to talk about."

"After we meet with Claude tomorrow, I don't want to talk about this again until next week. I want to enjoy the holidays with my family."

"Fair enough, babe."

"How was the trip?"

"I think we may need to let some folks go at that office. Not around the holidays though."

"Yeah, you're talking to someone with that story."

"They haven't made that decision, Lonnie. You're still employed." There was a moment of silence. "I'll be home late tonight. We'll talk with Claude tomorrow. I love you."

"I love you too." Neither of our declarations of love was very passionate. They were simply said out of necessity. A declaration that we were still in it, not excited about the current situation, but sticking it out.

Dad's pep talk yesterday brought me some peace. That

peace led to decent sleep. When I woke the next morning, David was lying there next to me, sleeping soundly. I'm so thankful he doesn't snore. Hey! Look at me practicing gratitude right out the gate today! I began to plan what things I wanted to tackle on my extended vacation. For sure I'd need to transition Eva to formula. I had never followed up on getting a housekeeper. I also had never followed through on going to the gym. That was plenty to work on.

I got up and made breakfast while everyone was still sleeping. Eva was the first to rouse and then Johnny. I fixed Johnny's plate and breastfed Eva.

"Mom, are we going to get supplies for building our gingerbread houses today?"

"We sure are. Papa is coming over this afternoon to sit with you all while your dad and I go to a meeting."

"Is it about the video?" he asked innocently.

"It is, honey. But no worries, we'll get it worked out."

"So are you famous?"

"I don't think so." I chuckled at that thought.

"I wouldn't mind being famous. Famous people are rich."

"Not all famous people are rich and not all rich people are famous."

"Really?"

"Really." You could see his little mind working on an alternate scenario in which he could be both. DJ came upstairs with still sleepy eyes.

The boys were looking forward to the break from school. We chatted about things they wanted to do over the break, and I added them to the calendar on my phone. I was free, so let's do them all.

After breakfast, I decided to take myself up on the challenge to work out by going for a walk. I changed Eva, got both of us dressed warmly, and headed to the garage. Getting her ready to go out was a process. I put her in her car seat, zipped up the cover, and snapped the car seat into her stroller. When I opened the garage door, the brisk winter air stung my cheeks.

All Good Things Must Come To An End. Or Do They?

I pulled the canopies on the stroller together to further protect her from the chill in the air. I began my brisk walk through the neighborhood. I was going to start with twenty minutes. I've always enjoyed exercising, not so much the act of doing it, but the potential results. With my mom dying at a young age, physical fitness was important to me as well as healthy eating. I can't claim to being faithful to either of these, but I respect them both and comply at least half of the time.

As thoughts flooded my mind, I found myself pushing a little harder, past a brisk walk into a light jog. That lasted about two minutes before I had to reduce my speed back to brisk walking. Nice try, postpartum, nearly middle-aged woman. I started heading back toward the house at the ten-minute mark. The walk eased Eva to sleep, so I took advantage of her nap to get showered and dressed when we returned to the house. About thirty minutes before we were to leave for our meeting, David and I sat down to discuss how we wanted justice to look for us.

"So what are we trying to build our case around?" David asked.

"Honestly, I just want her to be found guilty of damaging my reputation. I've lost friends. My job is in jeopardy. My child is having to defend me at school. I want justice for that. It doesn't change my reality, but it makes her feel the pain she's dealt me."

David continued to write. "Okay. Defamation of character. What should we ask for in return for her damaging your reputation and publicizing your private information?"

"At the least, legal fees and any lost wages."

"That's fair. My research suggests we can ask for at least seventy-five percent more than what we want to be compensated for," David said.

"That sounds excessive."

"Lonnie, our lives have been disrupted. There's no price tag that can be put on the friendships you lost, the years of longevity at your job, and the peace of our family." His tone was aggressive. I hadn't stopped to think about how all this was affecting him.

"I'll let you and Claude work that out. I trust you." The doorbell rang, and I heard DJ open the door for Dad.

"Let's get ready to go," David said as he gathered his notes.

I felt like a child who broke a neighbor's window playing baseball and now my parent had to fix my mistake. I hadn't felt this way until now because I had been so engulfed in my own emotions. But now I saw the weight of this on David.

"Thank you for taking the lead on the legal actions, David. I'm sorry you're in this position with me. This is my doing, and I don't want you to feel like you have to be responsible for me."

"Lonnie, your dad looked me in my eyes on the day I married you and said, 'I will always be there for her, even if you're not.' He declared to me that day that he was your safety net. But I knew I loved you more and that one day you would look to me as your safety net. Your dad is the epitome of a true man, and I've had to work real hard on myself to even come close. Now I'm not comparing myself to him, but I am declaring to you that I will always be here for you. I am your safety net, and I take that role seriously."

Mic drop. I had nothing to say. I would let him be my safety net.

Contingency Plan

Claude greeted us as soon as we arrived. He escorted us to his office, and we got right to business. I updated him on the situation at my job. David shared how we saw justice being served on our behalf.

"The one hurdle in this case is proving who created the account in your name and if this woman from your support group has any connection. A wrong has definitely been committed. We just need to prove who did it," Claude explained.

He asked about witnesses and what role they played in the story. He said he would try to obtain a statement from each of them. I let him know that some of the witnesses were no longer speaking with me, so I wasn't sure if they would provide a statement.

"There are ways to work around that. Let me handle that part. We need to obtain a record of phone calls. Maybe the person placed a call or text from your phone."

David immediately logged into the account for our phone provider to get the info Claude requested.

"We can also check social media to see if there is any mention of the video. Looking at comments may give us a lead. I'll get my aide working on this. We have enough to go ahead and get the complaint filed with the court, so we'll try to have that done by the end of day since the long holiday weekend is coming."

The rest of the meeting he explained how the process

would go with a lawsuit and warned that it could take a while to settle, but he would work diligently to get this resolved.

"Will you please notify us when it's been filed?" David requested.

"We will do that. We'll also handle notifying the defendant, who at this point will be Tish McBride," Claude said. He provided us with a few more details before the meeting ended.

David didn't say much on the way home. I had him stop at the grocery store so I could get gingerbread house supplies.

"Before I go in this store, I need you to tell me what you're thinking and feeling. I know you are not okay."

"This is a lot, Lonnie. I know it's a lot for you, but it's a lot for me too. I'm not upset with you. I just want to make sure we are covering ourselves well."

"What can I do for you?"

He thought for a few moments then said, "You said that after that meeting you didn't want to talk about this until next week. I'd like that. I just want to enjoy my family."

"Me too." I reached over and put my hand on his thigh. He put his hand on top of mine.

"I need to pick up gingerbread supplies."

"I'll go in with you. You always bring home candy I don't care for."

The tension dissolved as we shopped for candy. Well supplied, my family enjoyed an evening of building gingerbread houses, having pizza for dinner, and settling down to watch a movie.

Christmas Eve Day we had brunch with my family and then swung by Sheryl's house to exchange gifts. That evening at home, we read the Christmas story together. Everyone got to open one gift.

Christmas morning was as electric as usual. The kids were anticipating some really exciting gifts. They ripped through the paper and boxes pulling one item after the next from the wrappings, excited to get a new phone and a new game system.

We even got footage of Eva pulling at some paper. I opened one of David's gifts to find a beautiful journal with a pen. The note read, "Keep telling your story." He glanced over at me and smiled.

After gifts and breakfast, everyone got ready to head over to Dad's house. Linda's car was already in the driveway when we pulled up to his house. The boys ran straight for the tree searching for boxes with their names as soon as we got inside. We watched the kids happily opening their gifts. David and I gave Dad and Linda their gifts, and Dad gave us our gifts. The last gift of all he gave to Linda.

She carefully opened the rectangular box. Inside was a case that looked like it held a bracelet. She opened it and inside there was a ring. When she looked up, my dad got down on his knee next to where she was sitting.

"Linda, I've been a long time without a better half, and I'm sure that you are my better half. Will you marry me?"

She cried and wrapped her arms around his neck. I screamed and jumped up and down. David patted my Dad vigorously on the back while the boys cheered.

"I thought you'd never ask. We're too old to be dating forever," she said with a big smile. "Yes, I want to be your better half."

I admired the ring, and we all hugged and recounted the details of the moment and started planning the wedding. It was a happy family moment.

Christmas break kept everyone busy and happy on through the New Year celebration. The week was full of family time and fun memories. When the end of the week arrived, anxiety about my meeting on Monday started to creep in.

On Monday we were all back into the routine. Dad came over, David and the boys headed out to work and school, and I was heading out to face judgment. In all the years I'd worked for this company, never had I walked into the building uncertain if I would come back. I stopped by my office before making my way to the conference room where everyone was gathered.

There were five people in the room, two from the legal team, Will, Brian, and John. I sat down and greeted the group.

The meeting started with Will extending his sympathy for me having to go through this situation. The legal team asked me to recount the events including and surrounding the posting of the video. Brian explained how the videos could potentially impact Mendallmen. And last, our CEO John Bianco brought the verdict.

"Lonnie, you have worked here for a majority of your career, and you've contributed to the growth of this company over the years. We value your presence, but unfortunately we must take disciplinary action in response to this video. We are asking you to step down from the AVP position. We have a director position coming available at Main Branch that we are encouraging you to consider. We are terribly sorry for the impact this crime has had on you and your family, but it is in Mendallmen's best interest to pursue this path. Do you have any questions?"

"What will my new take-home pay be and is there any chance of returning to this position?"

"We will direct that question to HR. If the position becomes available again in the future, you'd be a great candidate. But for now we have a few replacements in mind."

"I'd recommend Julia for the position." Who would have seen that coming? Not me.

"We will take that into consideration," Brian said.

"When do I have to decide if the director position is a good fit for me?"

They all looked at me, surprised that I would consider not taking the position on the spot.

"You have until the end of today. At the end of the day, we'll need you to clear your office. If you decide the position is a good fit, we'll see you tomorrow morning at Main Branch. If you decide it is not a good fit," he paused, "this will be your last day," Brian said. He asked the legal representatives to have the job description forwarded to me.

"Lonnie, this is meant to be a disciplinary action in response to this unfortunate event. It in no way reflects your current performance in the position. Typically there are performance improvement steps that precede a move like this, but due to the potential risk Mendallmen could face as a result of your videos being exposed, this was the best resolution. We know you are valuable to the company, and we want you to stay."

"I appreciate the consideration. Who will be my contact with my final decision?"

"You can call me, Lonnie," Will said.

"Thank you all." I stood and exited the conference room. The emotions flooding my soul were intense. One part of me said take the demotion and move on with your life. You need the money to keep your current lifestyle afloat. It shouldn't hurt the bottom line too much. Then I was enraged that they would expect me to gladly accept *punishment* for someone else's actions. This wasn't something I initiated. And the company would not suffer one bit from a video that didn't even mention the company name. Then there was a part of me that said set yourself free from the pressure of trying to balance a work and home life that together are too weighty. There are other options available to you.

I wasn't in my office for five minutes before Will came knocking on the open door of my office.

"Lonnie, are you seriously thinking of quitting?" He asked as if that idea was unthinkable.

"I need to weigh my options, Will." How preposterous of you all to think I was just going to say yes.

"Lonnie, please accept the offer. We genuinely don't want to lose you. We had to address this, and it's better for this to be done up front than in response to any potential backlash."

"The key word there is potential, Will. If absolutely nothing happens to this company because of my misfortune, then what was my demotion based on? Voicing my opinion about a work situation? Every person in this building and in your building and any other business on this globe has employees that go home or to a bar or their kid's little league game and releases the tension of their workday to someone. Including you."

"I get it. I hope you can see past this and stay with us." He left my office without saying anything else. What was there left to say?

I made two phone calls, one to David and one to Dad. By lunch time I had all my things packed in boxes. I drafted an email to the directors of my branch, Will, Brian, John, and a separate one to Grace.

Dear colleagues,

As many of you may know, I was recently the target of a petty crime that has led to the defamation of my character. It was determined by Mendallmen leadership, in an effort to diminish any negative publicity that could be aimed at the company as a result of my misfortune, that I would step down from the AVP position of South Branch. I was offered a director position at Main Branch to maintain my employment with the company.

In advance, I offer apologies if this company experiences any ill will because of the crime committed against me. I would also like to acknowledge the privilege it has been to work with you in the capacity as AVP and in every other position I've held over the years. Today will be my last day with Mendallmen Inc, as I will not be accepting the director position that has been offered. Thank you all.

Best Wishes,
Lonnie Peterson

Both Dad and David arrived at my job to help me load all my things in the car. When David came in, he embraced me.

"We're going to be okay, Lonnie. I promise."

"I'm not afraid, David. This will work out in my favor."

As Dad and David carried the last boxes out, I sent the email. I turned off the lights in my office and left that building for the last time. We were about a mile away from the building when the phone calls started coming in. I turned the ringer off and stared out at the highway in front of us. I was experiencing that feeling you get when you're driving a familiar route with your conscious mind instead of your subconscious. I was feeling that way about my life right then too. I didn't know where I was. Everything was unfamiliar, yet this was the path I've been on for months.

Dad and David had driven separately to the office. Dad took my things home, and I rode with David. When we passed our exit, I knew he was intending to take me somewhere to talk.

"David, I really just want to go home," I said. I was completely emotionally exhausted.

"I'm going to take you home, but I want you to go home feeling good about yourself."

I was fixing my lips to oppose the idea, but I didn't have the energy. We pulled into a shopping center, and he parked at the curb in front of a spa. He got out and walked around to the passenger side to open my door. He escorted me into the spa and handed me over to the ladies of the establishment.

"I'll be back at two. Everything is already setup for you and paid for." He blew me a kiss and slipped out the door.

Well, no need to fight him on this one. Now *this* was the best thing that had been offered to me all day.

By Wednesday we heard back from Tish, who also enlisted the help of a lawyer. Of course, she was denying she played any role in the publication of the video. So we officially entered the discovery phase of the lawsuit process. My only concern was getting Grace to speak on my behalf. She was the one who suggested that Tish take my phone to the support group. I decided that I would leave all of that up to the lawyer.

Linda asked to have lunch with me on Thursday.

I assumed she was either wanting some bonding time or to talk about wedding plans. But that lunch put me on a trajectory that was completely unexpected.

"Why'd you pick this place?" I asked Linda as I sat across from her in a booth at a quaint little coffee shop.

"This is where your Dad and I first had coffee together. I get good vibes being here." She smiled.

"Has my dad shared my current situation with you?"

"He did, Lonnie. And that's why I wanted to have lunch with you."

I was somewhat confused. I couldn't figure out what would intrigue her about my professional demise.

"I know this is a very difficult time for you," she began, "but I wanted to talk with you early in your transition to see if I can provide some advice."

"I'm all ears. I have no idea what I'm going to do. To be honest, I didn't plan on even trying to figure anything out until next week. I'll need to update my resume and start looking for positions. I just don't want to deal with that this week. I need a mental health week."

"That's just it. I want to talk to you about how you can turn this situation into a victory."

She got my attention. I hate losing, and this situation so far was looking to be a TKO.

"You know that I've worked my whole career in the financial sector. I've had the opportunity to work with major corporations, startups, and nonprofits in taking their businesses to another level through successful fundraising. While working with these companies, particularly the startups, I was exposed to the stories behind their success. The origins of their ideas and businesses. What drove them to pursue their products or services. When your dad told me your story, and we watched the videos . . ."

"You watched the videos?!" I dropped my head. "Did you all eat popcorn, while watching me spill my life into my phone?"

"Yes, we watched the videos and no, there was no popcorn. But there was an idea." Linda leaned in, "What if you became a video blogger. It was not intended for the whole world to peek into your life, but when they did, they told their cousin, their coworker, the person sitting next to them on the train. If your story was that interesting to share, then go ahead and share. Whoever put the videos out there just gave you free publicity that you never would have given yourself."

I sat there and looked at Linda, then looked out the window, then back at Linda. After a few rounds of this, I shook my head. "I don't have anything to talk about that's new or different."

"The thousands of views your videos received say different," Linda said with confidence.

"When would I have time to do that once I go back to work?"

"You made time to make the videos that went out on the internet, didn't you? And the point I'm getting to is that you don't have to go back to work. People are making their living online. You're not giving yourself credit. From the short time I've known your dad and you, I have seen you not only have something to say, but people listen when you say it."

When she said that, two memories came to mind. One was the conversation with David's cousin at Thanksgiving dinner. The other was a conversation LeeAnn and I had when she made a comment about me being a voice of reason. My mind started churning. I remembered the first day at breastfeeding support group and how I shared with Grace my own troubles with breastfeeding as a new mom.

"Linda, I think you have a point. But I don't know if I'm cut out for that."

"That's totally understandable. Most successful entrepreneurs didn't see themselves cut out for entrepreneurship. They simply had a passion about something and defied the odds and failures until success was theirs."

"Were you also a motivational speaker in your decorated career?" I asked, peering over my cup of coffee.

"I've given a speech or two and countless come to Jesus talks, similar to this one." She grinned. "It's moments like these where greatness is birthed. You should think seriously about this. Before you send any resumes, let's talk again. Can we do that?"

This chick was serious. It couldn't hurt to talk again about this, but I couldn't see it happening. The videos are what got me in this predicament. Why would I fuel this type of fire? The burn hurt.

"Sure, we can have lunch before I send any resumes. Enough talk about me. Have you and Dad set a date?"

That night, Linda's proposition kept me awake. What if she was right about video blogging? Many people have watched me already. The thief took the time to make me an account on a video platform. I could use it. That'd be a slap in her face. I made a mental list of things I could talk about and all the new topics that would come as Eva got bigger, as DJ and Johnny got older, as a new entrepreneur. I was letting my thoughts get away with me. I cleared my head and closed my eyes to go to sleep, this time with success.

The following week I had to disclose to Claude names of any and everybody who would have information about what happened with my phone, the relationship with Tish, and my character in general. I gave a lot of names from the support group. I gave Will's name. David, Lisa, and Jackie would definitely speak on my behalf.

"Claude, if I kept the account on the video platform and used it, would that be a conflict with this lawsuit?"

"Yes."

"If I started making videos with a new account, would that be a conflict?"

"What are you thinking of doing?"

"I was thinking about starting a vlog, just about life and some of my experiences and how others can get through similar situations."

"I don't know if now would be the best time. The account is in your name. It may look like a marketing stunt if you start posting new videos. The concept sounds interesting and you do have a *following*, and you could benefit from the crime against you. I like the idea, but not now."

"Okay."

I didn't dismiss the idea, but I heeded his advice and put a cap on the idea. I met with Linda again about two weeks after our first lunch. She made a pass at me again regarding the vlogging. She even threw out the idea of podcasting! I loved her ideas, but I let her know what Claude said about the timing. She could see his point of view.

"I just hate for you to lose momentum."

"Do you think he'd let me post an apology explanation video?"

"I'd ask him. It would help keep everyone tuned in until this lawsuit is over. The only thing about lawsuits is that they can drag out. Let's pray that isn't your experience."

"I second that," I said and raised my coffee mug in agreement. "You agreed I could send resumes after this meeting, so don't be surprised if I'm working in a week or two.

"Have you thought about staying home with Eva until she's one?"

"I have. I think we could swing it, but I'm so conditioned to working, I don't know if I'd enjoy being at home."

"Outside of the current circumstances, have you enjoyed being at home this last month?"

"Truthfully, it has been refreshing. But for the long haul, I don't know if it would work out. And I don't want to get rusty. My industry is fast-paced."

"I just want you to think about all of your options."

"Thank you, Linda. I appreciate your thoughtful input on my situation. So, back to you. Last time we talked you and Dad hadn't set the wedding date. Have you talked about a date yet?"

By February Claude was wrapping up depositions. There were a few left, one of which was Grace's. She hadn't responded. That concerned me. What if something was wrong and I knew nothing about it. I hated not being able to talk to her. Maybe I should contact her. I took the chance and called and, of course, it went to voicemail. After the beep I squeezed all my thoughts into the limited time the voicemail allowed.

> *Grace, this is Lonnie. I wanted to check in on you and Jackson. I apologize that you were involved in all my mess. I genuinely care about you and getting to know you was a rewarding experience. Thank you for letting me be a part of your life for the past few months. I hope you and Jackson are well. Feel free to call me anytime.*

I got teary eyed as I hung up. It was the best I could do. I hadn't tried to call LeeAnn, but I wanted to so badly. I missed our lunches at that little place after support group. She always meant what she said, and she said our friendship was suspended, indefinitely. But what did I have to lose? I called her.

As I waited for the voicemail to kick in, I nearly had a heart attack when she answered my call.

"This is LeeAnn."

"Hi LeeAnn, it's Lonnie."

"What can I do for you?"

"I wanted to tell you I regret that you were involved in the release of the videos, and I want our friendship to come off of suspension."

"Lonnie, you were a friend. One of the best I've come by in a long time. But that cut deep. I know I'm eccentric, but I thought you could understand and respect that."

"I understand and respect you, LeeAnn. My account of you in the videos was my experience of the wild woman I just met that totally intrigued me. I said nothing that was degrading."

"You exposed me, Lonnie."

"I was exposed, LeeAnn. I was the target and the fact that you were hurt is not something I'm proud of. I miss our friendship."

We sat quietly for a moment.

"I don't know, Lonnie."

"Think about it. If you call me back that would bring me so much joy. If you don't, I will understand."

"Thank you. Bye, Lonnie"

"Hope to hear from you soon, LeeAnn."

Now I'd gone from teary-eyed to just flat out crying. I missed my breastfriends!

David came in the room to hand me his phone. I wiped my eyes and asked who was calling.

"It's Claude. He's got a lead."

I grabbed the phone.

"Lonnie, we have potentially good news. There's a lady from the support group named Bobbi who gave some valuable information during her deposition."

"That's Tish's sidekick. What did she say?"

"She said that Tish told her about the video and said that you got what you deserved. Bobbi claimed that's all Tish said. That sounds like a motive to me."

"Wow. So what's next? How soon can we wrap this up?"

"That's hard to say. We'll see if Tish is willing to settle out of court. If not, we'll file to get a trial date."

"What's the likelihood that she'll settle out of court?"

"If the cost of going to trial and losing doesn't motivate her, then she's as crazy as everyone has painted her to be. She doesn't have a strong story for what she did with the phone between it being given to her and it being returned to you. Your phone was not in the possession of anyone else and mysteriously the contents of your phone wound up on the internet shortly after being in her possession."

"Bring home a victory for us, Claude."

"I will do my best, Lonnie."

February rolled by and life was starting to get back on track. I did find another job. It was something to make money, not anything I really enjoyed. My baby was starting to crawl. She was so much fun. Even though I wasn't breastfeeding anymore, we still spent our evenings and mornings together in the rocking chair, staring into each other's eyes and enjoying the peacefulness of those quiet times. David and I decided to go ahead and put her in daycare since Dad would be a newlywed soon. Dad fought us on that decision, but we knew it would be best. He missed holding his baby girl every day. I told him he had another girl he could hold everyday (wink wink).

Dad and Linda set a date in late March for the wedding. I had a late start on the postpartum exercising, but for a nearly middle aged woman, I looked all right in my dress. Linda has good taste. No ugly bridesmaids would be in this wedding. Linda loves traveling, and Dad had never been on a cruise, so guess who would be going on an Alaskan Cruise for their honeymoon? I was so excited for Dad. Linda made him so happy. She brought such vibrancy to his life, which I loved seeing. I couldn't wait for the wedding.

This whole lawsuit naturally put a strain on my marriage. It was never dire, but things were not as sweet as they had been before. The stress had stripped away a precious layer that we had taken for granted for so many years. We both knew it, but the cloud of this lawsuit made it difficult to repair. David continued to travel, and I got better at managing everything while he was gone. Our marriage was just floating in the current of our life. We both wanted desperately to make our way back to the shores of passion, but it was as if we were stranded out in the water, unable to overcome the pull of the current.

One afternoon Claude notified us that Grace had agreed to a deposition. She gave a detailed account of that evening, and it locked in the time frames that the phone was in Tish's possession. The only missing piece was who made the video. Tish admitted she had the phone but denied making the video. When asked if she knew who made the video, she denied that as well. But Claude and his team were persistent. They started digging deeper to see if Tish had connections with anyone savvy in video editing and social media. It wasn't until mid March that they finally struck gold.

Given the short amount of time the phone was in her possession, it was unlikely that she hired someone to post the videos. The legal team was able to find a young man related to Tish who just happened to be a college sophomore majoring in media and communications with a concentration in technology. When they brought him in for questioning, he was initially uncooperative, but when Claude began laying out the consequences for producing and posting those videos, the young man revealed what we all knew to be true.

Tish was his aunt and she gave him a little spending money over the Christmas break to "be creative" with the videos and post them online. He swore that he had no idea that his aunt knew the lady in the videos.

When Claude shared this with us, he mentioned that we could file a suit against Tish's nephew as well. We didn't want this video to ruin another life, so we decided against that. He was young and was put into a bad situation not knowing all the details.

"Do you think she'll settle out of court?" David asked.

"If she cares about her nephew, she will."

"Let's settle this, Claude. We need to move on with our lives," David said.

Claude moved forward on pursuing a summary judgment. The case was solid enough for us to win.

Emerge

The moment we had all been anticipating came on a Saturday afternoon in late March. The room had large sliding windows that led to a balcony overlooking the mountains in the distance. There were a hundred and twenty close family and friends gathered to celebrate Dad and Linda tying the knot.

The air was a little chilly but the beauty of this moment backdropped against that stunning view made everything perfect. When the minister presented Mr. and Mrs. Lee, he instructed the groom to kiss the bride. They must have been practicing this kiss. They looked way too comfortable.

We danced the night away with everyone delivering best wishes to the newlyweds. At the end of the night, the couple had their final dance on the balcony, now lit by gentle strands of tiny white lights. It was a beautiful sight. We sent them off in their limo to start their new life together. I cried like a baby, but it was a happy cry. The lady who did my makeup knew what she was doing, because my face was still looking good despite the tears and snot.

Monday I was sitting at my desk sporting huge bags under my eyes from lack of sleep with all the weekend's festivities when I got a call from David.

"Hey, babe, how's your day?" I asked.

"It's real good, Lonnie. Tish is going to settle."

I was flooded with emotions. Relief, anger, joy, peace, sadness. "What happens next?"

"We negotiate the settlement."

"How long will that take?"

"Until both parties agree with the terms."

"After we pay Claude, you and I need a vacation."

"I agree."

When all was said and done, the settlement covered my lost wages, our legal fees, and a small amount for punitive damages. It was over. But the relationships that were damaged in the process were still either nonexistent or in limbo. I decided to create a video explaining the details behind the videos and extending a public apology to those who were exposed in the videos. I used the same ID that the original video was posted under to catch as many people as possible. I ended the video like this:

> **Although the intention of the original video post was negative and done without my knowledge or permission, going forward the videos will be positive. From this point forward, you will hear my thoughts on everything from being a working mom to breastfeeding to relationships. Many of you already have received an unintended slice of my life. Now I'm intentionally going to share more. I hope you'll join me.**

The video didn't go viral, but it received plenty of views. I started with a weekly vlog post. Once I got into the rhythm of doing the weekly posts, I bumped it up to twice a week. With help, I began optimizing my channel so it generated revenue. Several things led to another, and I found myself speaking to small groups and taking on sponsors.

Within a year I said goodbye to my job and started a podcast based on my vlog. People I met were connecting me with all types of thought leaders on the topics I liked to present to my audience. Today I was very excited to have one of my favorite podcasters on my podcast. I didn't know what I was in for.

> *"Today we're going to hear from life coach Cindy J. Cindy, teach us everything we need to know about repairing relationships."*

> *"Thank you, Lonnie, for having me on your podcast. I want to do a live demonstration on how we typically coach our clients on relationship restoration. I did a little research on you, and I have conferenced another person for our session today."*

I usually am in total control of the podcast, so this was unexpected.

> *"Every one, let me introduce LeeAnn."*

> *"Hello, everyone out there."*

> *"Lonnie, do you want to tell us how you know LeeAnn?"*

This just got real. I answered Cindy J with truly heartfelt words:

> *"It would be an honor to tell you about this special lady."*

Cindy walked LeeAnn and me through our process of restoration. That episode elicited laughs, tears, tension, and peace. And at the end, restoration. LeeAnn and I agreed to meet up the following day. It would be the first time we've seen each other since we were all together in that hospital room supporting Grace and Jackson.

The following day I arrived at Hot Spatula, the little restaurant LeeAnn and I frequented after breastfeeding support group gatherings. I walked in and she flagged me down. As I approached the booth, I saw LeeAnn, Rachel, Sasha . . . and Grace. I'd been one giant ball of tears the last two years of my life, but this reunion was worth every tear. I held Grace the longest. I looked her in her eyes and said I was sorry. Something I had longed to do.

Two hours went by as we caught up on each other's lives. Sasha had a little boy, and he joined us for lunch. With her schooling now complete, Rachel had a job that she was proud of and thriving in. Grace was still at Mendallmen, Jackson was doing well, and her dream of purchasing a home had come true. LeeAnn was steadily growing her business and had taken on some big clients in the city. Overall, they were happy and thriving. Everything I had hoped for all of them.

"But look at you, Lonnie, big time podcaster," LeeAnn said.

"I wouldn't say big time, at least not yet."

"You're always blazing the trail, Lonnie. I wanna be like you when I grow up," Rachel said.

"You all are too much. I think the bond we made in the support group made me see a part of myself that wasn't being used because I was set in my routine of life. You all had a big part to play in this." I lifted my glass, "To breastfriends."

We all laughed and lifted our glasses to toast the revival of our friendship. As we left, I pulled Grace to the side.

"Seeing you was the best thing about today."

"I'm glad to see you too, Lonnie. I'm still loving it at Mendallmen, and I have you to thank for that."

"I wanted to make you aware that I've partnered with a local company that manufactures unique breastfeeding supplies. They've offered me an opportunity to be the sole distributor in this region. I want to give a portion of all proceeds to a charity in honor of you and Jackson. Is there one that you would prefer?"

"Wow, what an awesome opportunity. Well, Jackson has asthma, so maybe you can give to organizations that focus on asthma."

"I will do that."

"Thank you for always thinking of me and my family."

When we got outside, the ladies were discussing our next meeting.

"We should be systematic about this," said Rachel. "How about we stick with the second Saturday of January, April, August, and December."

Everyone seemed okay with that, and so the band was back together. Along the way we added a few new friends to the group, including David's cousin Sherrie.

This particular second Saturday in August, we were meeting up for our regular Breastfriends outing. It had been three years since we reunited. Today we met at a movie theater in town. We were the only ones permitted to go in Theater 6 this afternoon. We were privileged to have a private viewing of a movie that was slated to come out in a week. We all sat down in the middle of the theater with our popcorn and drinks.

"This better be good," Grace said.

"Yeah, if it's not, I'm suing you," said LeeAnn.

"Well, I'll have plenty of money to settle with you out of court," I said.

The movie we were viewing was our story through my lens. I was approached by a gentleman a couple of years ago about taking my experiences post-Eva and putting them on the big screen. And here we were, about to watch a reenactment of how we met and grew the bonds between us. We all knew how we would be depicted in this film, but I don't know if any of us were truly ready to see ourselves from this vantage point.

"I hope we're still friends after this," LeeAnn called out as the lights dimmed.

I looked down the row and smiled. Breastfriends Forever.

ABOUT THE AUTHOR

Florencia Robertson is a working mom and wife who finds joy amidst the demands of her multidimensional life. She holds a Doctorate of Clinical Sciences and has worked almost two decades as an occupational therapist in clinical, academic, and leadership roles. Writing, one of her creative outlets, is where she uses her unique tone to share anecdotal and fictional experiences of a working mom. There are always similarities in how professional moms live. Sharing these experiences can empower those who read or listen. After all, she can't be the only one who's left the house wearing shoes from two different pairs.

You are invited to visit
FlorenciaRobertson.authorsites.com.

www.ingramcontent.com/pod-product-compliance
Lightning Source LLC
Chambersburg PA
CBHW070128080526
44586CB00015B/1600